★ 12 TEXAS AGGI

NUMBER 150

Williams-Ford Texas A&M University
Military History Series

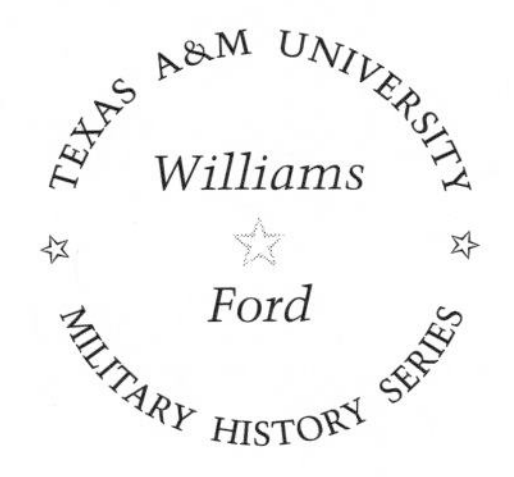

From World War I to Vietnam

JAMES R. WOODALL

Maps by Anne Boykin

TEXAS A&M UNIVERSITY PRESS

College Station

Copyright © 2016 by James R. Woodall
All rights reserved
First edition

This paper meets the requirements of
ANSI/NISO Z39.48-1992 (Permanence of Paper).
Binding materials have been chosen for durability.
Manufactured in the United States of America

Library of Congress Cataloging-in-Publication Data

Woodall, James R., 1929–
12 Texas Aggie war heroes: from World War I to Vietnam / James R. Woodall;
maps by Anne Boykin.—First edition.
pages cm—(Williams-Ford Texas A&M University Military
History Series; Number 150)
Includes bibliographical references and index.
ISBN 978-1-62349-319-6 (cloth: alk. paper)— ISBN 978-1-62349-430-8
(paperback)— ISBN 978-1-62349-322-6 (ebook) 1. Agricultural and Mechanical
College of Texas—Alumni and alumnae—Biography. 2. Texas A&M University—
Alumni and alumnae—Biography. 3. Agricultural and Mechanical College of
Texas. Corps of Cadets—Biography. 4. Texas A&M University. Corps of Cadets—
Biography. 5. Veterans—Texas—Biography. 6. Heroes—Texas—Biography.
7. United States—Biography. 8. United States—History, Military—20th century.
I. Title. II. Title: Twelve Texas Aggie war heroes. III. Series: Williams-Ford Texas
A&M University military history series; no. 150.
LD5309.W66 2015
378.764'242—dc23
2015032287

This book is dedicated to
my wonderful wife, Gloria,
and my four fabulous daughters—
Susan Gardiner, Carol Ann Honeycutt,
Melissa Carpenter, and
Martha Jane Page.

A nation reveals itself
not only by the men it produces,
but also by the men it honors,
the men it remembers.

JOHN F. KENNEDY

★ CONTENTS ★

★ FOREWORD ★

Dr. Robert Gates, while serving as president of Texas A&M University, described the school as a "unique American university." Since the day he made that statement, it has been repeated over and over in publications, speeches, and conversations as people try to describe the university, its students, and its former students. Having observed and experienced A&M up close, Dr. Gates recognized that there was something truly unique about A&M's history, spirit, and traditions, about its students and former students.

Part of the special feeling he had about students and former students, no doubt, related to the Corps of Cadets and the gallantry and great leadership skills of A&M former students who helped fight our nation's wars for more than 115 years. Over that time, the university provided far more than its share of "soldiers" for the military services. Aggies, it seems, are eager to serve, both in peacetime and when our freedom is threatened. From them have come many heroes: some who made the ultimate sacrifice, some who were awarded the Medal of Honor, and many who won awards like the Distinguished Service Cross, Navy Cross, Air Force Cross, Silver Star, and other medals of valor.

It is best we not forget our heroes, for they give us courage, hope, strength, and someone to rally around and follow—especially in time of war. Where would the United States be without great men like Washington, Pershing, MacArthur, Rickenbacker, Doolittle, Patton, Nimitz, Abrams, Stockdale, Schwarzkopf, and others? These are but a few of the highly decorated men who will forever stand as genuine American military heroes. Each in their own way provides an example of courage and leadership that bears study and remembrance.

Texas A&M University has its own list—a long list—of heroes who have demonstrated great courage, valor, strength, tenacity, perseverance, and leadership in combat. Most readers are familiar with the heroics of Maj. Gen. Earl Rudder and Lt. Gen. James Hollingsworth. But who are the other most notable Aggie heroes? The latter are who Col. Jim Woodall (USA, Ret.) introduces in his book *12 Texas Aggie War Heroes: From World War I to Vietnam*. The number twelve is special with

Aggies, which explains why his top-ten list of heroes was expanded to twelve.

Colonel Woodall did an enormous amount of research, analysis, and evaluation to identify the men he would include on such a list. Medal of Honor winners were deemed to be in a separate category and thus were chronicled in his first book, *Texas Aggie Medals of Honor: Seven Heroes of World War II*. The men he presents here were not desk jockeys or behind-the-scene types but frontline combatants who saw the enemy face to face, experienced the heat of battle, and witnessed death and destruction at its worst. In such conditions is where heroes emerge. Each man selected exhibited raw courage and bravery of the highest level.

Colonel Woodall's twelve heroes are slam-dunk selections. Any one of us might repeat his research and come up with a slightly different list of individuals, but I doubt it would vary from his list by more than one or two names. Who could dispute the courage and bravery—the heroism—of men like George Moore (Class of 1908) of Corregidor fame; John Hilger (Class of 1932), who piloted one of the B-25s on the famous Tokyo raid of 1942; Ray Murray (Class of 1935), a tough marine who distinguished himself during the cold and costly Chosin Reservoir battle in Korea; and George Gay (Class of 1940), who became the sole survivor of a navy torpedo squadron at Midway. Then there is Jim Hollingsworth (Class of 1940), A&M's most decorated soldier and one of the most decorated men in US military history, and Earl Rudder (Class of 1932), who scaled the cliffs at Normandy. I will not mention the other men on Woodall's list here, but I can assure you that they are heroes of the same order.

During his research, Colonel Woodall took on an additional task, to identify every Aggie who had received one of our nation's second-highest awards for valor—the Distinguished Service Cross, the Navy Cross, or the Air Force Cross. He identified sixty-five men in this category and lists them in Appendix 2 by service and the war in which the award was earned. The appendix also includes another seven men who are believed to have been awarded one of these medals but await verification. To these Aggie heroes, and scores of other Aggies who distinguished themselves in battle, we owe a deep debt of gratitude. We marvel at their courage and celebrate their exploits—may they long be remembered.

We can only ponder why these men were so heroic. Possibly it was due to circumstances, maybe it was because of the good training and discipline they learned at home, or perhaps it was due to a strong faith acquired through a religious experience. I suspect much of it had to do with the training and schooling they received at Texas A&M University. It makes me think all the more that Dr. Gates indeed got it right when he declared Texas A&M to be a unique American university.

THOMAS G. DARLING '54
Major General, USAF (Ret.)
Commandant, TAMU, 1987–96

★ PREFACE ★

You could say that the number twelve is a mystical number for students and former students of Texas A&M University. The fascination dates back to January 1922, when an underdog Texas Aggie football team was playing Centre College, the nation's top-ranked team. As the game progressed, the Aggies suffered several injuries and before the end were using their last reserves. Coach Dana X. Bible remembered that a former player, E. King Gill, was in the press box helping reporters identify players. Gill was called from the stands, suited up, and stood ready to go on the field if needed. When the game ended and Texas A&M had won 22–14, Gill was the only reserve left standing on the sidelines for the Aggies. Although he did not get to play, Gill had accepted the call to help his team. He came to be thought of as the "Twelfth Man" because he stood ready for duty in the event his teammates needed assistance. The entire student body at Texas A&M now considers itself the Twelfth Man and stand during all football games to show their support for the team and their willingness to be called upon if needed.

This tradition took on a new look in the 1980s when Coach Jackie Sherrill started the Twelfth Man Kick-Off Team, composed of regular students selected through open tryouts. This unit performed very well and held opponents to one of the lowest yards-per-return averages in the conference. Later Coach R. C. Slocum changed the team to have only one non-student-athlete representative on the kick-off team, a practice that continues to this day. Gill has been honored with a statue that stands in the plaza next to Kyle Field, the university's football stadium.

Texas A&M is also known for its service to country. For example, some 20,000 Aggies served in the armed forces during World War II, 14,000 as officers, a greater number than those from the US military academies. Seven Aggies have been awarded the Medal of Honor, and at least sixty-five others have been awarded the Distinguished Service Cross, Navy Cross, or Air Force Cross, the nation's second-highest awards. This book details the lives of twelve Aggies whose records indicate they were genuine war heroes. The citations for their awards are included as Appendix 1. The project to identify more of these individuals continues, the results to date included in Appendix 2. This is the first time such a list has been compiled and published.

The initial process for selecting the twelve was to solicit nominations from military historians familiar with Texas A&M and from several former students who have an interest in military history. When these were tabulated, there was general agreement on most of those chosen. Several former students who had long and distinguished military careers were nominated, but the book is about Pattons, not Eisenhowers. The selection of the twelve is admittedly subjective, and some readers might have named someone else. This is completely understandable: one only has to read Henry Dethloff and John Adams's *Texas Aggies Go to War* to see that many, many others would qualify for inclusion in this book. The final selection was entirely the purview of the author.

Due consideration was given to an individual's military decorations. Most, though not all, were awarded the Distinguished Service Cross or Navy Cross; the lives of the seven Aggies awarded the Medal of Honor were detailed in *Texas Aggie Medals of Honor: Seven Heroes of World War II,* and this book is a companion to that work. Award of military medals is an imperfect system, especially where medals for valor in combat are concerned. Many acts of valor go unrewarded for the lack of witnesses, who may have been killed or wounded and evacuated and never again located. There is also the problem of administrative failures. Awards are still being made for valor in previous wars because the original recommendation was misplaced or for other clerical reasons.

Of the twelve selected heroes, seven became general officers in later years, but only George F. Moore was a general at the time of his cited action. All twelve survived their war but are now deceased.

This book covers the period from World War I to the Vietnam War. Two men served in World War I and World War II and two others served in three wars—World War II, Korea, and Vietnam. All twelve served with distinction and should serve as an inspiration to readers. Ronald Reagan once asked at a D-Day ceremony at Ponte du Hoc, "Where do we get such men?" One answer is you get such men from places like the Corps of Cadets at Texas A&M University.

★ ACKNOWLEDGMENTS ★

Over the more than three years spent writing this book, many people have provided encouragement and support. There were some who made significant contributions, and I would like to thank them for their help.

First, I want to thank my family for their interest in the book and for their support. My wife, Gloria, provided insightful suggestions as she corrected the first draft. My daughter, Carol Ann Honeycutt, served as my editor and literary advisor, making a major contribution to the manuscript. My grandson, Steven Page, a student at Texas A&M, was always willing to dash over to Granddad's house to provide much-needed computer support. Another daughter, Melissa Carpenter, was pressed into service helping solve computer problems when she visited from San Antonio. I also want to thank my daughters Susan Gardiner and Martha Page who were here during a difficult period to provide support so I could continue writing.

The first document needed for each of the men profiled in this book was the Application for Admission to Texas A&M. This provided the basic information for telling the story of the individual, including parents' names, high school attended, high school activities, and other pertinent information. My thanks to Don Carter, Texas A&M University registrar, and his assistant, Cindy Smith, for their help and support.

Once again Anne Boykin volunteered to prepare the maps for me. Her father, the late Calvin Boykin, contributed his research on Gen. A. D. Bruce.

As with *Texas Aggie Medals of Honor*, Rebecca Ann Jordan, niece of Lt. Lloyd H. "Pete" Hughes, who was awarded the Medal of Honor in World War II, made a major contribution by providing genealogical information for each of the heroes. She also did research on the individuals and found several items that helped tell their stories.

Documents from the Texas A&M University Archives were essential to completing this book. Robin Hutchison and her staff were always willing to promptly cart out the files requested. She also alerted me to the oral histories available, which proved a tremendous help in writing the stories of Jay Robbins and James Hollingsworth.

I am very grateful to Cheryl Hightower, librarian at Allen Academy in Bryan, Texas, for her assistance in documenting the assignment of Bruce as commandant of that academy.

I am also grateful to Tom Mucia, son of Hilger's navigator-bombardier on the Tokyo Raid, who provided several photos associated with the raid. My thanks also go to Tom Brott, librarian at Sherman High School, for providing information about Hilger's activities during his high school days.

A special word of appreciation goes to Regan Schaupp, Tex Hill's grandson, who provided several photos that are included in this book. He is the coauthor of his grandfather's book, *Tex Hill, Flying Tiger.*

I am particularly grateful to Jack Teague, Olin Teague's son, and Terri Toler, his granddaughter, who gave me access to their relative's military records. Terri never hesitated to lug several boxes of documents to my house and even bring them back when I needed to do more research.

It was my good fortune to make contact with the family of Raymond Murray. His wife, Zona, wrote a book about the general's service, and the family graciously provided me a copy. I enjoyed getting to know Zona, son Jim Murray, and daughter Sherry Smeltzer. They were very giving in providing photos and details of Murray's career. I should also thank Rigo Ortiz of Mercedes, Texas, for providing information from the Mercedes High School yearbook about Murray's high school activities.

I am very grateful to Frank Muller, Hollingsworth's aide in Vietnam, for his memories of the battle at An Loc and for providing documents from that period. I should also mention Victoria Elieson, director of the Sanger Public Library, and Sue Laswell and Linda Hewlett, both of Sanger High School, for their contributions to the Hollingsworth story.

A special thanks goes to Lane Callaway, Eighth Air Force historian, Barksdale Air Force Base, Louisiana. He provided valuable support in researching the air force heroes and put me in touch with other air force resources.

As always, the staff at the Sam Houston Sanders Corps of Cadets Center at Texas A&M were very supportive. I think of the Corps Center as the "Jewel in the Crown" of the campus. Jeff Gardiner and his staff never hesitated to respond to my numerous requests for books from the center's library. Lisa Kalmus, curator of the center, was a valuable asset. She provided photographic support in assembling images for the book to include the Rudder and Hollingsworth statues on the campus.

Among the many persons who agreed to interviews, I wish especially to thank Douglas Kendrick, Marion Pugh's brother-in-law, for the background information he provided. Thanks also to Barney Welsh, a longtime friend of Pugh, and to Sue Shaw, librarian at North Side High School.

Jerry Cooper, former editor of the Association of Former Student's *Texas Aggie* magazine, provided extensive material used in writing the Robert Acklen chapter. He also was instrumental in developing the list of Aggies awarded the Distinguished Service Cross, the Navy Cross, and the Air Force Cross. Acklen's sister, Carolyn Bender, also provided additional material concerning her brother.

The staff of the Corps of Cadets Association, Bill Gutierrez, Monica Zavala, and Dennis Davenport, were helpful in gathering images from the *Longhorn* and *Aggieland* yearbooks.

Credit for including the list of Aggies awarded the Distinguished Service Cross, the Navy Cross, or the Air Force Cross in the book goes to John Adams. It was his suggestion. Thanks also go to Henry Dethloff for his support and advice. He was always willing to give his time to help.

★ 12 TEXAS AGGIE WAR HEROES ★

★ 1 ★

Defender of Corregidor

GEORGE F. MOORE

CLASS OF 1908

George Fleming Moore was born in Austin, Texas, on July 31, 1887, the son of John M. and Estelle Moore. George had an older brother, Fleming, born in 1884. The family increased in 1890 with the birth of a sister, Susan, and in 1896 with the birth of another brother, John. The father was an attorney who passed away in 1902. Moore's grandfather and namesake was George Fleming Moore (1822–83), who served as chief justice of the Texas Supreme Court in 1866–67 and 1878–81. The family was living in Edna in September 1904 when George applied to Texas A&M to study civil engineering. While a student there, his family moved to Fort Worth.[1]

In the fall of 1904, Texas A&M's student body numbered 414, all members of the Corps of Cadets. The corps consisted of a nineteen-man

Moore played tackle and guard on the Texas A&M football team.
Courtesy Texas A&M University Yearbook

band and a battalion of four companies, with many of the cadets housed in tents due to a shortage of dormitories. Moore was assigned to Company A his first three years and then to Company B his senior year, serving as a cadet second lieutenant. He acquired the nickname "Maud," after a mule in a popular cartoon strip, when he kicked a football over Ross Hall. He also displayed his prowess on the football field, playing tackle and guard, and received varsity letters in that sport in 1907 and 1908.[2]

Moore was active in student activities, with membership in the Ross Volunteers, the Swastika Dancing Club, and the "T" Association. He was also the associate business manager for the *1908 Longhorn*. Other activities included serving as athletic manager of the senior class, president of the company football association, and manager of the Company A baseball team. Accompanying Moore's student portrait in the *1908 Longhorn* was this tribute:

> Maud is another of the '08 men on the team. He worked faithfully to gain his place and kept it up after getting it. He stayed by the side of Dutch Schmidt persistently and is a good student of the game. He is a quiet and mild-mannered but a steady fighter; no wonder, remember what encouragement he had from the fair sex on the sidelines. Neff's effective coaching was quite a help to Moore and though he was lighter than Schmidt and his companions, he was on to the ropes and made hard work count.
>
> He came from the Panther City and will probably locate there soon after he gets his sheepskin. The corps votes him a ladies' man, but in the Oklahoma game he was voted a football man. Maud is another loss to next year's team. . . . He goes to classes sometimes, but was never known to stay during the whole period.

The young graduate worked in the Fort Worth city engineer's office for a year before entering the US Army. The commandant of cadets during his junior and senior year was Capt. Andrew Moses, a coast-artillery officer. This may have influenced Moore's selection of coast artillery as his branch of service.[3] Moore was commissioned a second lieutenant in the Coast Artillery Corps on September 25, 1909, and promoted to first lieutenant on May 21, 1912. In 1915 he attended the Coast Artillery School and was a distinguished graduate. He was promoted to captain on May 15, 1917.

In September 1917 Moore was assigned to the 19th Field Artillery Regiment at Fort Sam Houston, Texas, and in March 1918 transferred to the Office of the Chief of Ordnance, War Department. During this period he served as a major and then as a lieutenant colonel. From 1923 to 1925 he saw service in the Philippines with the 59th Coast Artillery Regiment (see map 1). He attended the Artillery School Advance Course in 1927 and the Command and General Staff College in 1928. His next assignment was to return to the Philippines to study the harbor defenses of Manila. He returned to Washington, D.C., in 1930 for an assignment in the Office of the Chief of Coast Artillery. Moore attended the Army War College in 1934 and was a classmate of Jonathan Wainwright, who would be his commander in the Philippines during World War II.[4]

Moore served as commandant of cadets at Texas A&M from 1937 to 1940.
Courtesy Texas A&M University Yearbook

During his two tours in the Philippines, the military installations on the island of Corregidor, at the entrance to Manila Harbor, were improved, with tunnels blasted into the solid rock under Malinta Hill and upgraded roads, utilities, and water supply (see map 2). These years were prosperous ones for those in civilian life but not so for those in the military, where salaries were little above the pay rate during the Civil War. In addition, as happens whenever the country is not threatened by war, the army was held in disdain. Soldiers and officers were viewed with contempt, as incompetents who clung to secure jobs in the military because they could not make it in civilian life.[5]

In the fall of 1937, Moore was ordered to Texas A&M University to serve as the professor of military science and tactics and commandant of cadets. His selection was influenced by a request from former classmate Joe Utay, now a member of the A&M Board of Directors.

Moore returned to a much changed campus and Corps of Cadets. The corps numbered 4,933 students organized into the Aggie Band and six regiments (infantry, field artillery, engineer, cavalry, coast artillery, and composite), with forty-three company-sized units. The Reserve Officer Training Corps staff was composed of seventeen officers and forty enlisted men. Military training was offered in seven branches: infantry, field artillery, engineer, cavalry, coast artillery, signal corps, and chemical warfare.

Moore was faced with the persistent impediment to the growth of the corps, the lack of adequate dormitories. With the support of Pres. Franklin D. Roosevelt, his son Elliott (a member of the A&M Board of Directors), and Jesse H. Jones, administrator of the Reconstruction Finance Corporation, the college obtained a two-million-dollar loan to build twelve dormitories and a mess hall. Moore provided the board with timely information on the location of each dormitory and its construction progress. To maximize the number of new rooms within the slim budget, the four-story brick-and-concrete buildings were designed to be very spartan, with few if any amenities.

With the threat of war as background, Moore looked to reorganize cadet training to better align it with active-duty military standards. The training in each specific branch would be closely monitored to comply with army guidelines and to better prepare cadets for summer camp and active-duty service after graduation. Moore's demand for excellence reinforced the respect cadets held for him.[6]

The reality of war came suddenly to the campus just three days after the Nazis invaded Poland and on the same day, September 3, 1939, that England and France declared war on Germany. Moore's only daughter, Anne, was returning from Scotland with a tour group aboard the British liner S.S. *Athenia*. The ship was sailing from Glasgow to Montreal when it was sunk by a German U-boat. Moore and his wife, Lucille, spent many anxious hours awaiting news of their daughter's fate before finally learning that she was rescued after enduring eight hours in the cold and rough North Atlantic. She returned to College Station in early October to a near-hero's welcome.[7]

In the fall of 1940, Moore was ordered to the Philippines to serve as commander of harbor defenses at Manila and Subic Bays, with headquarters at Fort Mills on Corregidor Island. His command also included four other fortified islands—Carabao (Fort Frank), Caballo (Fort Hughes), and El Fraile (Fort Drum) at the entrance to Manila Bay and Grande (Fort Wint) near the entrance to Subic Bay. He selected thirty-five graduating seniors out of the 1940 class to precede him to the Philippines.[8]

Corregidor consists mostly of volcanic rock, with the most prominent terrain feature, Malinta Hill, located near its center. Commonly referred to as the "Rock," the island has roughly the shape of a tadpole, with the high, round head on the west end, and is about three and a half miles long and just over one mile at its widest point. The western area was known as "Topside" and contained most of the large-caliber coastal batteries on the island. It was also the location of Moore's headquarters, the parade ground, and the Mile Long Barracks, a two-story stone building said to be the world's longest barracks at the time.

Topside tapers east down to the next plateau called "Middleside," which was the location of the hospital, officer and noncommissioned-officer quarters, the Officer's Club, and schools. It also contained the station hospital, the post stockade, several warehouses, and more barracks and quarters. Farther down the slope just to the west of Malinta Hill was the lowest part of the island, called "Bottomside." It contained the terminal for the island's trolley system and the village of San Jose, where the island's workers lived. East beyond Malinta Hill stretched the long, twisted tail of the island, which contained a small airfield, Kindley Field.

The tunnel complex under Malinta Hill had been blasted through from one end to the other. The main tunnel, constructed in 1932 of reinforced concrete, was 1,400 feet long and 30 feet wide, with walls arching 20 feet to its ceiling. At regular intervals twenty-four dead-end laterals, each 150 feet long, stretched out from either side of the tunnel. A twenty-fifth lateral led to another tunnel complex housing a 300-bed hospital.[9]

When Moore was ordered to the Philippines, relations between the United States and Japan were deteriorating. On July 26, 1941, Japanese assets in the United States were frozen and an oil embargo implemented against the island nation. That same day Gen. Douglas MacArthur, since 1936 the military adviser of the Philippine Commonwealth and architect of the Philippine Army, was recalled to active duty and given command of US Army Forces in the Far East (USAFFE). In addition, the Philippine Army was called into US service.[10]

The standard plan for defense of the Philippines (War Plan Orange) stipulated that in the event of a Japanese invasion, US and Filipino

12-inch disappearing gun on Corregidor. *Courtesy John Ross*

forces would withdraw to the shelter of the Bataan Peninsula and Corregidor. From these positions, guarding the entrance to Manila Bay and denying its use to the Japanese, the defenders would hold out until the American battle fleet could break through with reinforcements. MacArthur considered Orange to be a defeatist plan and was determined to actively oppose the invaders wherever they landed. This meant that instead of stocking Bataan with supplies and equipment as called for in the original plan, all materials were moved forward to support a major effort to destroy enemy forces as they came ashore.[11]

On November 25 MacArthur appointed Major General Wainwright, then commanding the US Army's Philippine Division, as commander of the North Luzon Force, which at the time consisted of four Philippine divisions. These units had been recently activated and were undermanned, underequipped, and had little combat training.[12]

Because of the International Date Line, war came to the Philippines on December 8, 1941. The first strike fell against Clark Field, where American warplanes, just returned from a photo-reconnaissance flight, were caught on the ground. Losses of men and material were heavy, with eighteen B-17s, fifty-three P-40s, and three P-35s destroyed. An additional twenty-five to thirty miscellaneous aircraft were also wrecked.[13]

On December 10 Japanese advance troops landed at Aparri on the north coast of Luzon and at Vigan on the northwest coast. The main landing came on December 22 at the Lingayen Gulf. It was now clear that MacArthur's plan would not work, and the general ordered the withdrawal to Bataan. This meant that the supplies that had been moved to the front now had to be turned around and moved south, which proved impractical. For the rest of the campaign, the Bataan defenders would be seriously hampered by extreme shortages that would leave them starving and ill equipped to resist Japanese assaults.[14]

On December 24 MacArthur declared Manila an open city and departed the capital with his family and staff by interisland steamer for Corregidor. When the party arrived, they were met on the dock by Major General Moore, who escorted them to Malinta Tunnel. The dark, stinking tunnel was lit by flittering lights and packed with Filipinos celebrating a midnight mass. Moore led MacArthur and his family to a partitioned section of Lateral No. 3, where some cots had been prepared for their use along with a few items of furniture, army-issue chairs, and a desk. MacArthur demanded that better accommodations would have to be found for his family. The next morning Moore turned over his Topside cottage to the new arrivals.[15]

As US and Filipino forces withdrew into the Bataan Peninsula, the Japanese helped Wainwright by not altering their plan to first seize Manila and then continue the pursuit of their enemy. This gave the defenders time to complete their withdrawal and prepare their positions.[16]

The defense of Bataan officially began on January 7, 1942. Wainwright assumed command of the West Sector of the Bataan Defense Force, which became I Philippine Corps. The East Sector, redesignated II Philippine Corps, came under Maj. Gen. George M. Parker Jr., until then commander of the entire Bataan Defense Force. A Bataan echelon of MacArthur's headquarters on Corregidor allowed the general to exercise close control over operations on the mainland.[17]

The opening Japanese attacks on the peninsula were repulsed as were later amphibious flanking attacks. In February the Japanese suspended their offensive as their forces had become so depleted as a result of malaria. In addition, a division had been withdrawn from Bataan and sent to help in the attack on the Dutch East Indies. The Americans were unaware of this situation so no counterattack was attempted.[18]

On January 24 MacArthur called a staff conference and said that he was discouraged about the situation on Bataan, his attitude suggesting that he believed the position would soon fall. He ordered Moore to begin the transfer of food from the peninsula to Corregidor, further depleting Wainwright's already meager supplies. On February 3 MacArthur ordered Moore to make sure that he had enough food to feed 20,000 men on half rations until June 30. At the same time, Wainwright was receiving disturbing reports about the effects of the prolonged half-ration diet on his soldiers. He soon issued orders to begin killing the horses and mules to feed his men. The starving, diseased-ridden men were soon reduced to eating carabao, monkeys, lizards, and whatever else they could find.

On February 23 President Roosevelt ordered MacArthur to relocate to Australia to assume command of all US troops in the Far East. The War Department assumed that Wainwright would take charge of forces in the Philippines, but MacArthur had other plans. Prior to his departure, the general appointed newly promoted brigadier general Lewis C. Beebe as deputy chief of staff of USAFFE, allowing MacArthur to retain control of the US forces in the Philippines. He ordered Allied forces organized into four commands—Mindanao, Visayan, Harbor Defenses, and Luzon Force. Wainwright would command only the Luzon Force and would remain on Bataan.[19]

Originally, MacArthur's evacuation was to be by submarine, but since such a departure would be delayed by five days, he decided to travel to Mindanao by PT boats. In addition to his wife, son, and the child's nurse, he selected seventeen officers of his staff to accompany him. The party was escorted by Moore to the North Dock to board the four waiting vessels of Lt. John D. Bulkeley's Torpedo Boat Squadron 3. Before embarking, MacArthur turned to Moore and said, "Keep the flag flying," then, firmly shaking the major general's hand, added, "I am coming back." The PT boats departed Corregidor after dark on

March 12 and reached Mindanao the morning of the fourteenth. On the seventeenth the group was flown to Australia aboard B-17s.[20]

On the afternoon of March 20, the War Department informed Wainwright of his promotion to lieutenant general and his appointment as commanding general of all troops in the Philippines. The new command was designated US Forces in the Philippines. Early the next morning he turned over the Luzon Force to Maj. Gen. Edward P. King, formerly MacArthur's artillery advisor. Wainwright, accompanied by his aides, departed Bataan at about 8:00 a.m. for Corregidor, eager to assume his new command. The general told his aides: "Lee marched on Gettysburg with less men than I have here. We're not licked by a damn sight."

The next morning Moore took Wainwright on an inspection tour of the island. As they were driving along the South Shore Road, the air-raid sirens sounded. The driver quickly pulled over, and the generals went to the nearest shelter, which Wainwright entered only after Moore insisted. As soon as they got inside, a string of bombs exploded at the entrance. If they had delayed another thirty seconds, both men might have been killed.[21]

To man the beach defenses, Moore had the 4th Marine Regiment, which had served many years in China before being withdrawn to the Philippines in late November 1941. The unit's commander, Col. Samuel L. Howard, assumed command of these defenses. As more men reached the island, they were assigned to Howard's positions. By the middle of April, after the influx of troops from Bataan, the colonel had under his command about 4,000 men, of whom only 1,352 were marines; the rest came from the US Navy, the Philippine Army, and the US Army. This group constituted a heterogeneous force of doubtful strength, for few had any infantry training.[22]

By the end of March, Japanese forces against Bataan were reinforced with more than 22,000 fresh troops as well as more aircraft and many more guns. For five days the Corregidor defenders heard the continuous artillery and mortar fire from the mainland. Then suddenly, on April 9, an awesome silence descended over the peninsula. General King had surrendered.[23]

After the war Moore was quoted in a newspaper article as saying: "All that night and on the day after the surrender, refugees from Bataan poured into Corregidor by boats, rafts, bancas (native small craft), and

12-inch mortar on Corregidor. *Courtesy John Ross*

any other means of keeping afloat across the two-mile channel. The night sky was illuminated for hours as ammo stores and various installations were blown up."[24]

Peering through binoculars from a vantage point atop Malinta Hill, the general saw long lines of captives walking north from Mariveles along the East Coast Road. These were the defeated defenders of Bataan, Americans in their khaki uniforms and Filipinos wearing their blue fatigues. White flags of surrender dotted their columns. Observers on Corregidor did not know it at the time, but they were witnessing the beginning of the greatest atrocity of the Pacific War, the Bataan Death March. Some 70,000 men began the trek north, but only 54,000 of them arrived at Camp O'Donnell, not far from Clark Field.[25]

Corregidor itself had been subjected to daily air raids, but beginning on April 9, Japanese aircraft made multiple raids daily. The greatest threat came from land-based artillery, now in easy range of Corregidor and the fortified islands from the tip of Bataan. Despite the damage inflicted by the shelling, Fort Mills retained an impressive display of firepower, particularly heavy mortars and mobile 155s, as did nearby Fort Drum and Fort Hughes, with their heavy guns.

With April 21, San Jacinto Day, approaching, Moore asked Maj. Tom Dooley, Aggie Class of 1935 and Wainwright's aide-de-camp, for a list of Texas Aggies assigned to the Rock. Dooley provided the names of twenty-four men (with their class year), later updated to twenty-five:

Maj. Gen. George F. Moore '08
Maj. Tom Dooley '35
Maj. Paul A. Brown '29
Maj. John V. King, associate member of The Association of Former Students
Capt. Chester A. Peyton '33
Capt. Stockton D. Bruns '35
Capt. Roy M. Vick Jr. '35
Capt. Wilbert A. Calvert '38
Capt. Willis A. Scrivener '37
Capt. Henry J. Schutte Jr. '39
Capt. Graham M. Hatch '31
Capt. Jerome A. McDavitt '33
Capt. William M. Curtis '32
Lt. John McCluskey '36
Lt. David Snell '37
Lt. Lewis B. Chevaillier '39
Lt. Carl Pipkin '40
Lt. Clifton Chamberlain '40
Lt. William A. Hamilton '40
Lt. Charlton Wimer '39
Lt. William Boyd '38
Lt. Andy James '40
Lt. Urban C. Hopmann '39
Lt. Stanley Friedline '40
Sgt. Hugh Hunt '38

The popular legend of the "1942 Corregidor Muster" is that the Aggies on the island gathered together on April 21, 1942, and "drank a toast in water to the heroes of the Texas Revolution of 1836." But this never happened; the island was under intense bombardment and air attacks during the period, and it was not possible for the defenders to leave their posts during these final days.

Moore's intent had been to discuss with those Aggies he could contact the tradition of San Jacinto Day. Instead, the general used the list to conduct a roll call—in army terms, a muster—of Aggies present on the Rock during the Japanese siege. Dooley persuaded a United Press correspondent to file a story that included the list of those who had "mustered." The April 1942 story from Corregidor told the American public (erroneously) about Texas Aggies celebrating San Jacinto Day while under siege. It more accurately informed the families of those listed that the men were still alive and still fighting.[26]

By May 5 the island was broken and blasted; almost all of its artillery had been destroyed. The guns covering the beaches were gone as well as the searchlights, barbed-wire entanglements, and machine-gun emplacements. There were almost no beach defenses remaining on the north side of the island, the side facing Bataan.

By 10:30 p.m. Japanese landing barges had neared Corregidor while the island remained under heavy artillery fire. The 4th Marines manning the beach defenses slaughtered the first invaders, but the enemy kept coming and soon established a position ashore. Moore ordered reserve units from other parts of the island into the battle, but they were unable to push the enemy back.[27]

Casualties had been severe during the night, and it was impossible to get the wounded to the hospital through the heavy enemy fire. When dawn broke, there was not a building standing on Corregidor. The US counterattack had been checked, and there were no more reserve forces. When Wainwright learned that the Japanese had put tanks ashore, he knew the fate of the island was sealed. He called Moore to his headquarters and as soon as he walked in asked, "Should we surrender now or wait?" Moore did not hesitate, replying, "There should be no delay." A broadcast to the Japanese announced that at noon on May 6, a white flag would be displayed in a prominent position and all firing would cease. The Japanese commander, Lt. Gen. Masaharu Homma, refused to accept the surrender of Corregidor only, insisting the capitulation include all US forces in the Philippines. The next day Wainwright and some staff officers were taken to Manila by the Japanese and required to broadcast a surrender message to Maj.

Gen. William F. Sharpe, commander of the Visayan-Mindanao force. Following this, Wainwright and some of his immediate staff were held at the University Club, now converted to Japanese officers' quarters.[28]

A few days after the surrender, the generals and senior colonels still on Corregidor were taken by boat to Manila and driven to comfortable quarters in the University Club. They remained there for a month, well fed and courteously treated, until the surrender of American units scattered throughout the southern Philippines had been completed. Then the Japanese drove them to a small camp at Tarlac in central Luzon, where treatment by their jailers was less gentle. Altogether, fifteen generals, about one hundred colonels, and approximately sixty enlisted men were held at Tarlac. The prisoners were constantly humiliated and sometimes beaten by their guards. Officers were not required to work, though, and were spared even humdrum tasks since the Japanese assigned them captive enlisted men as orderlies.

On May 23 the remaining American and Filipino prisoners on Corregidor were taken by motor launch to three small tramp steamers that took them to Manila. They were paraded through the streets of the city on display to the local populace. After a march of about six miles, they arrived at Bilibid Prison.[29]

At Tarlac the senior-officer group was joined by those from Camp O'Donnell and Bilibid Prison. The Japanese placed 180 prisoners of war (POWs) in a barracks that once housed eighty Philippine Army recruits. General officers received a cot each, with heads against the wall and sides so close together that they had to climb in over the foot. Other officers were assigned to wooden double-decked bunks with no springs, mattresses, or blankets.

The food at Tarlac was much worse than at Manila and consisted principally of rice, with an ounce or two of pork or beef thrown in once every week or two. It was not nearly enough to restore the health of men already weakened by the starvation rations of Bataan and Corregidor and subsequent imprisonment. The meagerness of rations became such that an officer was appointed to divide the food as impartially as possible. The craving for sustenance was so intense that the group stood over this man while he apportioned the daily rations. Finally, the officer said he could not do the job any longer and quit. The squad then voted for Moore to take over the task. He accepted on the condition that he could attend to the splitting of the rice and soup behind a closed door without the supervision of his starving comrades.

In mid-August the senior-officer group was moved by train to Manila and then by truck to a pier, where they boarded a large ship. Wainwright and King were the only Americans on board being treated as something other than cattle, Moore and the other POWs being jammed in the hold. The officers slept on two long wooden shelves extending out from the walls and arranged one over the other, providing each man about two and a half feet of space. No bed clothing was provided, and the toilets were primitive.[30]

After a two-day voyage, the ship arrived at Takao on the west coast of Formosa. The next day the prisoners were transferred to a small, dirty coastal steamer that took them to Karenko, a small port on the island's east coast, where they were marched through the city. When they arrived at the prison camp, the POWs were forced to strip down to their underwear. The clothing was eventually given back, though not the shoes, each man instead receiving wooden Japanese clogs, none of them a proper fit. The treatment at Karenko was uneven and arbitrary, sometimes reasonably good but at other times grim and harsh. Prisoners were subjected to indiscriminate beatings and clubbings; generals were not exempt. Some of the enlisted men were beaten as many as three times a day, and it was a rare sight to find one whose eyes were not blackened. The prisoners were punished for many undetermined infractions of rules, many of which were often made up on the spur of the moment.[31]

The prisoners began to receive pay that could be used to purchase food and other items in a store the Japanese opened. The pay scale was that of the Japanese Army and ranged from 395 yen for a general officer to less than 20 yen for a sergeant. Some mail from home was received as well as occasional Red Cross packages.[32]

The routine at Karenko was grim and monotonous. Each day opened with a roll call and a bow to the emperor of Japan, followed by a breakfast of two-thirds cup of rice and a bowl of vegetable soup. Lunch and dinner were essentially the same. The officers were organized into ten-man squads for most activities—eating, roll call, bathing, and monthly weighing. Most disturbing was the constant slapping for minor infractions, the requirement to salute all Japanese, and the menial labor they were required to do.[33]

In the fall of 1942, the monotony was broken with the arrival of 357 British, Dutch, and Australian officers and enlisted men as well as some high-ranking civilian officials who had been captured in Hong Kong, Singapore, Borneo, or the East Indies. Lt. Gen. Arthur E. Percival, commander of the British forces at Singapore, led them into camp.

In April 1943, 117 of the highest-ranking officers and civilians—general officers, governors, and chief justices—were sent thirty-six miles south to a new camp at Tamazato. The colonels were left behind. Conditions at Tamazato were an improvement in many ways. No work was required, and the prisoners were allowed a degree of independence in running the camp while permitted to take over the kitchen. Two weeks after arriving there, the men received Red Cross packages that contained corned beef, liver paste, cocoa, salt, bacon, marmalade, chocolate, cheese, candies, and even American cigarettes.

The generals suffered no beatings at Tamazato, though some guards kept up mild harassment and hazing. The same rules remained in effect, though, particularly the requirement that all prisoners must bow low before every Japanese soldier, no matter his rank.

In early June 1943 the prisoners were divided into two groups. Wainwright, Moore, King, Percival, and a few others remained at Tamazato, while the others were sent to an unnamed destination. Two and a half weeks later the generals' group was taken by train to Karenko, marched to the dock, and herded aboard a small, filthy freighter. The next stop was at Muksaq, in northern Formosa, where they would spend the next sixteen months. The new camp's buildings were made of rough pine boards on a hill above a valley of rice fields. The structure housing the POWs was a long one-story affair, with a straight hall down the center and eight small rooms to each side. Each room had an easy chair, bamboo cot, and a table for meals and writing. The prisoners were given more rice than during the early days of captivity and were also given vegetables. They were able to buy a little clothing, which they wore over the Philippine summer uniforms they had on when captured.[34]

On the night of October 5, 1944, the POWs were taken to Taihoku and put on a train that arrived at Heito, near the southern tip of Formosa, the next day. The following day the group was taken by truck to a nearby airport, where planes were waiting to fly them to the southern end of Kyushu, southernmost of the four main Japanese home islands.

Arriving in Japan on October 7 at the large city of Beppu, the prisoners were taken to a hotel, where they were delighted to find all of the American generals last seen at Tamazato in June 1943. The entire group was taken to a seaport and packed like fish into a small ship. The vessel took them to Pusan, Korea, where they were placed aboard a train that took them to Sheng Tai Tun in western Manchuria. The weather was freezing, and the long stay in the tropics had acclimated them to much-warmer temperatures. None had overcoats or any warm clothing.[35]

The barren camp had once been occupied by Russian troops guarding the Manchurian railway. Once assigned to rooms, the first order of business for the men was to get the old Russian stoves working. The fire had to be constantly stoked because of the poor quality of the coal. And their first meal made everyone realize that they had moved out of the rice-growing regions, for it contained real white bread and a thick vegetable cake mixed with maize or millet. It was a hard life at Sheng Tai Tun, there being no work to do and walking outside in the piercing gales being too rigorous. Warm clothing was not available, so prisoners could not move far from the stoves. There also was no hot water or soap for washing. The kitchen, bathhouse, and latrine were thirty or forty yards away from the barracks across open land.

On December 1, 1944, sixteen senior generals along with their orderlies were ordered to pack up again. Their next stop was near Sian in northeast Manchuria. This was an unpleasant POW camp, and the nine months spent there were a mind-numbing agony of cold, hunger, and boredom in the winter and unbearable heat, hunger, and boredom in the summer. The food was never sufficient and the taste of what was available was poor. Breakfast was a kind of soup mush; lunch was a thin, watery soup; and supper was vegetables and soybean curd. Red Cross packages to supplement the diet were few and far between. Although the guards did not beat the prisoners at Sian, there remained a constant harassment.[36]

The prisoners first learned of the war's end on August 16, 1945, when one of the interpreters told an American corporal the news and that Russian troops had entered Manchuria. The next morning at roll call, the camp commander read aloud in Japanese from a prepared script and then nodded to the interpreter. The interpreter said, "By order of the Emperor the war has now been amicably terminated." Laughter broke out in the ranks, and it seemed that it would never stop. The long ordeal was over.

At the War Department in Washington, Gen. George C. Marshall and his staff were concerned about Wainwright; no one knew where he and the other Bataan and Corregidor senior officers were. Their worry was that the Japanese might execute him at the last moment in a fanatical act of reprisal.

Throughout China and Manchuria, teams of Office of Special Services (OSS) personnel parachuted into every known POW camp. They soon learned that Wainwright, Moore, and other generals were held at Sian. On the morning of August 17, OSS major J. T. Hennessey and four members of his rescue team arrived at the Japanese camp at Hoten, just outside Mukden. Several of Wainwright's friends were there and bombarded the OSS men with questions about the war. Breaking away from the crowd, the major went to the camp commandant's office to inquire about Wainwright. He learned that the general was one hundred miles away at Sian. Hennessey summoned Maj. Robert F. Lamar, a flight surgeon, and Sgt. Harold Leith, a specialist fluent in Russian and Chinese, and made plans to leave for Sian the next morning, arriving there on the morning of August 19. The guard at the gate notified Lieutenant Marui, the camp commandant, who received Lamar gratuitously in his office. The major asked to see the prisoners, but Marui refused. He pressed the issue, demanding to see them at once and threatening reprisals; the two men argued for some time. Then the lieutenant offered a compromise: Lamar could see Wainwright now and the others in the morning. A few minutes later a tall, emaciated figure appeared at the doorway; the major had trouble recognizing the man as Wainwright from the photos he had seen. The general remained at the door, for a prisoner did not enter the commandant's office without permission, until Marui beckoned him into the room. Wainwright stepped inside and bowed low to the lieutenant. Lamar rose and offered the general his chair, a gesture that offended Marui: "He must remain standing," he shouted. Finally, Marui relented to the major's insistence, and Wainwright sat down in the same room as a Japanese soldier for the first time in three and a half years. "General," Lamar said, "you are no longer a prisoner. You're going back to the States."[37]

Lamar tried to contact Major Hennessey, but his radio was not working and the telephone lines had been destroyed by the advancing Russians. He decided to go to Mukden and return with a convoy of vehicles to take the prisoners out, explaining the plan to Wainwright and promising that he would return in two days. The POWs remained in the camp waiting for his return. The only thing that had changed in the meantime was that the Japanese distributed all the Red Cross parcels they had been hoarding. A third day passed since Lamar's departure and he still did not appear. In Mukden Lamar had been trying for two days to arrange transportation, but the Russians in charge there were not interested in American prisoners one hundred miles away.

On August 24 a Russian unit entered the camp. Using Sergeant Leith as interpreter, Wainwright made a deal with the Soviet colonel to accompany them to Mukden, with the understanding the Americans would provide their own transportation. He then ordered Marui to supply two buses and a truck for the former prisoners. The lieutenant, "afraid of the Russians, said, 'Yes sir.' Wainwright was shocked to hear these words from a Japanese soldier."

That evening the Russians led the convoy of troops and ex-prisoners out of Sian. Expecting to reach Mukden the next day, the Americans were disappointed when they realized the column was lost. The next day, when one of the buses got stuck in the mud, the Russians threatened to abandon Wainwright and his companions. Then someone spotted a narrow-gauge railroad line and learned from a Chinese local that the spur connected to the main track to Mukden. Minutes later a small engine hauling three cars came along, which the Russians flagged down. A heated discussion with the train drivers followed, but after the soldiers brandished their weapons, the Japanese crew agreed to transport the Americans to the main line.

The prisoners loaded their few belongings and bade farewell to their liberators. The little train started off, but before it was out of sight of the convoy, the engine jumped the track. The Russian colonel drove up and said he would go ahead to the main line and see if he could find another train for them. At daybreak on August 26, the replacement arrived and took the group to the main line, where they learned there would be no train to Mukden until late that evening. After a while the colonel grew tired of waiting and commandeered a train that was bound for another destination. At 7:00 p.m. they all departed, reaching Mukden at 1:30 on the next morning. The group of officers was flown to Chungking later that day.[38]

Lt. Gen. Albert C. Wedemeyer greeted the former prisoners at the Chungking airport and took Wainwright, Moore, Jones, and Beebe to his home, where he provided them with a luxurious bath and had

General Moore, center, returning from captivity. *Official US Army Photo*

their tattered clothing replaced with his own fine uniforms. That afternoon, in a deeply moving ceremony on the lawn outside the American headquarters, Wainwright, Moore, and Jones were awarded the Distinguished Service Cross.

Wainwright was invited to participate in the formal surrender ceremony aboard the USS *Missouri* in Tokyo Bay on September 2, 1945. He was accompanied by Percival, Beebe, his aides Dooley and Pugh, and his enlisted aide, Sgt. Hubert Carroll. The general also took along those who had been with him when he surrendered the Philippines.[39]

The day following the ceremony in Chungking, Moore, King, Jones, and several others flew to Manila and then on to San Francisco and Washington, D.C. Moore made the long trip back to the United States and his family for a well-deserved period of rest and recuperation after five years overseas. Thirty-nine months of that time had been as a prisoner of war living in harsh conditions, suffering mistreatment, and subsisting on near-starvation rations.[40]

Maj. Gen. George F. Moore returned to the Philippines after the war and served as commander of the army forces of the West Pacific. *Official US Army Photo*

After regaining his health, Moore's next assignment was in Hawaii as commanding general of the US Army Middle Pacific forces. He was not able to enjoy living in Hawaii for long, however, because in late October 1946 General MacArthur ordered him to Manila to assume duties as commander of army forces in the West Pacific. This sudden change came as a result of problems in the Philippines. There were claims of poor morale among the American soldiers, complaints against their behavior, and reports of theft and black-market activities. In May 1947 Moore announced that 145 US Army personnel, including thirteen officers and three civil-service employees, had been found guilty of theft or black-market offenses in the Philippines over a fifteen-month period. On December 31, as a result of command shifts in the Pacific ordered by President Truman, MacArthur announced that Moore was given the new title of commander of the Philippines and Ryukyus rather than of West Pacific ground forces.[41]

On October 12, 1947, Corregidor was transferred to the Philippine government in a ceremony attended by Moore and about four hundred invited guests. Among them were thirty survivors of the five-month siege and fall of the island in 1941–42. As the American flag was lowered and the Philippine flag raised, it marked the first time since the Spanish took it over to establish a fortress in 1793 that Corregidor was again in Filipino possession.[42]

Moore's last official act in the Philippines was to present a check for $46,889,000 as an advance for payment of claims to Filipino guerrillas and former soldiers. Pres. Elpidio Quirino honored the general with a state banquet in recognition of his success in repairing the strained relations between the US Army and Filipino civilians, which were at the lowest ebb in many years when he had assumed command in 1946.

In July 1948 Moore was succeeded by Maj. Gen. Jonathan W. Anderson. He returned to San Francisco to serve as deputy commander of the Sixth Army under Gen. Mark Clark. Retiring in 1949, he made his home in Burlingame Hills, California.

Maj. Gen. George F. Moore's military decorations include the Distinguished Service Cross, Distinguished Service Medal, and Republic of the Philippines Distinguished Conduct Star.

On the night of December 2, 1949, Moore drove to a tree-dotted field near Hillsborough, a suburb of San Francisco. He shot himself in the right temple, his body found by the local police with a .38-caliber service revolver in his hand. Moore left a note at his home for his wife, but it was not made public. The local chief of police said the general was known to have been despondent because of ill health resulting from his years of imprisonment by the Japanese.

Last rites were held at the Golden Gates National Cemetery, San Bruno, California. Moore was survived by his widow, Lucille, and a daughter, Mrs. Burton H. Browne, of New York.[43]

Expressing the feelings of all of the surviving prisoners of war, Gen. Albert Jones said, "We who went through similar experiences and who find we are unable to remember things and get the shakes, etc., can sympathize with the view point that he feared he was losing his mind."[44]

★ 2 ★

Father of Fort Hood

ANDREW D. BRUCE

CLASS OF 1916

"I wasn't born in Texas, but I got here as soon as I could" would have been an appropriate bumper sticker for Andrew Davis Bruce's automobile if they had existed when he was growing up. Born in Saint Louis, Missouri, on September 14, 1894, the son of John Logan and Martha Washington Smith Bruce, he attended school in that city and received his high school diploma from Kentucky Wesley Academy in 1911.

When his father purchased land holdings during the earliest development in the lower Rio Grande Valley, the family moved to Mercedes, Texas, and later to San Antonio. Bruce enrolled in Texas A&M in the fall of 1912, majoring in dairy husbandry. He was one of more than 235 freshmen entering the 868-strong Corps of Cadets that year and became a member of Company A. His junior year Bruce was the regimental color sergeant and the adjutant on the corps staff his senior year. He was also active in student publications, serving as assistant editor of the *Battalion*, the school newspaper, and as assistant manager of the *1914 Longhorn*, the school yearbook. Bruce served in leadership positions on committees to plan banquets, balls, and hops. He was a member of the Ross Volunteers, an honor military organization in the Corps of Cadets named after Lawrence Sullivan Ross, a Confederate general, former governor of Texas, and former president of Texas A&M. The *1916 Longhorn* contained a biographical sketch of Cadet Bruce that stated: "A. D. that military man, had one of his ambitions realized when he was made captain and adjutant of the regiment, the highest ranking Captain on the campus. He deserves the rank, for his attention to military as well as other duties has been faithful. 'A. D.' is a student of dairy husbandry, and everyone knows it, for that is one topic he takes great delight in discussing. The head of this department early realized Bruce's ability along dairy lines, and, as a result, he has been a student assistant for three years. Bruce is a man with a mind of his own, determined, studious, and yet never so busy that he would not give assistance when approached, often offering assistance where it was badly needed."

Events on campus in 1912–13 resulted in a student strike, and in January 1913 the full faculty ordered the immediate dismissal of twenty-seven cadets for hazing underclassmen. Among the group were numerous student leaders. A large number of cadets petitioned the administration to review and overturn the order. Officials responded that failure to comply would be considered a breach of cadet rules and grounds for dismissal.

The cadets accused of hazing were dismissed. Additionally, the 466 cadets who signed the petition in their support were dismissed for insubordination. Bruce was among this larger group, which would be known thereafter as the "466 Club." The 466 Club had a page in the college yearbook for the next three years. Disgusted with the handling of the situation, other cadets prepared to leave en masse. The corps held an unscheduled "final" dress parade, with the seniors lining up as they would have in the graduation dress parade and the underclassmen marching past. This "strike" ended when the 466 cadets were given amnesty in exchange for a pledge that they would abstain from all forms of hazing.[1]

Graduating with a bachelor of science degree in dairy husbandry on June 13, 1916, Bruce was commissioned an infantry second lieutenant. After the United States declared war on Germany, he was ordered to report to Camp Funston at Leon Springs, Texas, twenty miles northwest of San Antonio. On June 16, 1917, he received a commission in the Regular Army and the same day was promoted to first lieutenant. He was assigned to the First Officers Training Camp (similar to today's Officers Candidate School) at Camp Funston as an instructor.

Bruce's service in the Great War began in France with the 2nd Infantry Division (see map 3). That command was organized on October 26, 1917, at Boutmont as a "square division." Composed of two infantry brigades of two regiments each, the division was unique in that it had one US Army and one US Marine Corps brigade. The 3rd Brigade (army) contained the 9th and 23rd Infantry Regiments and the 5th Machine Gun Battalion. The 4th Brigade (marine) contained the 5th and 6th Marine Regiments and the 6th Machine Gun Battalion. Artillery support was provided by the 2nd Field Artillery Brigade, comprising the 12th, 15th, and 17th Field Artillery Regiments and the 2nd Trench Mortar Battery. Engineer, Signal Corps, and other units were also in support. Division strength was 25,484 officers and men, including 16,546 infantry. Later it was decided that more machine guns were necessary, and one machine-gun company was added to each regiment. Additionally, the 4th Machine Gun Battalion was activated to provide general support to the division.

It was obvious that the United States could never get its arms industry up and running fast enough to equip the military forces heading to Europe. Generally speaking, almost all of the military equipment for these troops, including artillery pieces, machine guns, automatic rifles, trench mortars, and grenades, came from the French. The United States not only paid for these items but also provided the needed raw materials to French industry. American machine-gun units (including Bruce's) used the Hotchkiss machine gun as their basic weapon.

Bruce attended the machine-gun school at Gondrecourt, and after completing the course, he was assigned to the 2nd Company (later Company A), 5th Machine Gun Battalion, as its commander. The company was stationed in the village of Soulaucourt on the banks of the Meuse River. Billeted in a room over the Café Morel, the lieutenant turned a backroom of the house into a classroom where he provided instruction on tactics and firing computations, including geometry, trigonometry, and algebra for indirect fire, learned at the machine-gun school. The evening lessons carried into the night and were usually followed by a nightcap of eggs, fried potatoes, and wine from Mme. Morel's kitchen.[2]

The initial training in Europe was provided by French officers and mainly covered trench warfare, but that concept was soon dropped. Gen. John J. Pershing, commander of the American Expeditionary Force, decided that US troops would not fight from the trenches as the Europeans but would fight "standing up and going forward." It would be maneuver warfare in its most basic design. Each division would train for three months and then interact with French divisions in a quiet sector. In March 1918 in the Verdun area, American infantry battalions began rotating into the French front lines to get some battle experience.[3]

As his company was beginning the march to the front, Bruce discovered that several of his troublesome troops had talked a French civilian into selling them cognac, the consumption of which made several unfit for duty. The lieutenant gave orders to souse every drunk in the town washbasin until the man was fit to march. A few noncommissioned officers voiced opposition and a mutiny threatened.

As the company marched out of the village, singing, shouting, and cursing broke out among the scattered squads. After a half-hour's march, Bruce called a halt. Mounted on his horse, he rode to the center of the company and addressed his men, appealing to their pride in their organization and telling them of the job to be done and the need for discipline. He was greeted with groans. Bruce then stated:

> A Company, you're going to soldier! Many of you are influenced by drink and don't realize what you're doing, but the non-commissioned officers who fail to obey orders from now on will face General Courts-Martial for mutiny. You men will face no court—listen carefully!
>
> I am going to lead the company. We are going to march. If order is restored before we reach the support position we will halt there. But, if this noise and this refusal to obey continues, we will march straight through the lines to the Boche trenches. I'll take you over the top and give you the fight you are looking for, and any man who drops will do so because of a bullet—wounded from the front or shot as a deserter behind. Squads right, March!

The threatened mutiny was over and order restored. The commanding officer meant what he said, and the men knew it.[4]

The trenches, prepared for extended service, were supplied with duck boards for the floors and sandbags for the parapets. Doors to dugouts opened into the trenches and were well reinforced with timber. The dugouts themselves were constructed to accommodate from ten to fifty soldiers, with bunks built one section above another. And all of the dugouts were infested with lice, known by the Americans as "cooties."

The frontline training program continued until commanders determined that the division had experienced combat and could be pulled out to refit and recover. The move out began in mid-May, but on the thirty-first the division was committed to the Château-Thierry sector to stop the German advance on Paris. Heavy fighting in June to drive the enemy from Belleau Wood resulted in heavy casualties in the 2nd Infantry Division, especially in the 4th Brigade. But the Americans had demonstrated their ability to stand in battle against the best of the German troops. In early July the division was replaced by the 26th Infantry Division and moved to a reserve position.[5]

In mid-July the 2nd Infantry Division was placed under French control for an advance in the Soissons sector. It was during this action that Captain Bruce was cited for bravery at Vierzy, where "he made a personal reconnaissance ahead of his troops through heavy flanking machine gun fire. He pushed forward to the outpost lines through heavy artillery and machine-gun fire to keep in touch with all of his platoons."[6]

The division was withdrawn from the Soissons sector in July after suffering heavy casualties. In a quiet area along the Moselle River, the 2nd received replacements for the men lost at Soissons. On August 27 Bruce was selected to command the 4th Machine Gun Battalion and on September 20 was promoted to major. On September 26 the American First Army, with the French Fourth Army, launched attacks on the southern German front. This was the Meuse-Argonne campaign, the final effort of the war. The most strongly held part of the enemy line was Blanc Mont Ridge in the French sector. The position gave the Germans unlimited observation of the ground that any attack must cross. Every attempt by the French to take the ridge had ended with severe losses and complete failure.[7]

At 5:50 a.m. on October 3, the two brigades of the 2nd Division jumped off in the attack on Blanc Mont. By 9:00 a.m., after heavy fighting and severe losses, the first divisional troops reached the top of the ridge. That same day Bruce "made a personal reconnaissance on the left flank of his division through heavy shell fire and continual sniping and gained information which enabled him to place his battalion to cover an exposed flank." The next day the entire ridge and the surrounding area was under the control of the Allies. On October 6 the first elements of the 36th Infantry Division arrived and were placed at the disposition of the 2nd Division; that night it took over the front line. Bruce's battalion was given the mission to protect the right flank and became heavily involved in the fighting advance of the 36th. With fourteen divisions, the Americans continued to press the Germans until the Armistice.[8]

The war was barely over when the 2nd Infantry Division and five others designated for the Army of Occupation began preparations for the march into Germany. The men began their march to the Rhine River on November 11. They passed through the territory until recently occupied by the Germans, with residents of each country along the route warmly welcoming their deliverers. The Americans were headed for the Coblenz area, with the British moving farther north and the French farther south. The occupying forces were to cross the German border no earlier than December 1, so for a few days the men just sat and waited. The 4th Machine Gun Battalion billeted in Irlich on the eastern bank of the Rhine across from Andernach.

Potential trouble from the still-organized German Army was anticipated, especially as unfavorable changes to the terms of the Armistice became obvious. Guards were posted at all bridges. In January 1919 orders even prescribed what each unit would do in the event of a surprise attack. Once these security measures had been put into place, the 2nd Division resumed their training. The Germans were exhausted after four years of war, however, so nothing came of the anticipated problems.

The 2nd Infantry Division returned to the United States in July and August 1919, and the men enjoyed a long-overdue parade in New York City followed by another in Washington. The division then returned to its permanent station at Fort Sam Houston in San Antonio.[9]

In May 1919 Bruce had been promoted, becoming one of the youngest lieutenant colonels in the army at the age of twenty-three. But after returning to the States, he received a peacetime adjustment in rank and became a first lieutenant again, soon promoted to captain. Bruce married Roberta Linnell Kennedy on June 28, 1920. He attended the Infantry School at Fort Benning, Georgia, in 1923 and after graduation served as an instructor at the school. He then completed the Advanced Course at the Field Artillery School at Fort Sill, Oklahoma. Returning to Fort Benning in 1925, he served on the Infantry School Board, was involved in weapons development, and then served as a company commander in the 29th Infantry Regiment. A son, Andrew Davis Bruce Jr., and a daughter, Linnell Bruce, were born during his tours of duty in Georgia.

In 1928 Bruce was assigned as the professor of military science and tactics at Allen Academy in Bryan, Texas. Allen Academy was the oldest boy's preparatory school in Texas, established in Madisonville in 1886 and moved to Bryan in 1899, offering four grades of high school instruction and one year of college. In 1923 the army's adjutant general designated it as one of the essentially military schools to undergo the honor-rating inspection by the War Department. During the following years, the academy received the honor rating and in 1927 became the first school in Texas to receive the rating of "honor military school." Allen's principal, Nat B. Allen, cited this achievement as instrumental in increasing enrollment to 241 students the following school year.

The officer Bruce replaced, Capt. George W. Griner, had been at the school for four and a half years, in that time endearing himself to the student body, the faculty, and the citizens of Bryan. It was believed that largely through his efforts, Allen Academy received and retained the proud distinction of an honor school.

The War Department inspection team's arrival in April 1929 was advertised extensively. Pathe News filmed the inspection, showing the actual tests through which the cadets were put to obtain the honor rating. A copy of the finished production was purchased by the academy and shown in local theaters. When the East Texas Chamber of Commerce held its annual convention in Bryan in May 1929, the film was shown to the delegates, who were invited afterward to view the inspection scenes. After all of the publicity, and to the chagrin of Principal Allen, the academy did not retain the honor rating in 1929. The relationship between Captain Bruce and the faculty and students had not been harmonious, and losing the rating was unacceptable to the institution. At the request of the principal, Bruce was relieved of his three-year assignment after only the first year, and Captain Griner once again was detailed to the school. In the spring of 1930, Allen Academy was once again endorsed by the War Department as an "honor military school."[10]

This blemish on Bruce's military record was not serious enough to prevent his attending the US Army Command and General Staff College at Fort Leavenworth, Kansas, in 1931. Instruction at the staff college remains an essential step in the career progression of an army officer. Following graduation, Bruce was assigned to the 33rd Infantry Regiment at Fort Clayton in the Panama Canal Zone. While there, he served as an infantry company commander and later as a battalion operations officer. His time in Panama gave him an appreciation of jungle warfare that would prove valuable in later years.

On November 1, 1934, Bruce was promoted to major, and the following year he continued his military education at the Army War College at Washington. Following graduation, he was selected to attend the Naval War College at Newport, Rhode Island, graduating in 1937.[11]

In 1940, when the German Blitzkrieg overran Denmark, Norway, and Belgium, followed by the invasion of France, President Roosevelt and members of Congress finally became aware of the need to increase the size of the army and of the military budget for new weapons. Lawmakers first voted to increase the Regular Army to its full strength of 280,000 men, then to 375,000. After the fall of France, the War Department recommended an army of 1 million men by October 1, 1941, and two million by January 1, 1942.

On May 14, 1941, Maj. Gen. Lesley J. McNair, the commander of General Headquarters, Field Forces, ordered the creation of a "planning and exploring" command to pursue research. Placed in charge of the unit was Lieutenant Colonel Bruce, a young member of the War Department's general staff. After a series of conferences addressing the tank threat on the battlefield, Bruce submitted a detailed memorandum that called for separate antitank battalions. General McNair acted on the recommendation by establishing an antitank center under War Department control.

On November 27 the department ordered the activation of the Tank Destroyer Tactical and Firing Center. It called for the activation of fifty-three tank-destroyer battalions under the direct control of this new center. This essentially created a new arm of service whose task it would be to develop tank-destroyer doctrine, equipment, and training.

McNair insisted that Bruce be named first commander of this unit; the army's chief of staff, Gen. George C. Marshall, agreed.

The temporary location of Bruce's new command was Fort Meade, Maryland. There he began assembling an organization that would formulate, develop, and make recommendations to the War Department concerning tactics and training methods for tank-destroyer forces, cooperate in developing new weapons, and organize and operate the Tank Destroyer Tactical and Firing Center, the Tank Destroyer Board, and the Tank Destroyer School. In line with his new responsibilities, Bruce was promoted to colonel. Right away he began evaluating the various places that had been recommended as the location for a camp where training could take place. This would have to be a new post, for no base operated by the army was suitable for the needs of his new command.[12]

On December 19 Bruce and a few of his top officers, all dressed in civilian clothes, left Washington to make a quiet and hurried inspection of several potential sites. When the group arrived in Temple, Texas, to make unannounced and incognito visits to Killeen and Gatesville, they were surprised to be met by Frank Mayborn, publisher of the *Temple Daily Telegram*, and members of the Defense Projects Committee, a local group dedicated to securing an army camp in the local area. (The Santa Fe Railroad agent in Washington had learned of the trip and alerted Mayborn about it.)

On January 10, 1942, the army announced that the new Tank Destroyer Center would be located at Killeen and would require 109,000 acres, making it the largest military post in the US Army, on which some 1,800 buildings would be erected at a cost of $35 million. Until the land was acquired and temporary buildings constructed, headquarters would be in Temple. By February 17 there were some thirty officers and several civilian employees in the small Texas city. In recognition of the tremendous responsibilities now given to Bruce, on the thirteenth the army had promoted him to brigadier general.[13]

On March 12, bids were opened for actual construction and contracts let. On the thirty-first the 893rd Tank Destroyer Battalion arrived to erect a field camp near Gatesville with material salvaged from abandoned Civilian Conservation Corps sites. Two weeks later the 753rd Tank Destroyer Battalion arrived, and training began even as civilians were still living on many parts of what would become the army reservation.

Tank Destroyer headquarters at Camp Hood, Texas, in 1942.
Public domain (Post card from personal collection)

Although Bruce and his entire command had moved from Temple to the main cantonment near Killeen on August 12, it would not be until September 18 that ceremonies marked the official opening of Camp Hood. On August 17 the Advanced Unit Training Center was activated, with the mission to organize and train new tank-destroyer battalions. The Tank Destroyer School was also organized to provide specialized technical training to officers and enlisted men. By the end of 1942, the units had trained and shipped out six tank-destroyer battalions and had begun the instruction of seven more.[14]

Because of the rapid increase in size and scope of the command at Camp Hood, on September 23, Bruce was promoted to major general. On May 25, 1943, he was notified that he was to become an infantry division commander. The general was relieved of command of the Tank Destroyer Center and transferred to the 77th Infantry Division. By this time most of the tasks assigned Bruce in November 1941 had been accomplished. The Tank Destroyer Center, including excellent firing ranges and maneuver areas as well as housing facilities for 80,000 troops, had been built, while thousands more men were bivouacked in the field. An administrative structure had been planned and then

Early tank destroyer. M3 half-track with mounted 75-mm cannon.
Courtesy the author

---

carried into reality. Sound tactical and training doctrine had been formulated and suitable weapons had been developed. All this had been accomplished with a speed unknown in American military history: just eighteen months had passed since the order to create the Tank Destroyer Tactical and Firing Center and train battalions. Tank destroyers became virtually a separate arm of the army, equal to infantry, armor, and artillery. By early 1943 there were 106 active battalions of tank destroyers.[15]

The 77th "Statue of Liberty" Infantry Division had been reactivated on March 25, 1942, at Fort Jackson, South Carolina. It had amassed a distinguished combat record in World War I. After activation, the division participated in the Louisiana Maneuvers in early 1943, and on May 27, when Bruce assumed command, it was at the Desert Training Center in California. The division returned to the East Coast and was based at several locations, with headquarters at Camp Pickett, Virginia. The three infantry regiments (305th, 306th and 307th) and the division artillery rotated between training areas at Indiantown Gap, Pennsylvania; Camp Bradford, Maryland; and the West Virginia Training Area.

Maj. Gen. Andrew D. Bruce commanded the 77th Infantry Division in the Pacific. *Official US Army Photo*

Bruce insisted that his soldiers wear leggings, use helmet liners, and carefully police barracks and outside areas, earning the nickname "Old Man Leggings, Liners, and Landscape." Throughout its training, the 77th Division had a reputation for leaving its camp and maneuver areas clean and thoroughly policed.[16]

In February 1944 the entire division assembled at Camp Pickett, Virginia, to prepare for overseas deployment. During March 8–13, the men moved by train to Camp Stoneman, California, where they loaded aboard navy transports for the journey to Hawaii. Bruce flew to the islands by clipper and was waiting on the dock to watch the troops file down the gangplanks and board waiting trucks and miniature railway cars for runs to camps on the northeast side of Oahu. Scattered among several camps, the men began an intensive program of jungle and amphibious training. Top-secret documents received by headquarters indicated that the division would be committed to Saipan, Tinian, or Guam. The staff began to plan for employment in any of these areas.

With the capture of Saipan and Tinian, the focus now shifted to Guam (see map 4). A US possession prior to its capture by the Japanese on December 12, 1941, the island lies 3,320 miles from Pearl Harbor, 1,499 miles from Manila, and 1,595 miles from Tokyo. Guam is 34.5 miles in length and varies from 5 to 9 miles in width, with an area of 228 square miles. The southern and central portions are chiefly rolling hills culminating in a few rugged mountains. The occasional villages, plantations, and clearings are surrounded by dense woods and jungle. The northern part of the island is mostly heavy jungle, while unbroken coral reefs entirely surround it.

The American assault in 1944 was carried out by the III Amphibious Corps, with the 3rd Marine Division and 1st Provisional Marine Brigade making the initial landings. The 305th Regimental Combat Team (RCT) of the 77th Division was attached to the 1st Provisional Brigade and would land on the first day on orders of the brigade commander. The remaining 77th units would be in corps reserve.

The 305th departed Hawaii in early July and arrived at the island of Eniwetok on July 9, remaining afloat until joined by the rest of the division on July 17 before proceeding to Guam. The 305th made its landing on July 21 and assisted the 1st Provisional Brigade in taking Mount Alifan the following day. On July 22 the remainder of the 77th Division, less the 307th RCT, was ordered ashore to relieve the marine brigade on the entire beachhead line so it could reorganize and continue the attack.

The 3rd Marine Division met heavy resistance over difficult terrain in the drive from the north of Guam as it sought to close a gap between its beachheads and those of the 77th Division in the south. The capture of Mount Tenjo by the 77th was the final link in forging a single continuous beachhead for American forces. On the night of July 25–26, the Japanese lost an estimated 3,500 men in counterattacks against the now-unified beachhead.[17]

There was concern about the strength of enemy forces in the southern part of the island, and the 77th was tasked to conduct reconnaissance patrols in that area. Five patrols over a period of six days revealed that the majority of the Japanese had moved north, except for a few small groups still roaming the southern jungles.

With the southern part of the island basically secure, the attack to the north continued on July 31, with the 3rd Marine Division on the left and the 77th Division on the right. Both commands met only scattered resistance until August 2, when the army troops caught up with the withdrawing enemy at the village of Barrigada. The next day General Bruce pushed his army regiments forward through heavy jungles. In planning for the advance, he gave some attention to the problem of contact between units. On August 2 his main body had been out of contact with the 3rd Marine Division, and the drive northeast through the thick jungle would make lateral liaison more difficult. Bruce subscribed to the theory that in jungle fighting, close contact between units should not be insisted upon to the sacrifice of rapidity of advance and destruction of the enemy. Drawing on his experiences in Panama in 1933, the principles of jungle warfare he had developed there were later partly incorporated into the army manual on the subject. He also had impressed his theories on the 77th Division during training.

By nightfall of August 8, the end of the fighting on Guam was virtually at hand. The 3rd Marine Division had advanced to within a mile and a half of the sea, and the gains of the 77th Division around Mount Santa Rosa combined with the occupation of the entire northwest coast of the island by the 1st Provisional Brigade spelled the doom of the remaining Japanese. The end of organized resistance came with the capture of Mount Santa Rosa. On August 10 the corps commander announced the official conclusion of the campaign, though that did not mean the fighting was actually over. The soldiers and marines spent many weeks before they finally cleared out the enemy-infested jungles and mountains of Guam.

The 77th Division remained on the island in a large bivouac area on the hills east of the west-coast town of Agat. The troops spread out over the ridges, pitched pup tents, and built native-type shacks of bamboo and palm. The rainy season was on, and nothing was ever really dry. Clothing and equipment mildewed. The cart road running three miles uphill from Agat was a path of mud and practically impassable to vehicles. Food and supplies had to be hand carried at least two miles directly uphill through mud and rain.

Training now resumed. Patrolling exercises took place over terrain still traversed by occasional Japanese stragglers, adding realism to the training. A rifle range was improvised, and a weapons-training program was conducted by all units. All of this took advantage of lessons learned during the battle.

Eventually, the 18,500 men of the Japanese garrison were either killed or captured. American casualties as of August 10, 1944, came to 7,800 men, of whom 2,124 were killed in action or died of wounds. Of this total, the army accounted for 839, the navy for 245, while the remaining 6,716 were marines.

The 77th Division departed Guam on November 3 aboard navy transports bound for a rest area on New Caledonia. On November 11, though, when the force was four days from New Caledonia, radioed orders directed the convoy to turn northwest and put in at Manus in the Admiralty Islands. Arriving there on the seventeenth, most of the troops had an opportunity to spend part of a day on a recreation island where beer and activities were available. Two days later the division departed for Leyte in the Philippine Islands.[18]

American forces had surrendered Leyte to the Japanese on May 20, 1942. When on October 20, 1944, the US Sixth Army landed on the island, General MacArthur's promise to Maj. Gen. George Moore to return to the Philippines was fulfilled. Leyte roughly resembles a molar tooth, with the crown pointing toward Samar to the north and the roots toward Mindanao to the south. It is the eighth largest island in the Philippines, with an area of 2,785 square miles, an approximate length of 115 miles, and a varying width of 15–45 miles. Mainly volcanic in origin, a range of mountains forms the backbone of the island.[19]

The invasion force consisted of the X Corps, comprising the 1st Cavalry and 24th Infantry Divisions, and the XXIV Corps, consisting of the 7th and 96th Infantry Divisions. The beachheads were on the east coast of Leyte. Initially serving as the army reserve, Bruce's 77th Infantry Division came ashore on November 25. Although the beaches were secure by then, unloading cargo and equipment from the ships was difficult since there were no piers. The 307th RCT moved inland to La Paz to guard the roads and passes in the area. The rest of the division established beach defenses and conducted widespread patrols of the area. In addition, 1,300 officers and men were furnished to handle cargo for a task force preparing to capture the island of Mindoro.

Warning orders were received on December 1 alerting the division for a shore-to-shore movement and assault landing on the west coast of Leyte in the Ormoc area. The operation was intended to disrupt Japanese resistance, prevent further enemy reinforcement, and break down their supply lines and communications.[20]

The first wave of Americans hit the beach south of Ormoc on December 7 and moved inland against very little opposition. The entire force, including artillery and all supplies, was ashore in two and a half hours. The initial plan was to hold the beachhead until the arrival of supplies and reinforcements via a convoy due to arrive two days later, but owning to the light resistance, the speed with which the troops moved inland, and his desire to exploit the situation before the Japanese could counterattack, Bruce decided to continue the advance to the north.

Attacking along the road toward Ormoc, two RCTs met increased resistance. The terrain was favorable to defenders, with finger ridges extending from the east to the road and rice paddies bordering it on both sides. Reaching Camp Downes—a prewar military post south of Ormoc—the troops were ordered to continue the attack the next morning. As the men moved out, they encountered little resistance until the outskirts of Ormoc, where a steep ravine lay between them and the southern edge of the town. An enemy force, which had dug in on both sides of the ravine, had to be rooted out with bayonets, grenades, and mortars. Despite the determined resistance, American casualties were light. Fighting in the town was street by street and house by house. On December 10 Ormoc, now reduced to gutted buildings and rubble, was captured.[21]

General Bruce had been one of the earliest officers to recognize the value of the light aircraft in combat. While at the Tank Destroyer Center, he was quick to realize their importance in connection with the tank-destroyer battalions he was training. The general put his observations into effect on Leyte when he flew missions in a liaison plane to coordinate air strikes and artillery bombardments.

Bruce issued orders for the resumption of the offensive on the morning of December 13. The division objective that day was Valencia, located in the north part of the island. The 305th RCT attacked up Highway 2, while the 306th and 307th RCTs moved to the left through the jungle-covered mountains. This was a calculated risk that depended on the 305th pushing through to open the highway and affect a junction with the other two regiments. The risk paid off when the 306th RCT arrived at the road on the evening of December 17. The division continued the attack the next day and captured the village. On December 21 the 306th RCT made contact with the leading elements of the 1st Cavalry Division, linking organizations of the X and XXIV Corps. On December 26 MacArthur declared that, except for minor mopping-up operations, the campaign for Leyte was over. As with many of the general's pronouncements, though, this was not completely accurate. Some 15,000 Japanese continued to resist in a number of pockets in the mountains of central and northern Leyte. It was not until mid-February 1945 that the grim, dangerous task of reducing these holdouts was accomplished.[22]

The Leyte campaign lasted much longer than MacArthur had imagined but brought unexpected results. The Third and Seventh Fleets had effectively destroyed most of the remaining Japanese Navy. The warplanes and pilots lost trying to defend Leyte could never be replaced. Japanese army units committed to the campaign were among the best in the Philippines, and almost all of the estimated 65,000 troops were killed at a cost to the Americans of 35,000 dead.[23]

The 77th Division was still engaged in mopping-up operations when it was alerted to prepare for the invasion of the Ryukyu Islands on January 11, 1945. A planning group left for Hawaii, where it prepared the preliminary plans for the 77th's part in the coming campaign. Meanwhile, the soldiers continued to clear Leyte of Japanese stragglers and to prepare for the next battle. The division was relieved by the Americal Division on February 5 and during March 18–24 departed the Philippines for their next assignment.[24]

The Ryukyu Islands lie southwest of Japan proper and northeast of Formosa and the Philippines. The exposed peaks of submerged mountains, these islands stretch in an arc about seven hundred miles long between Kyushu and Formosa and form a boundary between the East China Sea and the Pacific Ocean. The chain consists of about 140 islands, but only 30 are large enough to support substantial populations.

Approximately in the center of the arc is a group of some fifty islands clustered around the island of Okinawa. The Kerama Islands lie in an area from ten to twenty miles west of southern Okinawa. Ie Shima rises just beyond the tip of the Motobu Peninsula on the northern part of the island. The entire Okinawa group is surrounded by seas warm enough to support coral, which surrounds all of the islands in a fairly extensive reef, some extending several miles offshore.

Okinawa is the largest of the Ryukyu Islands. Running generally north to south, it is 60 miles long and 2–18 miles wide, with an area of

485 square miles. It is entirely fringed with reefs, which on the western side lie fairly close to shore and is seldom over a mile wide, though on the eastern side these extend for some distance offshore. In 1940 the population of the island was 435,000 people, most of whom subsisted through small-scale agriculture.[25]

Lt. Gen. Simon B. Buckner Jr. of the Tenth Army would be the ground commander on Okinawa. His forces consisted of the US Army's XXIV Corps (7th and 96th Infantry Divisions), the US Marines' III Amphibious Corps (1st and 6th Marine Divisions), the 27th Infantry Division as a floating reserve, the 2nd Marine Division as a demonstration landing force, and the 77th Infantry Division as the western islands landing force. The 81st Infantry Division was the area reserve.

The employment of the 77th was a bold action that called for landing on the Kerama Islands six days prior to the main-force invasion of Okinawa. Four battalion-landing teams of the 77th went ashore first on March 26. The first unit to land was a battalion of the 305th RCT on Aka, an island of irregular shape, measuring 3,400 by 3,000 yards and rising in a series of ridges to two peaks. The Americans were met with sporadic and ineffective mortar and machine-gun fire, and they quickly overran the beaches and the town of Aka. Geruma, a circular island five-eighths of a mile in diameter lying south of Aka, was invaded next by a battalion of the 306th RCT. The men met no opposition except for long-range sniper fire and secured the island in three hours. The easiest conquest of the day was that of Hokaji, a small island just south of Geruma. A battalion of the 306th seized it without resistance. The fourth objective was Zamami, an island 5,500 yards long east–west and 400 yards at its narrowest point formed, except for a few low, flat areas along the southern coast, by a group of wooded hills rising to 450 feet. A battalion of the 305th stormed ashore but met little resistance until they reached the town of Zamami. From there a company of Japanese fled north into the hills, where they offered stiff resistance to the Americans for some time.

By late morning General Bruce realized that the rapid progress of his landing teams would permit the seizure of an additional island. Accordingly, he ordered a battalion from the 307th RCT to take Yakabi, essentially a rough and steep hill mass rising from the water measuring 1,500 by 1,200 yards. It had practically no beaches, but the buildings of a large copper mine clung to its slopes above the most passable landing site. Meeting only slight opposition, the battalion quickly overran it.

On March 27 the 306th RCT landed on Tokashiki, the closest island to Okinawa and the largest in the Keramas, six miles long north–south and about one mile in width. It was captured without opposition.

By the evening of March 29, all of the Kerama Islands were in American hands. The 77th Division had made fifteen separate landings during the operation. Casualties were low. From March 26 to 31, the men killed 530 enemy soldiers and took 121 prisoners at a cost of 31 Americans killed and 81 wounded.[26]

On Easter Sunday, April 1, 1945, forces of the Tenth Army, with four divisions abreast, assaulted the west coast of Okinawa. The entire landing took place with almost incredible ease. By nightfall the beachhead was 15,000 yards long and in places as much as 5,000 yards deep. The next few days the invading force advanced inland against light resistance. But it was a different experience for the supporting naval vessels, which were under constant aerial assault and suffered heavy losses due to bombing attacks and suicide planes.

Following the mopping up of enemy forces on the Kerama Islands, the 77th Division boarded ships and put to sea. The convoy moved 350 miles away from the Ryukyus to escape Japanese air activity. Bruce and his staff remained aboard the USS *Mount McKinley*, anchored in the Keramas, where they closely followed the battle on Okinawa. Soon they came to realize that the division's next target would be Ie Shima.

Lying off the northwest coast of Okinawa, Ie Shima constituted a massive, permanent "aircraft carrier" at the doorstep of Japan proper. This island, measuring five miles by two and a half miles, has a level plateau covering almost its entire area. The plateau is broken on the east by Iegusugu Mountain, which rises abruptly for about 600 feet and appropriately called "the Pinnacle" by soldiers. South of the Pinnacle lies the town of Ie, consisting of about three hundred houses. The Japanese had established an airbase with three landing strips, each more than 5,500 feet long.

Enemy strength on Ie Shima was unknown, with estimates ranging from none to 5,000 men. Even though the evidence indicated that the island had been evacuated, Bruce and his staff looked at the reports with suspicion. They believed that at least 2,500 Japanese still occupied Ie Shima. Therefore, the general objected to an army proposal that the 77th land two companies in daylight to reconnoiter the island. In fact, the Japanese had expended human labor on a vast scale to make pillboxes out of houses and tombs; to dig trenches, tunnels, and gun emplacements on ridges; and to conceal rifle pits, machine gun, and mortar positions in hedgerows. The numerous natural caves were strengthened by tunnels and firing positions.

Field Order No. 26 was completed on April 12. General Bruce had used a rule of "landing where they ain't" on Guam and Leyte to good effect, and he used this same principle in planning for Ie Shima. The poorer beaches on the south and southwest coasts of the island were selected for the invasion sites.[27]

The landings on April 16 were made without incident, and two battalions of the 305th and two battalions of the 306th were ashore before nine in the morning. Scattered resistance was experienced in most areas, but as the troops moved inland, enemy fire intensified. The airfield was quickly overrun, and by nightfall the 306th's assault battalions had advanced about 5,500 yards. The 1st Battalion of the 305th advanced another 800 yards, and the 3rd Battalion had moved 1,800 yards inland. During the night the Japanese launched a coordinated attack on the 3rd Battalion with a suicidal recklessness. Supported by mortars and artillery, the enemy was armed with small arms, sharpened stakes, bags of hand grenades, and hundreds of satchel charges. After five hours of desperate fighting in the dark, the surviving attackers withdrew, leaving behind 152 dead.

The next day the Americans continued their advance across the island. The strongest Japanese positions, aside from in or around the Pinnacle, were along a prominent ridge and in a small rise topped by a large concrete building. These positions came to be known as "Bloody Ridge" and "Government House Hill." For two days the 305th and 307th battered in vain against Bloody Ridge, south of the Pinnacle.

On April 18 Ernie Pyle, renowned war correspondent, was on his way to the 77th Division's front in a jeep when he was killed by a Japanese machine gun hidden in the terraced coral slopes along the side of the road. Only after three hours of intense patrol action was the enemy position destroyed. Pyle was buried in the division's cemetery under a crude marker that was later replaced by a permanent monument. Its inscription reads: "At this spot the 77th Infantry Division lost a buddy, Ernie Pyle, 18 April 1945."[28]

Bruce was determined to break the deadlock, and on April 19 he reconnoitered the eastern approaches to Iegusugu by sailing around the eastern end of Ie Shima in a patrol boat. From his floating observation post, the general was able to study the terrain as it would appear to attacking infantrymen. He concluded that the most promising direction for the attack would be across the favorable terrain north and east of the Pinnacle.

The main effort was launched against the strongest Japanese positions on Bloody Ridge in an attack by the 305th and 307th RCTs. After seizing Bloody Ridge and Government House Hill, the 77th overwhelmed enemy forces on the Pinnacle; by April 21 the final mop up of the island began. Many Japanese civilians fought to the end with the soldiers, most armed with grenades, though some had rifles and satchel charges. Several women, some dressed in Japanese uniforms, were among these civilian fighters.[29]

At 5:30 p.m. on the twenty-first, Ie Shima was declared secure. "The last three days of this fighting were the bitterest I ever witnessed," Bruce stated when the operation was over. Still, for another five days, elements of the 77th eliminated many remaining small groups of the enemy. During this period hundreds of Japanese were killed in and around the Pinnacle, in the town of Ie, and in caves along the coast.

An interesting side note of this operation comes from a speech Bruce delivered at the 1960 Aggie Muster on the Texas A&M campus. He stated: "I sent the following message to the Governor of Texas: 'The 77th Infantry Division, after a bitter pillbox-to-pillbox, house-to-house, cave-to-cave fight, planted our American flag on the highest point of the strongly defended mountain pinnacle on Ie Shima. Men from Texas planted a Texas Flag on Bloody Ridge of the pinnacle fortress (the scene of the heaviest fighting) in honor of those gallant Texans who gathered together at Corregidor to remember San Jacinto on 21 April 1942."

During the six-day battle on Ie Shima, the Americans killed 4,706 Japanese and took 149 prisoners. US casualties through April 24 were reported as 172 killed in action, 902 wounded, and 46 missing—a total of 1,120 men.[30]

The 305th Infantry remained on the island as a garrison force until May 7, the rest of the division transferring to Okinawa on April 27. On April 29 the 77th replaced the 96th Division in their frontline positions. In a bitter battle lasting until May 5, the 307th captured the "escarpment." The division then pressed slowly southward to the towns of Shuri and Yonabaru. On May 30 Bruce's men took three hills east of Shuri, battled past "Hundred-Meter Hill," and pushed into the ruins of the town. They then covered the rear of the 96th Division and mopped up remaining resistance in the Shuri area. On June 24 the division moved to bivouac positions north of Shuri and engaged in outpost duties and patrols. Even as Okinawa was declared secure on June 26, the 77th loaded for a move to the Philippines to stage there for the next operation.[31]

The division returned to the Philippines with the mission of hastily rehabilitating, reequipping, and planning for the part the command would have in the November invasion of the Japanese home islands. Upon arrival, the men had to build their own rest camp on the east coast of Cebu Island. They afterward enjoyed an extensive recreation program, which included games, swimming, sailboat racing, movies, and dances. Bruce took an active interest in the site's development. He personally designed many of the native-style buildings and selected locations for the four enlisted men's recreation centers before the camp was laid out in detail. He was determined that his soldiers should have a pleasant camp and an enjoyable stay on Cebu. Into the midst of this program came the news of Japan's surrender.

The 77th Division received orders to prepare for occupation duties in northern Honshu or Hokkaido. The men combat loaded, left Cebu on September 26, and arrived at Hakodate, Hokkaido, on October 4. Several different areas on the island were occupied by the various units of the 77th, and Bruce was appointed military governor. This was an orderly, peaceful occupation, and the residents caused no trouble. The Japanese army and naval forces had been almost entirely demobilized prior to the occupation, so the Americans' task in this regard was a matter of collecting and disposing of military equipment. The most pressing problem was dealing with the thousands of Chinese and Koreans who had been brought to operate the coal mines and farms in the home islands during the war. These people, who had been worked almost as slaves, seldom paid, and kept in undesirable living conditions, became restless after the Allied victory. They participated in some rioting and looting, and the laborers refused to work in the mines. The Military Government Section of the division made arrangements with Japanese authorities for their repatriation to their homelands.

During October and early November, 6,000 enlisted men and 600 officers from the 77th Division were sent home as a result of the Readjustment Program. This was a system that gave points for time in service, time overseas, combat awards, and other factors to determine when men might be mustered out. Thousands of replacements arrived from the United States, and the new men hastily assumed the duties of the homeward-bound veterans.

On February 28, 1946, Bruce departed to assume command of the 7th Infantry Division in Korea (see map 5). The assistant division commander, Brig. Gen. Edwin H. Randle, took over the 77th. Low-point men of the division began leaving for assignment with other units destined to occupy Japan for a longer period.

The 77th Infantry Division closed out its military affairs; transferred its property, personnel, and responsibilities to other units; and was inactivated on March 15, 1946. It had served four years, fought about two hundred days in three campaigns, had killed 43,651 Japanese troops, and had suffered almost 14, 000 casualties.[32]

Following the sudden end of the war, the problem of Japanese units in Korea became a concern. The US decision to land troops to accept the surrender of these enemy forces and to occupy Korea was taken only at the very end of the conflict. Barely twenty-four hours after the dropping of the Nagasaki bomb, the State-War-Navy Coordinating Committee reached a hasty, unilateral decision that the United States should participate in the occupation of Korea. The committee proposed that the Russians accept the surrender of Japanese forces north of the 38th Parallel and that US forces accept the surrender of those south of that line. Committee members were relieved when the Russians readily accepted their recommendation.

Bruce's new command, the 7th Infantry Division, had been on Okinawa at the end of the war and was ordered to Korea in September 1945. The division was understrength, with a low combat-readiness rating when it arrived on the peninsula. The first order of business was to establish a military government to replace the Japanese-run government while returning some 70,000 colonial civil servants and more than 600,000 soldiers and civilians to the home islands.

In April 1946, a month after assuming command of the 7th Division, Bruce returned briefly to College Station, where on April 21 both he and Gen. Dwight D. Eisenhower were awarded honorary LLD degrees. The ceremony coincided with the anniversary of the Battle of San Jacinto, when Texans under Sam Houston had defeated the Mexican Army and won Texas independence in 1836. Texas Aggies have long celebrated April 21 as Aggie Muster Day, and ceremonies are held worldwide. The 1946 muster was held at Kyle Field and featured Eisenhower as speaker.[33]

After commanding the 7th Infantry Division for eighteen months as a part of the Army of Occupation in Korea and having served for over three and a half years in the Pacific, General Bruce returned to the States. His next assignment was as deputy commander of the Fourth Army at Fort Sam Houston in San Antonio. He had long considered Texas his home and had maintained his permanent residency in the state during his military career. At Fort Sam Houston he became heavily involved in the training activities over a five-state area of the Reserve Officers Training Corps, the National Guard, and the Organized Reserve Corps.

His next assignment was as commandant (president) of the Armed Forces Staff College at Norfolk, Virginia, where he reported on July 6, 1951. Upon his departure, the Fourth Army commander, Lt. Gen. Le Roy Lutes, wrote in Bruce's efficiency report, "He is well rounded in professional attainments; particularly handling civilian compliment activities, Fourth Army, in a superior manner; qualified to command corps or army; recommend promotion to lieutenant general." On July 30 Bruce received his third star.[34]

The Armed Forces Staff College was created in 1946 under the direct control of the Joint Chiefs of Staff to educate selected officers of the army, air force, navy, and marines in joint and combined operations. As the commandant, Bruce could draw on his experience with supporting marines during World War I and working closely with all services during World War II. As a graduate of the Naval War College, he was well grounded in the naval service. He devoted his efforts at the college to furthering armed-forces coordination. Approaching age sixty, he was preparing for retirement when he received a telephone call from a longtime friend, William B. Bates, who discussed an opportunity at the University of Houston.

In the years since World War I, veterans of the First Officers Training Camp (FOTC) had formed an organization to maintain friendships with their wartime comrades. Regular conventions were held, and during one at the Rice Hotel in Houston in 1947, Bruce had had a long visit with Bates, a friend since their days at the FOTC and a member of the Board of Regents of the University of Houston.

Upon learning that the general was approaching retirement, Bates convinced Hugh Roy Cullen, Houston financier and chairman of the board of regents, that Bruce should be offered the presidency of the University of Houston. Cullen called the general on June 12, 1954, to offer him the post effective September 1. Bruce told Cullen that he was deeply honored and asked for a few days to consider the situation. He had already determined that he would accept the presidency if offered, but an ingrained sense of decorum told him that a delay of a day or two might be proper. The following Monday, he telephoned his acceptance to Cullen.

On August 31, 1954, Lt. Gen. Andrew D. Bruce, after thirty-seven years of service and two world wars, retired from the US Army. Appropriately, the retirement ceremony was held at Fort Hood and was attended by his many friends from Killeen, Temple, and Central Texas. All came to honor the man who they knew as the "Father of Fort Hood" and who had done so much for the economy of Central Texas.[35]

The University of Houston was founded in 1927 by the Board of Education of the Houston Independent School District as Houston Junior College. Classes were initially held at night in the high schools and by day in local churches. It was planned that the junior college would expand to a four-year program as soon as it showed consistent growth and fiscal stability. Four-year status was attained in 1934, and the name was changed to the University of Houston.

Bruce became the third president of the university in 1954. One of his first decisions was to create the post of vice president for academic affairs and provost to help him upgrade the academic quality of the institution. Immediately the university began working to erase the marks of its early origins in the public-school system. Also included in changing the image was eliminating the junior-college division and all correspondence courses. The quality of the faculty and requirements for student performance were upgraded.

In 1956 Bruce proposed that the regents create a chancellor-and-president system, promoting his provost to president so that he could become chancellor. Since the university was operating almost entirely on tuition, Bruce believed that as chancellor he could devote more time to fundraising. On December 10, 1956, at the regular meeting of the board of regents, Dr. Clanton W. Williams was named president of the university and Bruce was named chancellor and chief executive officer of the university system.[36]

Three years later Bruce requested that the regents seek full support for the university to become a part of the state system of higher education. There was hidden, but substantial, opposition to this from the University of Texas, Texas A&M University, Texas Tech University, and the other state-supported colleges. After a hard-fought legislative battle, though, the Texas legislature passed the necessary bill in 1961 for the University of Houston to become a public institution beginning in 1963. The chancellor celebrated the victory by announcing his retirement effective August 31, 1961.[37]

Bruce moved to Temple and opened an office, his friends of Camp Hood days welcoming him with a semblance of ruffles and flourishes. From his office he served as a development and public-relations consultant to business and industry in the region. But in 1963 he moved to Southern Pines, North Carolina, to be near his daughter.

Lt. Gen. Andrew D. Bruce's military decorations include the Distinguished Service Cross, Distinguished Service Medal, Navy Distinguished Service Medal, Legion of Merit, Bronze Star, Air Medal, and Purple Heart. Foreign awards include the French Legion of Honor and three awards of the Croix de Guerre. From the Republic of the Philippines, he received the Legion of Honor.

General Bruce, chancellor emeritus of the University of Houston, died suddenly at a hospital near his Southern Pines home on July 27, 1969. He was interned in Arlington National Cemetery in Washington.[38]

★ 3 ★

Doolittle Raider

JOHN A. HILGER

CLASS OF 1930

In 1909 Sherman, Texas, was a quiet, small town of a little over 10,000 people located in Northeast Texas seventy-five miles north of Dallas and about ten miles south of the Oklahoma border. Named after Gen. Sidney Sherman, a hero of the Texas Revolution, it boasted several flour and cottonseed mills and was also a railroad center for the region. It was also an educational center, with several small colleges, and was known as the "Athens of Texas."

John Allen Hilger was born in Sherman on January 11, 1909, to John Fredrick and Emma Dye Hilger. His father was a stonecutter at the local marble quarry. The third of four sons in the family, he grew up in the town and attended Sherman public schools. In high school his student activities included the Pep Squad, Hog Club, Forensic Forum, Glee Club, and Hi-Y Club. In 1926 he was the assistant business manager for *Hi-Talk*, the school newspaper. He participated in class football in 1925 and 1926. The senior class of 1926 was the largest for Sherman High School up to that time, with 133 students.[1]

Hilger applied for and was accepted to study mechanical engineering at Texas A&M. He arrived at the university on September 13, 1926, and was assigned to Company B, Infantry, in the Corps of Cadets. At that time the corps numbered 2,395 cadets and was organized into an Infantry Regiment of three battalions with three companies each and a Composite Regiment of the Artillery Battalion of four batteries, the Cavalry Squadron of four troops, the Signal Corps Battalion of three companies, and the Air Service with two flights.[2]

By his junior year, Hilger was a sergeant in his cadet company and a member of the American Society of Mechanical Engineers and the Toonersville Reviewers. He dropped out of college in September 1929 but returned two years later. Again in Company B, Infantry, he served as a cadet lieutenant his senior year. Hilger received his bachelor of science in mechanical engineering in June 1932 and was commissioned a second lieutenant in the Infantry Reserve.[3]

Hilger entered the Army Air Corps Flying School in February 1933. After receiving his wings in February 1934, he was placed on active duty in the Air Corps as a flying cadet. In February 1935 he was commissioned a second lieutenant and in October 1936 received his regular commission. His first duty assignment after completing pilot training was at March Field, California, where he served as a pilot, assistant base adjutant, and commander of the base photographic section. He was promoted to first lieutenant in October 1939.[4]

On March 12, 1937, Hilger married Virginia Botterud in a simple ceremony in San Pedro, California. His brother, Ensign Ted Hilger, served as best man. Later as a navy lieutenant, Ted Hilger was aboard the USS *Houston* when it was sunk on February 28, 1942, in a naval battle in the Bali Strait. Rescued by the destroyer USS *Pillsbury*, he was declared missing in action and later dead after the *Pillsbury* was sunk the next day.[5]

In May 1940 John Hilger was transferred to McChord Field, Washington, and became commander of the 89th Reconnaissance Squadron in September. In the fall of 1941, he took his unit to Daniel Field in Augusta, Georgia, where they participated in the Carolina Maneuvers. Following the Japanese attack on Pearl Harbor, his unit was assigned to antisubmarine-patrol duty along the Pacific coast. He continued this mission until February 1942, during this time receiving promotion to captain and later to major.[6]

Hilger with brother Jack, who was lost at sea in the Pacific in 1942.
Courtesy Cushing Memorial Library and Archives, Texas A&M University

---

Plans to strike back at Japan were being examined by the military staffs in Washington. On the evening of January 10, 1942, Adm. Ernest King, chief of naval operations, went to the Washington Navy Yard and boarded the *Vixen*, a former German yacht that served as his flagship and second office. Earlier that day President Roosevelt had expressed to him the desire to strike Japan as soon as possible.

After dinner, US Navy captain Francis S. Low, a submariner and operations officer on King's staff, asked to speak to the admiral in private. He presented an idea to have twin-engine army bombers fly off a navy carrier and bomb Japan. The plan was submitted to King's air-operations officer. After several days of research, a thirty-page handwritten analysis concluded that the North American B-25 was the only plane that could carry out the proposed mission. The staff also concluded that the newly commissioned USS *Hornet* would be the ideal carrier to transport and launch the B-25s. The *Hornet* was due to sail from Norfolk, Virginia, to the Pacific in February. Its decks were wide enough to accommodate the medium bombers, and the ship could steam at about twenty-five knots. The *Hornet* could be brought to within about four hundred miles of the Japanese coast before launching the bombers. Since the B-25s could not be retrieved by the carrier, they would have to fly across Japan and on to friendly fields in China.[7]

The navy staff approached Lt. Gen. Henry H. "Hap" Arnold, who did not tell them that the army was already working on the possibility of flying army aircraft off a carrier. Arnold called in Lt. Col. James H. "Jimmy" Doolittle to be briefed on the concept. Returning to his office, Doolittle studied the basic question about which medium bomber should be used and also decided that the best choice was the B-25. Reporting back to Arnold, Doolittle was given command of the mission.[8]

The 17th Bombardment Group and Hilger's 89th Reconnaissance Squadron were designated as the source of the mission's personnel. Both units had recently been transferred to Lexington Field in Columbia, South Carolina, where they were undergoing B-25 combat training. On the flight to Columbia, they stopped at the Mid-Continent Airport in Minneapolis, Minnesota, to have modifications made to the aircraft to increase fuel capacity.

After this work, when the aircrews first climbed into their B-25s, they were surprised to see that the interior looked like a Rube Goldberg contrivance. Inside, a 225-gallon fuel tank made by US Rubber Company of Mishawaca, Indiana, was fitted into the bomb bay, a 160-gallon rubber bag was lodged in the crawlway, and a 60-gallon tank was fitted into the area where the lower turret had been removed. Up in the nose the Norden bombsight was missing, replaced by a simplified, twenty-cent instrument designed by Capt. C. Ross Greening. A vertical plate with graduations marking elevations and a slide that moved up and down, this mechanism was substituted for the high-level precision bombsight since the attack was to be done at extremely low level. Two wooden broomsticks simulating .50-caliber machine guns protruded from the tail, a ruse to forestall enemy attack from that quarter.

Doolittle visited the men in South Carolina and asked for volunteers for a special mission. He said it would be dangerous, important, and interesting, but he could not tell them anymore about it. They all

Crew 14 of the Doolittle Raiders on the USS *Hornet.* Left to Right: Lt. James H. Macia, Maj. John A. Hilger, S.Sgt. Jacob Eierman, Lt. Jack A. Sims, and Sgt. Edwin V. Bain (killed in action in Italy in 1943). *Official US Navy Photo*

volunteered and within a week, twenty-four crews picked by Doolittle received orders to fly to Eglin Field in Valpariso, Florida.

Wanting an experienced deputy to take over during his absences, Doolittle asked Lt. Col. William C. Mills, commander of the 17th Bombardment Group, for a recommendation. Mills suggested Hilger, a no-nonsense perfectionist. Hilger's job was to get the men and planes assembled at Eglin and set up a training operation. He was joined there by four fellow Aggies: Lt. Robert M. Gray, Class of 1941, of Killeen; Lt. William M. Fitzhugh, Class of 1936, of Temple; Lt. Glen C. Roloson, Class of 1940; and Lt. James M. Parker, Class of 1941, of Houston.

During the first days at Eglin, Doolittle took Hilger and three other senior officers aside and told them the general nature of the mission, providing as few particulars as possible. He explained why the B-25 had been selected, the main objective of the raid, and how the planes were to be carried within range of their targets. Doolittle also emphasized the urgency of the training and that secrecy was of the utmost importance to the mission.[9]

The training at Eglin was fast paced, and with time lost due to weather, practicing the short takeoffs was given first priority. The runway was marked with a line denoting the starting position; the next line was at 450 feet, then another line every 50 feet thereafter up to 800 feet. Parallel lines painted down the field 50 feet apart aided pilots in keeping their ships straight during the takeoff roll. The crews engaged in gunnery and bombing practice and did long navigation missions of eight to ten hours over the Gulf of Mexico.

Lt. Henry Miller, US Navy, reported to Eglin Field from the Pensacola Naval Air Station to help train the pilots for carrier launches. He measured and timed each takeoff, critiquing each pilot afterward. The pilots had to adapt to new techniques that were contrary to everything they had been taught in flight training, but soon they were mastering the short takeoff.[10]

Training ended abruptly, and the unit was ordered to fly cross-country to McClellan Field near Sacramento, California, where the aircraft underwent final mechanical checks. From there they flew to an airfield near the Alameda Naval Air Station near where the *Hornet* was moored. The B-25s were towed to the dock and loaded aboard the carrier. On the afternoon of April 1, the *Hornet* sailed out of her berth at Alameda and dropped anchor in San Francisco Bay.

Task Group 16.2, commanded by Capt. Marc A. Mitscher, consisting of the *Hornet*, heavy cruiser *Vincennes*, light cruiser *Nashville*, the oiler *Cimarron*, and the destroyers *Gwin*, *Grayson*, *Meredith*, and *Monssen*, passed under the Golden Gate Bridge at 11:10 a.m. the next day and set a course for Japanese waters. Task Group 16.1, commanded by V. Adm. William F. Halsey, consisting of the carrier *Enterprise*, heavy cruisers *Northampton* and *Salt Lake City*, the oiler *Sabine*, and the destroyers *Balch*, *Benham*, *Ellet*, and *Fannin*, rendezvoused with Mitscher's group thirty miles southwest of the Hawaiian Islands to become Task Force 16 under Halsey's command.[11]

The weather for most of the journey was dreary, misty, and rainy. The aircrews went on deck daily to check their planes. The engines were turned over every other day to keep them tuned up. To keep in practice, kites were flown and the gunners fired at them with the top-turret guns. Doolittle held a daily meeting to lecture on gunnery, navigation, first aid, and bombardment. A naval officer who had been an air attaché in Tokyo talked about the terrain of Japan and of ways to

B-25s on deck of the USS *Hornet*. *Official US Navy Photo*

tell Chinese people from Japanese. Though there was no time to learn Chinese, the crewmen memorized the phrase "Meg Wa Bing," meaning "American soldier."[12]

Doolittle's plan was to employ thirteen planes against the Tokyo area. Each element of three planes was given a sector to strike, with Doolittle flying unattached. The fourth element was to hit the Yokohama area, including the navy yard. Hilger flew in the fifth element, which would bomb Nagoya, Kobe, and Osaka with one plane to each target (see map 4).[13]

The date selected for the raid was April 19. On the fifteenth Halsey ordered the two oilers to refuel the carriers and cruisers for the run to the launching points. Doolittle called the crews together for a final briefing. He said that although the planned strike date was April 19, it looked like they would launch on the evening of the eighteenth. By dusk on the seventeenth, ammunition and bombs had been loaded, gas tanks topped off, and last-minute engine runs made. Deck crews moved the planes as far back as possible to provide maximum deck space for takeoff.[14]

At 3:00 a.m. the *Hornet* received a message from the *Enterprise* that radar had spotted two possible enemy ships at about 21,000 yards away. General quarters sounded, and all ships were ordered to change course to avoid detection. At 6:00 a.m. a scout plane sighted a small fishing boat, and Halsey ordered another course change. Shortly afterward, another small vessel was sighted at about 20,000 yards. When yet another small vessel was sighted at 12,000 yards, Halsey ordered it sunk and sent a message to the *Hornet* for Doolittle to launch his aircraft. The klaxon horn sounded, and Mitscher's voice blared over the loudspeaker: "Army pilots, man your planes!"

The B-25s were pushed into position and the gas tanks again topped off. There was no time for breakfast, but the crew rustled up some sandwiches. Each man was issued a pint bottle of whiskey for emergency use. At about 8:30 a.m. Doolittle was the first to launch. He did not linger in the area but headed straight for Tokyo. The other planes followed and headed individually for their assigned targets. Hilger was in ship fourteen, and the foul weather was getting worse. The rolling and pitching was so bad that it took fifteen men to hold the plane steady. Once off the deck he was followed by the other two planes in his element.[15]

Just prior to takeoff, Hilger told his crew: "The way things are now, we have about enough to get us within 200 miles of the China coast and that's all. If anyone wants to withdraw he can do it now. We can replace him with men who are going to be left aboard. Nothing will ever be said about it and it won't be held against you. It's your right. It's up to you." Not a man withdrew. With Hilger as pilot, his aircrew consisted of Lt. Jack W. Sims, copilot; Lt. James H. Macia Jr., navigator-bombardier; S.Sgt. Jacob Eierman, engineer; and S.Sgt. Edwin V. Bain, gunner. All would survive the war except Bain, who would be killed in action during the first US air raid on Rome.[16]

Once in the air, Hilger circled the ship once to check his compass, course, and drift. All the way to Japan, he never went above fifty or sixty feet and much of the time was flying at fifteen to twenty feet above the waves. Approaching the coast, the aircraft passed over several small boats, and the people stood on deck and waved. At this point in time, the Army Air Corps was still using the old-style emblem—a blue circle with white star and a red ball in the middle of the star—and perhaps this confused them.[17]

Hilger's plane came over Japan just above the tree line in a rural district with green fields and open country. The day was sunny, without a cloud in the sky. His objective was Nagoya, a big industrial center. The B-25 arrived about 1:00 p.m., and after circling the bay so as to come back and make the bomb run from the inland, the crew had no trouble locating the targets. The first was an army barracks complex near Nagoya Castle, an ancient landmark. According to plan, Hilger pulled his plane up to 1,500 feet at two hundred miles an hour so the improvised bombsight could be used. About the time the first bomb was released, some flak began to come in but not too close. The second target was a large arsenal or military depot, which was hit by the bomb dropped. The third was an oil-storage facility, which was also hit. The fourth and last target, the Mitsubishi aircraft plant, was hit with the last of their bombs. By now antiaircraft fire was increasing. With all of the bombs gone, Hilger took the plane back down to low level and out over the bay. Spotting some oil tanks on the waterfront, the bomber made a firing run using the .50-caliber machine guns firing incendiary bullets. The entire raid lasted about eight minutes.

Hilger turned the plane south for a run down the coast before heading to China. His main concern now was the fuel supply. Once over the China Sea, the plane turned west toward China. soon encountering fog patches and squalls that kicked up a thirty-five-mile-per-hour tail wind. If the tail wind held, he and his crew could probably make the China coast. The fog forced him to climb up to 500 feet, flying blind most of the time.[18]

With nightfall, he was flying completely blind, with no way of estimating drift or sighting on a star. Hilger took the plane to 7,000 feet to clear a mountain range known to be just inland from the Chinese coast. The crew listened for the direction-finding signals that were supposed to be in place to guide the planes to friendly airfields and watched for the signal markers that would identify these strips. Because of a series of mishaps and misunderstandings exacerbated by a lack of urgency on the part of the Chinese and Americans on the ground, the supplies and guidance systems were not in place.[19]

With less than an hour's worth of fuel left, Hilger told his crew to prepare to bail out. After giving the order, he made sure his men were all out before jumping at 8,500 feet. He had been in the air for thirteen hours and five minutes and had flown a distance of almost 2,300 miles.

Jolted when his parachute opened, Hilger fought to maintain consciousness. He discovered his musette bag gone, along with all of his rations, matches, and whiskey. Making his way out of the plane, he had accidentally unhitched his right-leg strap. This resulted in his slipping down in his harness and the loose strap slapping him in the nose, causing it to bleed. Floating earthward, he saw a hole in the fog, steered for it, and hit it square. It was not an empty hole, though, but a protruding mountain peak—Hilger slammed into it with a spine-jarring crash and lost consciousness. When he came to, he was lying on a 45-degree slope, and his parachute was snarled in the trees. With rain pouring down, he decided to remain on the mountain until daylight. Despite his sprained left hand and wrenched back, Hilger pulled his chute down and crawled up to a shelf on the slope. Spreading the silk over two bushes, he crept underneath and went to sleep.[20]

By jumping from the plane, the crew became scattered over the countryside. Fortunately, friendly civilians aided them; the men reunited the next day and were taken to a Chinese military post. There they enjoyed their first real meal since leaving the *Hornet*, with fried eggs, sweet sauce, bean sprouts, salt bread, and tea provided. Later they were taken by train and bus to Chucow, a large airbase built for the US Army. From there the men were flown by a C-47 transport plane to Chungking.[21]

The humiliation of the Japanese over the bombing of their homeland resulted in brutal retaliation against the Chinese. An expeditionary force of 100,000 men began a campaign of terror to discourage further collaboration, wasting and ravaging the land. In three months the Japanese rampaged two hundred miles through the heart of eastern China, destroying crops and exterminating every individual suspected of helping the American raiders. Entire villages through which the aviators passed were slaughtered to the last child and burned to the ground. More than six hundred air raids preceded the advancing army. Approximately 250,000 Chinese soldiers and civilians were killed in the three-month campaign of destruction.[22]

The recovered crews were united in Chungking (see map 6) and on April 30 were invited by the Nationalist Chinese leader, Generalissimo Chiang Kai-shek, and Madame Chiang to their palace to be decorated.

Hilger and Doolittle with Madame Chiang Kei-shek.
Official US Army Photo

All of the crewmembers present were decorated, and Hilger received the highest Chinese honor. The men eventually returned to the States. Doolittle was called back first and went to the White House to receive the Medal of Honor from the president and promoted to brigadier general. Afterward, he was successful in getting each raider a promotion to the next rank.

Hilger, along with several other raiders, soon made the long flight from China to the States. Their route was by way of New Delhi, Karachi, Cairo, Nigeria, Brazil, Trinidad, and Florida before finally landing at Bolling Field in Washington on June 17.

By the end of the month, enough of the Doolittle Raiders had returned to the United States to warrant a ceremony to present each the Distinguished Flying Cross. While in Chungking, they had been told of the award, but the medals were not presented because the American headquarters there did not have any. On June 27, 1942, at Bolling

Hilger with Nationalist Chinese officer. *Courtesy Tom Mucia*

Field, twenty-three raiders lined up against a backdrop of obsolete B-18 bombers to receive their medals from General Arnold.[23]

In July 1942 Hilger returned to the Texas A&M campus along with Ensign George H. Gay, the lone survivor of Torpedo Squadron 8 at the Battle of Midway. The Aggie heroes were received with wild ovations from the assembled cadets. Hilger said in his speech to them: "We did something which caught the public fancy and they have sort of raised us up on a pedestal. We would rather be thought of as soldiers. We were just the lucky ones who got to go. The one who did all of the planning had to stay behind."[24]

The Fourteenth Air Force was activated on March 10, 1943, but at that time it amounted to little more than a name change for Brig. Gen. Claire L. Chennault's China Air Task Force. More US bomber and fighter groups were slated for service in China, with plans calling for a force of eighty fighters and forty bombers of the Chinese Air Force to be commanded by Chennault. This force would become the Chinese-American Composite Wing (CACW), which would consist of Chinese aircraft and pilots trained under lend-lease and American pilots and technicians furnished by the US Army Air Force. Hilger was a

Hilger with cadets at Kyle Field in 1942. *Courtesy Cushing Memorial Library and Archives, Texas A&M University*

part of the first contingent that flew out of Miami on July 22 in a collection of Air Transport Command C-46s, C-87s, and C-54s. They arrived at Karachi Air Base in India on July 31 after the flight from Florida to Natal, Brazil; over the Atlantic, with a stop at Ascension Island; and across Africa and the Middle East to India.

The command system for the CACW was set up immediately. It called for duplicate US and Chinese commands all the way from wing command down to individual flight leaders in the squadrons. Most staff functions also were duplicated. Training began on August 5 in a collection of war-weary fighters and bombers.

The CACW combat units were the 1st Bomb Group (flying B-25s) and the 3rd and 5th Fighter Groups (flying P-40s.) The numerical designations were from the Chinese Air Force. Hilger commanded the 1st Bomb Group but was not permitted to fly combat missions because of his participation in the Tokyo Raid. Officials believed that if he was captured, the Japanese would execute him. Hilger commanded the bomb group until September 1943, when he was transferred to the staff of the commander in chief of the Pacific area, Adm. Chester A. Nimitz.

He spent the last eighteen months of the war serving in the western Pacific as a special-plans officer.[25]

Before taking off from the *Hornet*, Doolittle had promised the eighty men who were to accompany him on the raid "the best damned reunion you've ever had." The first reunion, more of a get-together, took place in North Africa, where Doolittle commanded the Twelfth Air Force, and was nothing like the gatherings to follow after the war. In 1947 the first "official" reunion was held in a Miami hotel on December 14, 1945, and apparently the veterans enjoyed themselves. The night watchman's report to his manager said in part: "I let them make a lot of noise, but when about 15 of them went into the pool at 1 a.m. I told them there was no swimming allowed at night. They were in the pool until 2:30 a.m. The Doolittle boys added some gray hairs to my head." There was no reunion in 1946 but one was held annually thereafter at sites around the country. The exception was in 1966, when the men decided that with so much left undone in Vietnam, they would skip the twenty-fourth anniversary of the mission. On May 5, 2012, seventy years after the raid, three surviving Doolittle Raiders met at the USS *Hornet* Museum in Alameda, California. Also attending were Doolittle's granddaughter Jonna Doolittle Hoppes and Republic of China Air Force lieutenant colonel Chu Chen, who as a teenager helped rescue and get to safety several crewmembers who bailed out over China.[26]

The final reunion was held at the National Museum of the US Air Force near Dayton, Ohio, on November 9, 2013. Three of the four surviving raiders sipped an 1896 cognac, a gift to Doolittle (who was born in 1896) from the Hennessy Corporation, from silver goblets. Each goblet is engraved twice, with one raider's name at the top and bottom. When a member dies, his goblet is turned upside down. The cognac was saved for the final reunion. Although the bottle was supposed to have been opened by the last survivor, because of their advanced age, the final four decided that 2013 would be their last reunion and opened the cognac. Hundreds of people, including family members of deceased crewmen, watched as the three attending raiders called out "here" at the name of each of the original eighty airmen. The final toast was to their departed comrades. The eighty goblets and case are now on display at the National Museum of the US Air Force.[27]

As for Hilger, in January 1946 he was assigned to US Air Force headquarters in the Pentagon and served as chief of internal policy, a

Brig. Gen. John A. Hilger. *Courtesy National Museum of the United States Air Force*

branch of the Plans Division. In August 1948 he was selected to attend the Air War College and, after graduation, was assigned as commander of the 307th Bomb Group located at MacDill Air Force Base in Florida.

On August 1, 1950, the 307th's B-29s deployed to Kadena Air Base, Okinawa. One week later the Superfortresses went into action over Korea. They attacked strategic targets in North Korea such as transportation and industrial facilities. In November the bomb group began a campaign against bridges spanning the Yalu River into Manchuria. The B-29s struck interdiction targets, including communication and supply centers, and supported United Nations ground forces by hitting gun emplacements and troop concentrations. (see map 5)

On November 8 "Hilger led an aerial attack against Sinuiju, a strategically important enemy stronghold and temporary capital of North Korea. Because of its location only 666 yards across the Yalu River from the Manchurian city of An-Tung, it was considered highly probable that Hilger's group would be attacked by antiaircraft fire from both sides of the river and by Chinese fighters from Manchuria. In order to assure destruction of this vital installation, as well as to prevent international consequences that could arise from American aircraft passing over or bombs landing in Manchuria, Hilger personally led his group."

The 307th Bomb Group became an unmanned organization on February 10, 1951, replaced by the 307th Bomb Wing. Hilger returned to MacDill Air Force Base in Florida and served as director of operations in the headquarters of the Sixth Air Division until he entered the National War College in August 1951.[28]

After graduating from the National War College, he was assigned as chief of the Allocations Division, Directorate of Operations, in the Pentagon. In July 1955 he was assigned as commander of the Air Force Operational Test Center, Air Proving Ground Command, Elgin Air Force Base, Florida. Hilger was promoted to brigadier general in October 1956 and continued to command the operational test center until June 1957. His next assignment was as commander of the US Air Force Group, Joint US Military Mission for Aid to Turkey, in Ankara. In July 1959 Hilger was assigned as chief of staff, Allied Air Forces Northern Europe, in Oslo, Norway. Two years later he was transferred to San Antonio, where he became the chief of staff of the Air Training Command at Randolph Air Force Base.

Brig. Gen. John A. Hilger retired from the US Air Force on November 30, 1966. Among his military decorations are the Distinguished Service Medal, Silver Star, Legion of Merit, Distinguished Flying Cross with Oak Leaf Cluster, Bronze Star, Air Medal with Three Oak Leaf Clusters, and Chinese Order of Yon-Hwei.

Afterward, he accepted a position with the Atomic Energy Commission. Hilger retired from that agency in early 1982 and moved from Las Vegas, Nevada, to the Air Force Village in San Antonio. Shortly after arriving in Texas, he met with a group of Doolittle Raiders for lunch to welcome him back. He had the group laughing as he recounted his experience at the reunion of his Sherman High School class that he had recently attended.

Hilger died in San Antonio on February 3, 1982. His body was cremated and his ashes scattered in the Pacific Ocean off the coast of Newport Beach, California.[29]

★ 4 ★

Rangers Lead the Way

JAMES E. RUDDER

CLASS OF 1932

At the sixtieth anniversary of the Normandy Invasion at Point du Hoc, Pres. Ronald Reagan asked, "Where do we get such men?" One such man was James Earl Rudder, who commanded the 2nd Ranger Battalion that captured Point du Hoc and who later led the 109th Infantry Regiment in the Battle of the Bulge.

Rudder was born on May 6, 1910, in Eden, Texas. His parents were Dee Forrest Rudder, a livestock-commission man, and Annie Clark Powell Rudder. Eden is a small town in West Texas, forty-three miles east of San Angelo and thirty-four miles west of Brady. The town was founded in 1882 and incorporated in 1911. It was an agricultural center for the area, which was primarily raising livestock—cattle, sheep, and goats. Eden's population in 1910 was about five hundred people.

Rudder's early education was in the town's public schools. He graduated from Eden High School in the spring of 1927. His high school activities included basketball and football. His stellar performance on the football team came to the attention of William J. Wisdom, football coach at John Tarleton Agricultural College (now Tarleton State College) in Stephenville, Texas. While on a recruiting trip to San Angelo, Wisdom stopped at the Eden pharmacy where Rudder worked behind the soda counter. The coach asked if the town had any football players, and the owner pointed out Rudder. The teenager protested that he had no money to attend college, but Wisdom vaguely promised a scholarship, saying, "Come on and we'll work something out." The "scholarship" he offered actually meant assistance in getting odd jobs around the campus such as waiting tables, mowing grass, cleaning classrooms, and other chores. Rudder enrolled at Tarleton in the fall of 1927. At the time all male students were required to participate in the Reserve Officer Training Program (ROTC) and be a member of the school's Corps of Cadets. They were also required to wear the prescribed ROTC uniform on campus and when going into Stephenville. Female students were required to wear school uniforms, blue chambray dresses by day and white dresses for evening entertainment.[1]

During his years at Tarleton, Rudder was a mediocre student but an outstanding football player, playing center on both offense and defense. He had a great love for football and decided that he wanted to coach after college. After attending Tarleton off and on as funds allowed for three years, he transferred to Texas A&M. Rudder was assigned to Company H, Infantry, in the Corps of Cadets. Eager for football, he played his first year at A&M on the freshman team due to conference rules for transfer students. Continuing to pay his way through college, Rudder had a variety of jobs. As part of his scholarship, he managed the soft-drink concession at football games for a 1/8 interest during his first year at A&M. He also was a waiter in Sbisa Hall, worked in the Aggieland Inn (a hotel on the campus), sold peanuts and candy on the honor system, and sold bookcases to freshmen and sophomores.[2]

The *1932 Longhorn* lists his activities as T Club, Sbisa Volunteers, Industrial Arts Club, Fish Numeral, and Intramural Wrestling champ. After transferring from Tarleton to A&M, Rudder changed his major from civil engineering to industrial education. He was a cadet captain on the infantry-regiment staff his senior year and graduated on June 4, 1932, with a bachelor of science degree in industrial education. Rudder also was commissioned a second lieutenant of infantry.[3]

Rudder played football for two years at John Tarleton and one year at Texas A&M. *Courtesy Texas A&M University Yearbook*

Because of the Great Depression, there were few jobs for college graduates. Unable to find work, Rudder returned to Eden, where he found employment with the state highway department digging ditches at twenty-five cents an hour. He began his coaching and teaching career at Brady High School in September 1933. Rudder and another Brady teacher, Margaret Williamson of Menard, a 1936 graduate of the University of Texas, were married in June 1937.

Rudder returned to Tarleton College in 1938, this time as a football coach and teacher. He remained there until 1941, when he was called to active duty in the US Army with the rank of first lieutenant. He reported to Fort Sam Houston and was assigned as commander of Company B, 38th Infantry Regiment, 2nd Infantry Division. In the fall of 1941 he attended the Infantry School at Fort Benning. In July 1942 he was assigned duties as a battalion executive officer in the newly formed 83rd Infantry Division at Camp Atterbury, Indiana. That fall and winter, he attended the US Army Command and General Staff College at Fort

Leavenworth, Kansas. Returning to the 83rd Division afterward, he was named assistant G-3 on the division staff.[4]

With the success of the first American Ranger unit in North Africa in 1942, additional units were authorized. The 1st Ranger Battalion was withdrawn from active combat and split up to form cadres for the 1st, 3rd, and 4th Ranger Battalions. Groups were also sent back stateside to help train the newly formed 2nd and 5th Ranger Battalions. The 2nd Battalion was activated on April 1, 1943, at Camp Forrest, Tennessee, one of the army's largest training bases during World War II.

Responding to a call for volunteers, thousands of men from all over the country reported to Camp Forrest. Those who did not meet the demanding physical standards required for service with the Rangers were soon on their way back to their unit. The 2nd Battalion was allotted three months to train an organization capable of performing combat duty using a program was based on the experience of the 1st Battalion. Its strength was twenty-seven officers and 484 enlisted men organized into a headquarters company and six rifle companies. Each company consisted of a headquarters of one officer and two men and two rifle platoons of one officer and 32 men each. Platoons were divided into two sections. Organizational turmoil, though, resulted in a series of battalion commanders, which did not improve the chaos.

Recognizing that a strong leader was needed for the battalion, Lt. Gen. Lloyd R. Fredendall, commander of Second Army and who, while commander of a corps in North Africa, had been impressed with the 1st Ranger Battalion, sought an appropriate officer. While inspecting the 83rd Infantry Division at Camp Atterbury, he noted the effective ranger training conducted by Rudder. When asked if he would volunteer for the Rangers, the Texan seized the opportunity.[5]

Rudder assumed command of the 2nd Ranger Battalion on June 30, 1943. Upon arrival, he called for a meeting with the troops. Sitting on the ground in the hot July sun, the men were introduced to their new chief: "I'm Jim Rudder, your new battalion commander. I've come down here to Camp Forrest so you can teach me how to become a Ranger. Company Commanders, take charge of your companies." The rangers were a little surprised by the brevity of the speech and thought that maybe this officer would not be so bad.

One of his first actions was to move the battalion out of their tent city and into wooden barracks, where they had showers and indoor toilets. Rudder instituted a monthly "gripe" session, during which every soldier was given a chance to make a complaint or a suggestion. One of the first complaints was about the food being served in the mess halls. Rudder sent the mess officer and some cooks to Cooks and Bakers School. When the food did not improve after they returned, he sent them back for more training. After that the food improved.[6]

Following months of intense and rugged training, in September the battalion was sent to Fort Pierce, Florida, to train at the Scouts and Raiders School. This course of instruction concentrated on the use of rubber boats and small assault landing craft (LCA, for Landing Craft, Assault). After two weeks of training, the battalion boarded trains for Fort Dix, New Jersey. Once there, the rangers were billeted in wooden-walled eight-man tents warmed by potbellied stoves. Rudder granted the men their first weekend passes. Following two days of hell raising in surrounding cities, the battalion began the final phase of training before going overseas.[7]

The men boarded the *Queen Elizabeth* and departed New York on November 23. In addition to Rudder's battalion, several other units were crammed into the ship. The rangers were detailed as military police for the voyage, a detail they resented at first. But the trip across the Atlantic, without convoy protection, was fast and uneventful.

On November 30 the *Queen Elizabeth* dropped anchor at Grenach, Scotland. Once ashore, the battalion traveled by train to Bude, Cornwall, a vacation resort on the western coast of England. The rangers were surprised to learn that they would be billeted in private homes, the command post located in a local hotel. Once settled in their new quarters, the rangers began a training program, including physical training, cliff climbing, hikes, section work, night exercises, and weapons firing.[8]

Christmas 1943 was a festive event. Rudder had asked his men to write home and request that their family send candy for the children of Bude. The rangers gave a party on Christmas Eve for 700 English children, complete with refreshments and gifts. On Christmas Day there was a USO show followed by a traditional Christmas dinner of turkey and all the trimmings. That night there was a dance, with a good band and an ample supply of liquor.

Two days after Christmas the battalion began its move to the small town of Titchfield, County Dorset, on the southern coast of England.

The intensive training program continued and included training with British commando units. Amphibious training with the Royal Navy included two weeks of intensive exercises on the Isle of Wight.[9]

Rudder continued to hold his gripe sessions, giving his men a chance to voice their opinions or complaints. At one of these a young ranger raised his hand and when recognized by the colonel stood and said: "Sir, most everybody has been issued a watch and I don't have mine yet. I wonder if you can tell me when I might be able to get me a watch?" Smiling, Rudder took off his own watch and gave it to the soldier, saying, "What about right now, son?"[10]

On February 14 the battalion returned to Bude, where Rudder had his hands full trying to keep up the morale of his men. The men had trained in Dorset until exhausted, expecting a cross-channel invasion that never came off. They were almost embarrassed to renew acquaintances with the families in Cornwall after bidding them farewell, when all thought they were off to invade France.[11]

The battalion continued training while plans for a cross-channel attack were being finalized at higher headquarters. The mission for the rangers would be to seize the German fortress on Pointe du Hoc and destroy the battery of six 155-mm French-made guns there. Pointe du Hoc was a (see map 7) triangular point of land jutting into the English Channel protected from the sea by cliffs eighty-five to one hundred feet high. The German artillery was placed to fire on what became known as Omaha Beach to the east and Utah Beach to the west. The guns also had the capability to reach offshore and wreak havoc on the incoming invaders.

Rudder and his intelligence officer, Capt. Harvey Cook, left for Portsmouth on March 15 to be briefed on the role his battalion would play in the invasion of Normandy. After returning to his headquarters, Rudder granted most of the rangers five-day passes, to be used by one company at a time. The men celebrated the first anniversary of the creation of their battalion on April 1. A few days later the unit departed Bude for North Devon, County Dorset, in southwest England, where they trained at the British Assault Training School, Braunton Camp.[12]

On April 27, 1944, the battalion moved to a bivouac area just outside Dorchester, where the men set up a tent city in an open field. They relaxed, slept, played cards, and generally allowed their nerves to settle down. Additional training here consisted of cliff climbing, competitive sports, and amphibious-assault exercises.[13]

The 2nd Ranger Battalion joined the 5th Ranger Battalion for a dress rehearsal of the invasion. At first the men of the 2nd were skeptical about the abilities of the 5th but soon discovered that their fellow rangers knew their business. A feeling of mutual respect began to develop between the two battalions.

Two days later the 2nd Battalion moved to Swanage, where the rangers were billeted in a school building on a hilltop with an enchanting view. Training continued with emphasis on cliff scaling and testing every available means of overcoming cliff obstacles. The M1919A4 light machine gun was proving a hindrance in scaling the cliffs, so many of these were replaced with the Browning automatic rifle (BAR). Although the BAR was heavy, it could be carried up a rope or ladder by one man and quickly put into action.[14]

The battalion moved to the staging area on May 19. Except for a few short road marches, the men spent their time relaxing, watching movies, and listening to music. On the night of the thirty-first, German fighter-bombers flew over the area. The men dashed for the cover of their foxholes, but none were seriously injured. The next morning they were moved to a different section in the staging area. Two days later the rangers trucked down to the Weymouth Esplanade to board their transport ships. The battalion sailed at 4:30 p.m. on June 5, the original date selected as D-Day; unfavorable weather had caused the invasion date to be changed to June 6.

For this mission, the 2nd and 5th Ranger Battalions were a part of the Provisional Ranger Group attached to the 116th Infantry Regiment, 29th Infantry Division, and under the command of Rudder. The plan called for three elements, designated Force A, B, and C. Force A consisted of three companies (D, E, and F) of the 2nd Battalion and would land at 6:30 a.m. (H Hour), climb the cliffs of Pointe du Hoc, and destroy the enemy guns. Force B, consisting of Company C, 2nd Battalion, was to land with the first assault wave on Omaha Beach, behind the 116th Infantry, and knock out enemy strong points near Pointe de la Percee immediately to the west. Force C (5th Ranger Battalion and Companies A and B of the 2nd Battalion) would wait offshore for the signal of success, then land at Pointe de la Percee. The ranger group would then move inland, cut the coastal highway connecting Grandcamp and Vierville, and await the arrival of the 116th Infantry before attacking west toward Grandcamp and Maisy.[15] (see map 7)

The operations plan called for Rudder to remain where he could best control the action of all three forces. He had intended to go ashore with Force C, but on the night of the fifth, an incident occurred aboard one of the transports that changed the situation. The designated commander of Force A, Maj. Cleveland A. Lytle (also the 2nd Battalion's executive officer) got drunk and punched the battalion medical officer. Rudder immediately arrested Lytle and, having no one available to replace him in command of Force A, assumed the post himself. The colonel thus would land with the three companies at Pointe du Hoc.[16]

Before H Hour, battleships, cruisers, destroyers, and other naval vessels steamed up and down the Normandy beaches, shelling the landing areas. Aboard the two Landing Ships, Infantry (LCIs) carrying Force A, the troops were awakened at 2:30 a.m. and served breakfast thirty minutes later. Around 4:00 a.m. the rangers loaded into ten LCAs, twenty men per craft. Each LCA was fitted with three pairs of rocket mounts to shoot climbing ropes to the top of the cliff. The men of the first wave also carried extension ladders.[17]

As the LCAs headed for shore, Rudder realized that they were on the wrong course. He ordered the British boatswain to turn the column westward, but time had been lost, the mistake costing the rangers thirty minutes. The craft were now running parallel to the cliffs and braving a gauntlet of fire from the German guns along the three miles of coast.

As a result of the navigation error, Force A was approaching the Pointe from the east instead of the north. Company D could not swing out from the column to reach the west side as planned in time to assault with the other units, instead deploying with the assault line and landing with the other companies. By this time, naval gunfire support on Pointe du Hoc had lifted, and the Germans had over thirty minutes to recover from the bombardment and to reoccupy their defensive positions.

As the force neared the beach, enemy soldiers could be seen on the cliff top. The rangers shot at them, and one German plunged off to the beach below. The rope-carrying rockets were fired about thirty-five yards from the cliff base, but only a few of the water-soaked ropes reached the top. Once ashore, some of the rangers began to free climb the cliffs but found the slippery clay surface was too much for them. Taking advantage of mounds of dirt along the base created by the preinvasion bombardment, the rangers used their extension ladders to reach the top of the cliff. As more men reached the top, more ropes were secured for the others to climb.[18]

When rangers reached the top, they did not wait for the rest of their units but moved out to their assigned objective in twos and threes. Using the many shell holes as cover, they drove the enemy from Pointe du Hoc and took several prisoners. But they found the battered gun positions empty of artillery. Preinvasion rumors of French Resistance reports that the guns had been moved proved to be true.

Naval fire support played a critical part of the rangers' early success. Observers on the destroyer HMS *Talybont,* which had taken part in the early bombardment, saw Force A taking the wrong course. As the rangers corrected course and came under fire from the cliffs, the *Talybont* moved closer to shore and raked the enemy positions with 4-inch and 2-pounder shells. Meanwhile, spotters on the destroyer USS *Satterlee* could see enemy soldiers on the cliff and opened on them with their main battery as well as machine-gun fire.[19]

Colonel Rudder initially established his command post on the narrow, rocky beach below the cliff but soon moved it to a crater at the top. Medics then set up an aid station at the base of the cliff. Rudder ordered a radio message be sent to Force C, under the command of Lt. Col. Max Schneider, to land on Omaha Beach. The message was not received, but Schneider, having waited thirty minutes beyond the prescribed time to land behind Force A, had made the decision to go ashore.[20]

Once Pointe du Hoc had been cleared of the enemy, two sections of Company E formed a defensive perimeter around the battalion command post. About thirty rangers from Companies D, E, and F moved down the exit road leading to the Grandcamp–Vierville coastal highway. Encountering artillery, machine-gun, and rifle fire, they fought their way to the highway and established roadblocks.[21]

Still searching for the missing guns, several patrols were sent out to find them. First Sgt. Leonard Lomell and S.Sgt. Jack Kuhn went down a country lane between two hedgerows. Lomell was in the lead, and when he looked over a hedgerow he saw five guns in an apple orchard. Ammunition was stacked nearby, but the crews were not with the unguarded guns, loitering instead about a hundred yards away. While Kuhn kept watch, Lomell used their two thermite grenades to disable two guns and smashed the sights on all five. The two sergeants then crossed the hedgerow and ran back to the Company D position for more thermite grenades. Returning to the guns, they disabled the remaining three.[22]

German defensive forces mounted two counterattacks during the afternoon of D-Day and another attack that night. All were repulsed, but enemy artillery and mortar fire continued throughout the first day. Casualties among the rangers continued to climb, and ammunition was running low. That afternoon Rudder sent a message by signal lamp via the *Satterlee:* "Located Pointe-du-Hoc—mission accomplished—need ammunition and reinforcement—many casualties." The only reinforcements during the next forty-eight hours were three paratroopers from the 101st Airborne Division who had been misdropped and had made their way through the German lines. In addition, two platoons from the 5th Ranger Battalion arrived at 9:00 p.m.[23]

The rangers at Pointe du Hoc were relieved around noon on D-Day plus two, June 8, by two battalions of the 116th Infantry Regiment and Force C (joined by Force B, having successfully completed their mission to capture Pointe de la Percee).

With his battalion together again, Rudder reorganized his command. Officers and key noncommissioned officers who were killed or wounded were replaced. After this reorganization, companies were assigned various areas to patrol to clear out any Germans who remained behind. The Americans continued to take prisoners and evacuate them to the ships offshore. The rangers took heavy casualties, though, and a number of them were taken prisoner. By the end of the battle, only ninety of the more than two hundred rangers who had landed were still capable of fighting.

After the war some writers on the fighting at Pointe du Hoc commented that it had all been a waste since the German artillery had been withdrawn. Had the guns not been knocked out by Lomell and Kuhn later, they still could have been used to shell Omaha and Utah Beaches. With a range of 25,000 meters, the 155s could also have wreaked havoc on the more than 5,000 ships offshore.[24]

For its actions at Pointe du Hoc, the 2nd Ranger Battalion was awarded the Presidential Unit Citation.

CITATION

The 2d Ranger Infantry Battalion is cited for outstanding performance of duty in action. In the invasion of France the 2d Ranger

> Infantry Battalion was assigned the mission of securing two separate sectors of the beachhead. Three companies of the battalion landed on the beach at Pointe du Hoc, Normandy, France, at 0630, 6 June 1944, under concentrated rifle, machine-gun, artillery, and rocket fire of the enemy. The companies faced not only terrific enemy fire but also mines and hazardous underwater and beach obstacles. Despite numerous casualties suffered in the landing, these companies advanced and successfully assaulted cliffs 100 feet in height. By grim determination and extraordinary heroism, large enemy coastal guns which had been interdicting the beach with constant shell fire were reached and destroyed. At the same time, the remainder of the battalion landed on the beach at Vierville-sur-Mer at 0630, 6 June 1944, directly under withering enemy rifle, machine-gun, artillery, and rocket fire. These companies suffered heavy casualties. Yet such was their gallantry and heroism that they would not be stopped in their advance, and despite mines, enemy snipers, and fatigue continued one mile inland to destroy a coastal battery of large enemy guns. This action secured the necessary beachhead for the forces that were to follow. The outstanding determination and esprit de corps of the 2d Ranger Infantry Battalion, in the face of tremendous odds, are in keeping with the highest traditions of the service.[25]

On June 25 the battalion moved to Foucarville, seventeen miles northwest of Pointe du Hoc on the Cotentin Peninsula, to serve as guards for German prisoners. The camp was intended to hold 20,000 prisoners but had twice that number. The battalion then moved on July 3 to a former German military post in a chateau near Beaumont-Hague, where they conducted day and night training. While at this location, men wounded on D-Day began to return for duty. Eight days later the rangers relieved a reconnaissance squadron in defense of the Beaumont-Hague Peninsula. The enemy held the Guernsey Islands just off the coast, but there was little German activity from that direction.[26]

The 2nd Ranger Battalion was attached to VIII Corps on August 17 and two days later trucked two hundred miles to the Brittany Peninsula. Brest, the second-largest port in France, had been bypassed in earlier attacks, isolating its 50,000 German defenders. Lt. Gen. Omar Bradley was concerned that these troops would raid the American supply lines and ordered VIII Corps to capture the city. Once at their destination, the rangers were attached to the 29th Infantry Division and during the campaign were given three missions: to secure the right flank of the division; to capture the Lochrist *(Graf Spee)* Battery of 280-mm guns; and to mop up Le Conquet Peninsula. The battalion's companies were soon scattered to support other units and engage in day and night patroling.[27]

The 2nd Ranger Battalion was back together by August 23, with tanks, tank destroyers, and two reconnaissance platoons attached. Two days later the attack on Brest began. The rangers began aggressive screening of the 29th Division's right flank. They were reinforced by 700 men of the French Forces of the Interior (FFI) and 162 liberated Russian prisoners the Germans had used as slave laborers. The Russians had their own leadership and were quickly armed and organized into a fighting force.[28]

The battalion attacked north toward the fortress held by the *Graf Spee* Battery. At times the resistance was fierce, at other times light, and many prisoners were taken. A patrol led by Lt. Robert Edlin captured a bunker guarding the huge fort. An English-speaking German officer agreed to take Edlin to the commander's office, where the lieutenant demanded the fort surrender. To emphasize his request, he pulled the pin on a fragmentation grenade and held it between the legs of the German commander, who agreed to surrender the post. Rudder thereafter accepted the formal surrender of the garrison, taking 814 Germans prisoner. Edlin was called "that fool lieutenant" by a forward observer, and the name stuck; it would later be the title of his memoir.

The next few days were spent mopping up the Brittany Peninsula. Germans surrendered in droves. As the rangers liberated towns, Rudder allowed the FFI to take the lead when marching in victory parades through the streets.[29]

After several moves across France, the 2nd Rangers arrived at Arlon, Belgium. There they engaged in training despite some German resistance in the area. On October 20 the battalion moved to Esch, Luxembourg, where it was attached to VIII Corps, First Army. The rangers enjoyed their time in Esch, the country's second-largest city, especially their billets in a former German youth camp in the middle of town.

On November 3 the battalion boarded trucks for Neudorf, Belgium, where they were attached to V Corps, specifically to Combat Command A, 5th Armored Division. The weather had turned nasty, with snow and rain alternating. After supporting a reconnaissance battalion, the rangers were attached to the 28th Division, which was fighting in the Huertgen Forest and had captured Schmidt in early November. A fierce counterattack drove the 28th back to Vossenack, and the division suffered heavy casualties but recaptured Schmidt (see map 8). The rangers replaced the battered 112th Infantry Regiment in the Vossenack area.[30]

During November 14–19, the 28th Division was relieved by the 8th Infantry Division, and the 2nd Battalion was attached to the 8th Division, the rangers continuing their role as regular infantry. The division was ordered to take Bergstein and the high ground at Burgberg, which the rangers remembered as "Hill 400." Also known as Castle Hill, it provided observation over the surrounding towns and countryside as well as the Roer River dams. The Americans did not realize the importance of Hill 400 to the enemy.[31]

On the morning of December 6, Rudder received a message to report to V Corps Headquarters. When he returned that afternoon, he announced that he was to leave the battalion and assume command of the 109th Infantry Regiment in Maj. Gen. Norman D. Cota's 28th Division. He promoted Capt. George Williams to major and gave him command of the 2nd Battalion. Under orders to move to Brandenburg, with Bergstein and Hill 400 (Castle Hill) as their objectives, the battalion mounted trucks for the first phase of the trip to action. The rangers dismounted at Kleinhau and marched on foot to Brandenburg. The weather was miserable, with cold rain falling. As the long column made its way down the muddy road to Bergstein, Rudder was on the road thanking each passing man and saying goodbye.

The battalion relieved elements of the 5th Armored Division, which occupied positions at the edge of Bergstein. Early in the morning of the eighth, the rangers quietly and swiftly moved into the rubble of the town and caught the Germans by surprise. After clearing Bergstein, the next objective was Hill 400.[32]

Hill 400 was taken when two ranger companies (D and F) made a wild bayonet charge at dawn and again caught the Germans by surprise. Once having seized the position, the Americans prepared for a German counterattack. The two companies had suffered heavy losses and could muster only thirty-two men between them. But they repulsed five counterattacks over a two-day period, during which the hill was hit by continuous artillery and mortar fire. The battalion held until relieved on the night of December 8 by a battalion of the 13th Infantry Regiment. While this was going on, Rudder was traveling to the Ardennes to join his next command.[33]

The colonel took command of the 109th Infantry Regiment on December 8. A US Army infantry regiment of World War II had 3,068 officers and enlisted men, commanded by a colonel, organized into a headquarters company, service company, cannon company, antitank company, and three infantry battalions. Each of these battalions had 35 officers and 825 enlisted men, commanded by a lieutenant colonel, and contained a headquarters company, three rifle companies, and a heavy-weapons company. A rifle company, commanded by a captain and having 6 officers and 187 enlisted men, comprised three rifle platoons and a weapons platoon. Each rifle platoon had three squads of 12 men each and was commanded by a lieutenant.[34]

The three divisions of Maj. Gen. Troy Middleton's V Corps occupied a quiet zone in the Ardennes and were responsible for a front of about eighty-five miles. The 4th and 28th Infantry Divisions were weary and casualty ridden from their part in the intense fighting in the Huertgen Forest in November, relieved by the newly arrived and untested 103rd Infantry Division on December 11. The Ardennes sector was used to rest, regroup, receive and train replacements, and replace equipment for units after service in the front lines. It was also a place where newly arrived units could gain combat experience without the risk of heavy fighting.[35]

On the northern part of the corps sector, the 14th Cavalry Group screened the area between the 99th Infantry Division (V Corps) and the 106th Infantry Division. The width of the 106th and the attached 14th Cavalry Group's sector was approximately eighteen airline miles. On the ground the actual defensive line they held was more than twenty-one miles in length. The 28th Infantry Division occupied the center of the corps sector, with a defense line of twenty-five miles, about three times longer than normally expected. Another newly arrived unit, the 60th Armored Infantry Battalion, 9th Armored Division, with no prior battle experience, was assigned a three-mile sector between the 28th and 4th Divisions. The 4th, on the south part of the corps sector, abutted Lt. Gen. George Patton's Third Army on the Luxembourg-French frontier.[36]

Cota deployed the division's three regiments on line. From north to south, the 112th, 110th, and the 109th were each responsible for about eight miles of front. The 112th was tied to the 106th Infantry Division in the north, while the 109th was only loosely connected by patrols, telephone, and radio to the 60th Armored Infantry Battalion to the south. It was obvious that such wide frontages could not be uniformly defended. Squad and platoon strongpoints were selected where good observation and fields of fire could protect the long gaps in the defense line. These were located at crossroads and strategically situated towns.[37]

The 109th had lost almost 50 percent of its soldiers in the November fighting, and since reaching the Ardennes the regiment had been brought to near 86-percent strength. Its soldiers were happy to be out of the hell of the Huertgen Forest and in a "quiet" sector where they had hot showers, fresh-laundered uniforms, and time to write home to loved ones. Passes to Paris or Luxembourg City also were available. Unknown to these men and to headquarters up to the highest level was that a large enemy force was prepared to attack.[38]

On the other side of the front, a mighty German counteroffensive was waiting out the final hours before its launch. The plan, devised by Adolf Hitler in mid-September, was to strike through the thin line of Americans in the Ardennes and drive to the Belgium port at Antwerp, splitting the American and British forces and, in Hitler's mind, compelling the British to sue for peace. The Germans had assembled three armies comprising thirty divisions, some of which were the best armored formations they had left. A quarter of a million men, hundreds of tanks, hundreds of self-propelled guns, and thousands of trucks, half-tracks, armored cars, and other vehicles stood ready to strike the Allied forces. In addition, the Luftwaffe had assembled one thousand planes to support the operation.

At 5:30 a.m. on December 16, a barrage of all calibers, up to and including 14-inch shells from railway guns, came crashing all along the Allied line. Intense fire came down on crossroads, strongpoints, and critical places whose coordinates were well known to the enemy. Taking advantage of almost-freezing temperatures, an early morning mist, and low, heavy cloud cover, the main German attack hit in the area occupied by the 106th Infantry Division and the 112th Infantry Regiment. On the eighteenth the 110th Infantry Regiment was almost wiped out and withdrew to the west. By the nineteenth two of the 106th's regiments had surrendered and the 112th was isolated from the division; after four days of fighting, the regiment joined the defenders at Saint-Vith.[39]

In the 109th's sector, the 2nd Battalion was on the left (north) of the line and the 3rd Battalion on the right, with the 1st Battalion in regimental reserve in Diekirch. Orders from division directed all units to "hold at all costs." Two companies of the 2nd Battalion were soon surrounded, and Rudder sent in a company from the reserve battalion to support them. All along the line enemy infantry infiltrated between frontline units and bypassed the strongpoints. By midmorning the 3rd Battalion's commander, Maj. Jim H. McCoy, a graduate of Texas A&M who had served with Rudder in the 2nd Infantry Division, was forced to commit his reserve to contain a penetration and protect the open left flank. By noon of the second day, the Germans had driven a wedge into the center of the 3rd Battalion's position, and all units were under heavy fire. With several platoons overrun, the battalion was fighting for survival.[40]

With darkness on December 17, commanders and their staffs had an opportunity to review events and plan for the coming day. Their main interest was to hold the line and survive. In the past two days the 109th had done reasonably well, but the cost was ever increasing as more German infantry and armor crossed the Our River. On the regiment's right, elements of the 9th Armored Division had fallen back and contact became tenuous. No air support had been provided and none was expected due to cloudy, rainy, and snowy weather. No reinforcements or support was expected for the next few days.[41]

By early afternoon on the eighteenth, Rudder made a decision on the action the 109th must take. He issued orders to withdraw to the west and defend at all costs the key terrain features and road networks the enemy needed to advance west and south toward Bastogne, Arlon, and Luxembourg City. After further analysis, the colonel concluded that this new defense plan would allow the Germans to defeat his isolated battalions in turn—a cohesive regimental defense position would provide a much larger problem for the enemy. Under Rudder's revised plan, all battalions would pull back to high ground (the Herrenberg) immediately northeast of Diekirch. There they would form a coordinated line anchored on the Sure River on the right, with the left astride the area's main north–south road, known as Skyline Drive.

The withdrawal began on that afternoon and early evening. By midnight the regiment had successfully regrouped to the stronger defensive position, but both flanks remained open and susceptible to attack. The 109th was on the southern shoulder of the German offensive and was expected to play a major part in stabilizing this portion of the American position. The 112th Infantry Regiment would help do the same to the north, but the 110th in the center had been hit so hard that it had disappeared as a military formation.[42]

It was almost noon on December 19 when the Germans attacked and drove the outpost line back to the main defense line some five hundred yards to the rear. By midafternoon Rudder determined that the situation would not permit the regiment to hold another day without danger of complete annihilation. He received the division commander's approval to withdraw that night. In its new position the regiment was attached to the 9th Armored Division for operations. In constant contact with the enemy, elements of the regiment were pushed back. On December 21 a liaison officer from the 80th Infantry Division of Patton's Third Army arrived to coordinate its relief of the 109th.

The next day the 80th Division took over the 109th's positions, and the regiment marched to an assembly area in the rear. At 11:00 a.m. on the morning of the twenty-fourth, VII Corps began an attack on the enemy and met little opposition. The 109th was soon back in familiar territory, moving into towns abandoned by the Germans. During daylight hours on Christmas Day, the regiment's attached tanks and tank destroyers reported eliminating at least twenty armored vehicles and two companies of infantry.[43]

By December 26 the regiment was finally reunited with the 28th Division and formed a defensive line south of Bastogne. During the Battle of the Bulge (as this sustained action became known), the 109th suffered 1,131 casualties, with the preponderance of losses in the infantry companies. During January 2–4, 1945, the regiment moved by trucks to a defensive sector on the Meuse River in France. It and the 112th both used the time to reorganize, while the almost shattered 110th was rebuilt. Reinforcements were pouring in to replenish the squads, platoons, and companies devastated by the surprise German attack. On January 17–18 the 109th Regiment was on the move again, traveling two hundred miles south to the Vosges Mountains and thence to the attack and reduction of the Colmar Pocket (see map 9).

The Vosges Mountain range is on the west side of the Rhine River Valley, with rounded mountains averaging about 3,000 feet in height and having heavily forested lower slopes. Upper ridges provide good observation of the Rhine Valley. In January 1945 the weather was bitterly cold, with knee-deep snow. Supply routes to frontline units in the area followed steep, winding, narrow roads, which were snow covered and often under enemy observation.

The 109th initially replaced the 15th Infantry Regiment, 3rd Infantry Division, at its frontline defensive positions among farmhouses in the bitter cold. The farm buildings were used by the soldiers for warmth, eating, and sleeping, while foxholes beyond were kept manned by rotating shifts. Daylight movement was severely restricted as the enemy had excellent observation of the area.[44]

On January 28 the 109th shifted to relieve the 7th Infantry Regiment. With this new position Rudder's men had exchanged the high Vosges snow and bitter cold for more moderate temperatures and less snow on the Rhine plain. The arrival of the 28th Division on the north line of the Colmar Pocket marked the final days of preparations by the First French Army to drive the Germans east beyond the river. The attack zone of the 109th included the city of Colmar. Rudder was directed to halt the regiment's advance once it reached the northern edge of the city so the honor of its capture would go to the French 2nd Armored Division. At 9:00 p.m. on February 1, the regiment attacked to seize the approaches to Colmar. By 3:00 a.m. they had reached the buildings on the outskirts of town. As planned, the French division swept past to enter the town. Following the liberation of Colmar, a victory celebration and parade were held. Rudder led the US contingent accompanied by Major McCoy, whose unit was the first to breach the German defenses of the town.[45]

When Rudder assumed command of the 109th, he was unaware that he later would be involved in one of the tragic events of World War II. On August 23, 1944, Pvt. Eddie Slovik was assigned to the regiment's Company G. Two days later the Germans shelled the company's position and Slovik vanished. The soldier returned to his unit in October and told his company commander that he was too scared and too nervous to serve in a rifle company—unless he could be assigned in the rear area, he would run away again. Slovik again left his position and turned himself in to military control on October 9. After being returned to the 109th, he wrote a confession to desertion. He was tried for desertion by general court-martial and sentenced to be shot to death.

General Eisenhower ordered Slovik executed on January 31, 1945, and that the sentence be carried out in the area of the 109th. Rudder was responsible to provide the soldiers for the firing squad and to witness that the execution was completed. Four soldiers from each of the three rifle battalions were selected for the firing squad. The site of the execution was Sainte-Marie-aux-Mines in the Vosges Mountains. During World War II, 2,864 members of the US Armed Forces were tried by general courts-martial for desertion. Forty-nine received approved death sentences, but only one was executed—Private Slovik.

After the execution Rudder sent the following message to the regiment:

> Soldiers of the 109th Infantry. Today I had the most regrettable experience I have had since the war began. I saw a former soldier of the 109th Infantry, Private Eddie D. Slovik, shot to death by musketry by soldiers of this regiment. I pray that this man's death will be a lesson to each of us who have any doubt at any time about the price that we must pay to win this war. The person that is not willing to fight and die, if need be, for his country has no right to life.
>
> According to record, this is the first time in eighty years of American history that any United States soldier has been shot to death by musketry for deserting his unit and his fellow man. There is only one reason for our being here and that is to eliminate the enemy that has brought the war about. There is only one way to eliminate the enemy and that is to close with him. Let's all get on with the job we were sent here to do in order that we may return home at the earliest possible moment.[46]

The colonel was soon back with his troops to continue the push to the Rhine. On February 3 the 1st and 3rd Battalions adjusted their positions in preparation for more-extensive attacks. That night the 1st Battalion launched an attack on Sundhoffen, capturing one hundred enemy troops. This was the pattern for the next few days, during which many prisoners were taken. The 75th Infantry Division, on the 109th's left, reached the Rhine on February 9. The Colmar Pocket was now

Rudder in victory parade in Colmar, France. *Official US Army Photo*

eliminated for all practical purposes. On February 12 the regiment was relieved by French forces and moved to an assembly area.

The regiment moved 165 miles north from the Colmar area on the nineteenth to a sector facing east toward the town of Schleiden, Germany. Operations here consisted mostly of combat patrols. On March 7, 1945, active combat for the 109th Infantry Regiment ended. From March 8 to April 21, the men engaged in rear-area security missions as other Allied forces moved east. By April 23 the 28th Division shifted to a new occupation area 215 miles to the south, relieving units of the 36th Infantry Division. The 109th's mission here was to maintain law, order, and security; secure main supply routes, railroads, and pipelines; administer displaced-persons camps; secure the west end of Rhine bridges; and to patrol the west bank of the river to prevent unauthorized crossings.[47]

On June 26 the division was alerted for redeployment to the Pacific. The 3rd Battalion was the first unit of the 109th to leave Europe, going to Boston on the transport ship *Excelsior*. The rest of the regiment boarded the transport ship *Mormacport* for transit to New York. On August 7 the ship carrying Rudder and the two battalions passed the Statue of Liberty, and the soldiers knew they were home. The reunited regiment was sent to Fort Dix, New Jersey, where plans were in place for the division's deployment to the Pacific. The troops were given thirty days of temporary duty at home, after which they were to report to Camp San Luis Obispo, California, for amphibious training and further military service.

The dropping of the atomic bombs changed these plans. The 28th Division was now ordered to assemble at Camp Shelby, Mississippi, for inactivation. While at Camp Shelby, Rudder was joined by his wife, Margaret. When the War Department invited the couple to participate in a transcontinental train tour to sell war bonds, the colonel turned over the regiment to his second in command, Lt. Col. Augustine O. Dugan. Active service in World War II for the 109th Regiment ended on October 22, 1945, and for the 28th Division on December 13.[48]

When Rudder was released from active duty in April 1946, the coaching job at Tarleton was waiting for him. Instead, he decided to stay in Brady and open a business with his friend Frank Corder. The Corder-Rudder Tire and Supply Store soon opened, selling General Electric appliances and Goodyear tires. In 1946 Rudder was elected mayor of Brady and served from 1946 to 1952, winning reelection in 1948 and 1950. He also continued to operate his ranch. He hired a foreman to oversee day-to-day activities but tended to the business side of buying and selling livestock as well as marketing the wool.

In 1946 J. J. "Jake" Pickle, Margaret Rudder's friend from her student days at the University of Texas, came to see Rudder to solicit his support for Allan Shivers and Lyndon B. Johnson. Shivers was running for lieutenant governor and Johnson, a congressman at the time, was considering a run for the US Senate. Shivers won the election and later became the governor of Texas. Two years later, after a visit from Johnson, Rudder agreed to manage his senate campaign in McCulloch County. This was the beginning of a long and personal friendship with the future president.[49]

In 1953 Rudder was employed by the Brady Aviation Company as public- and labor-relations counselor. The company had acute labor problems at the time, but under his guidance an amicable agreement was reached and maintained between labor and management. He was active in the Texas Democratic Party and was a delegate to state conventions in 1948 and 1950. In 1952 and 1954 he was chosen to be his district's member on the Democratic State Executive Committee. In 1954 he was appointed to serve on the Board of Public Welfare. Rudder's next challenge came when Governor Shivers appointed him commissioner of the General Land Office and chairman of the Veterans Land Board. These vacancies came about when the elected land commissioner, Bascom Giles, announced he would not take the oath of office. Scandals surrounded the Veterans Land Board, and a multiphase state investigation of alleged fraud and other irregularities in the $100 million program was underway. Giles was tried and found guilty of accomplice to felony, receiving a sentence of three years in prison. During Rudder's tenure, the office returned to a place of integrity and respect in the state government.[50]

Governor Shivers afterward handpicked Rudder for a position at Texas A&M, telling him "to go over there and straighten that place out." On February 1, 1958, the college's board of directors appointed Rudder A&M's vice president. Marion T. Harrington held the joint position of president of the A&M College and president of the A&M System. Rudder was in fact to be the real "president" and Harrington the "chancellor." The college was in the throes of change regarding two major issues: the admission of females and compulsory military training. In April 1963 the board of directors agreed to admit women on a limited basis but foresaw no changes for the Corps of Cadets. Rudder had a meeting with the entire corps in the G. Rollie White Coliseum to explain the situation, during which he was met with boos and hisses by the angry cadets, who chanted, "We don't want to integrate."[51]

Effective August 23, 1963, the Texas legislature approved a bill changing the name of the Agricultural and Mechanical College of Texas to Texas A&M University. When Harrington resigned effective September 1, 1965, Rudder became president of the university and president of the Texas A&M University System. In addition to his responsibilities on the main campus, he was responsible for the programs at Tarleton State College, Prairie View A&M College, the Texas Agriculture Research Station, the Texas Agricultural Extension Service, the Texas Engineering Extension Service, the Texas Engineering Experiment Service, the

Rudder visiting with Texas A&M students in their dormitory, October 29, 1969. Battalion, *Texas A&M University*

Texas Forestry Service, the Texas Maritime Academy, and the Texas Transportation Institute.[52]

On April 24, 1965, the Texas A&M Board of Directors eliminated the requirement for compulsory enrollment in the Corps of Cadets for entering freshmen. The board also authorized Rudder to use his "discretion" in the admission of women. As a result more applications from women were approved, and by the fall of 1969, all applicants who could meet the same academic qualifications as men were being admitted. In the fall of 1971, all pretenses were abolished, and women were to be admitted on an equal basis with men. After ninety-five years, much to

Rudder lying in state on the campus of Texas A&M University.
Courtesy Cushing Memorial Library and Museum, Texas A&M

Rudder upon retirement from the US Army Reserve on July 12, 1967. *Courtesy Nelda Green*

the chagrin of many former students and the majority of cadets, the all-male military college became a coeducational university.[53]

During the postwar years, Rudder remained active in the US Army Reserve. He earned promotion to brigadier general in 1954 and to major general in 1957, assuming command of the 90th Infantry Reserve Division in 1955. In 1963 he left the 90th to become assistant deputy commanding general for mobilization, Continental Army Command. He retired from the military in 1967 after thirty-four years of service.

Maj. Gen. James E. Rudder's military decorations include the Distinguished Service Cross, Distinguished Service Medal, Silver Star, Bronze Star with Oak Leaf Cluster, Purple Heart with Oak Leaf Cluster, French Legion of Honor and Croix de Guerre with Palm, and Belgium Order of

Rudder statue on the Texas A&M campus. *Courtesy Lisa Kalmus, Sanders Corps of Cadets Center*

Leopold and Croix de Guerre with Palm. His decorations are on display in the Rudder Tower on the campus of Texas A&M University.[54]

On January 29, 1970, Rudder suffered a cerebral hemorrhage and was taken to a hospital in Houston. He died on March 23 and lay in state in the Texas A&M System Administration Building on March 26. The funeral that afternoon was held in White Coliseum. In attendance were former president Lyndon B. Johnson, Gov. Preston Smith, Rep. Olin E. Teague, and numerous other dignitaries. Burial was in the College Station cemetery.

Historian Henry Dethloff summed up Rudder's time at Texas A&M when he said: "Rudder restructured, revitalized, and revolutionized the institution. He built a university where a college had been."[55]

★ 5 ★

Flying Tiger Ace

DAVID L. "TEX" HILL

CLASS OF 1932

During World War II, a group of American fighter pilots fought the Japanese in the skies over China and Burma. Some called them mercenaries, but this group of flamboyant, daring, and courageous flyers caught the attention of the American public at a time when the nation needed heroes. They were called the Flying Tigers. This is the story of one of those brave warriors.

Dr. Pierre Bernard Hill was a Presbyterian minister who was called to missionary work in Korea (see map 5). He left America in 1912 with his wife, Ella Thraves Hill; sons Sam and John; and infant daughter Martha to pursue his calling in the town of Mokpo, a coastal town on the southwestern tip of the Korean Peninsula. The family later moved to the ancient city of Kwangju, the capital of the South Cholla Province and located north of Mokpo, where David Lee Hill was born on July 14, 1915. In additional to his missionary work, Dr. Hill spent many hours at

Kwangju's hospital for lepers, disregarding the health risk to perform services for the unfortunate patients. (see map 5)

Korea's national administration was controlled by the Empire of Japan. This takeover had occurred in 1910, and the Japanese maintained military garrisons in strategic locations throughout the country. The occupiers were antagonistic to Koreans and foreigners alike. The Hill family was a double dose of irritation since they were both white and Christian. Several times Japanese soldiers would approach their house and demand to search for "contraband." Dr. Hill would fold his arms, plant his large frame in the doorway, and coolly inform the soldiers that the first man to lay a hand on him would die. Eventually, the angry soldiers would leave, somehow knowing that it was best not to test the tall American.

By the summer of 1916, the strain of their life and missionary work was taking a toll on Dr. and Mrs. Hill. Among other ailments, they suffered from toxemia in their teeth, a malady resulting from eating food grown in the Korean soil. Hill's doctor advised him to seek treatment in the United States since he would not find a competent dentist in Korea. After much prayer and consideration, Dr. Hill decided to request a furlough in the United States, which was granted immediately.

In September the family returned to America and settled in Virginia, where they stayed several months with Ella's father, Marse John Thraves, and his family. Thraves helped Dr. Hill locate a six-hundred-acre farm near Chula, which the family soon learned to work with the Thraves' help. Young David's first childhood memories were of performing his chores on the farm. Having left Korea when he was fifteen months old, he had no memories of that country. In the mild Virginia climate and with a diet of wholesome foods, the Hills' toxemia receded and their health improved.

Having been turned down for military service after the United States entered World War I, Dr. Hill looked for a place to minister. He was contacted by the elders of the Second Presbyterian Church in Roanoke, Virginia, who were looking for a "supply minister" since their regular pastor was away working with the YMCA in the war effort. Hill sold the farm and moved his family to Roanoke. After the war the regular minister returned, and the Hills relocated to Louisville, Kentucky, where the First Presbyterian Church was seeking a minister. Dr. Hill wanted to return to missionary work but was told that if he returned to Korea, so would the toxemia. He once again moved his family, this time to San Antonio, Texas, where he became the minister of the First Presbyterian Church.[1]

The church's manse was being renovated at the time, so the Hills would be staying in Kerrville at the Westminster Encampment for Young People, sixty-five miles north of San Antonio in the Hill Country. Westminster was a primitive camp of wooden-frame tents covered in canvas where the lack of electricity and indoor plumbing reminded the Hills of Korea. David grew to love the area, with so many hunting and fishing opportunities. After a month the family moved to San Antonio and a newly remodeled manse, spacious and upscale in the best part of town.

David entered the first grade at Travis Elementary School. He later attended San Antonio Academy, where he was subject to strict discipline enforced by the faculty and staff. The academy was a military school, and the students wore military uniforms.

After a couple of years in San Antonio, a member of the church offered the use of a summer house for a month or two in the small town of Hunt, near Kerrville. Dr. Hill gladly accepted the offer, remembering how much his boys had enjoyed the area. During this stay, David hunted and fished to his heart's content. The same offer was repeated for several summers after that, after which David considered the Hill Country his home. In 1925 Dr. Hill bought sixteen acres along the Guadalupe River near Hunt. The property was unimproved, so they set about building a new home. Ten-year-old David spent days on a nearby hill, quarrying rock for the walls. When these were up, he helped shingle the roof. The project was completed within a year, the house remaining in the family's possession for the next seventy years.[2]

David's fascination with flight began when a Mr. Moon, Dr. Hill's Korean helper, taught him to build kites. The boy soon began to make model airplanes using a straight stick and pieces of aluminum, with the makeshift propeller powered by a rubber band unwound from a golf ball. He was impressed by the Army Air Corps cadets from Kelly Field who came to his home to see his sister, Martha. He thought it would be great to fly an actual plane. His first airplane ride was when he and a friend slipped out of a church service and went to a local airfield, offering their collection money for a ride around the field. The pilot immediately understood the situation and agreed to take them on a spin, the boys grinning from ear to ear when they were back on the ground. As the two took off to return to church, the pilot thought to himself, "That boy is going to fly, even if he doesn't know it yet."[3]

The tall, lanky, fair-haired David was nearly thirteen when he graduated from the San Antonio Academy in the spring of 1928. He had excelled in school and had enjoyed the military structure of the academy. He then enrolled in the McCallie School, a prestigious military institution in the foothills of the Appalachian Mountains near Chattanooga, Tennessee. His older brother John had some years earlier attended McCallie and had described it in glowing terms.

David's longtime friend Bruce Martindale also enrolled in McCallie and accompanied him on the long train ride to Tennessee. They were roommates for their first two years. David, being one of the few cadets from west of the Mississippi and having a lanky gait and slow Texas drawl, soon picked up the nickname "Tex." Thereafter, except for family and the faculty, he became known as "Tex." His penchant for adventure, pranks, and mischief resulted in his being restricted to the school grounds many times.

During the summer vacations, Tex spent many hours hunting and fishing with his father. He also worked on expanding the family home and one summer worked for the Texas State Highway Department. The road project was improving the route between San Antonio and Fredericksburg. It was hard work in the searing Texas heat. Because of that, one day Tex hardly noticed when bitten by a spider, which turned out to be a black widow. He went home after work and began to have difficulty breathing. His older brother drove him to a hospital in San Antonio, where he was given a few shots. In a short while he felt the effects of the poison easing and was allowed to return home.

Dr. Hill was concerned about his son's conduct at McCallie and decided to enroll him instead in Main Avenue High School, though later attending Jefferson High School, both in San Antonio. After a year in public schools, Tex returned to McCallie, where he graduated in 1934. During his high school years, the young Hill participated in football, basketball, baseball, track, and boxing and was also a cheerleader. After graduation he had the idea of pursuing a military career and considered joining the navy. His father would not stand in his way but convinced Tex that getting a college degree would present unlimited opportunities. The young man agreed and sent his application to Texas A&M.[4]

Tex's sense of humor was evident in his application for admission to college. He wrote of his birth in Korea: "This unfortunate place of birth might have proved a handicap as I could never have become president of the United States. But for an ambitious person like me this fact has caused me little grief, for after all when one becomes president there is little room for advancement." He enrolled in Texas A&M in September 1934 and declared a major of chemical engineering. He found that the academic preparation at McCallie made it easy for him his freshman year, requiring only little study. He selected the cavalry for his required military science and was assigned to Troop A, Cavalry, in the Corps of Cadets. In 1934 the enrollment was 3,898 students, with 2,998 in the corps.[5]

Tex enjoyed the camaraderie in his outfit and the greater freedom that comes with college. He was close enough that he could go home some weekends during the year. He also enjoyed the many corps activities and events on the campus. At the end of his freshman year, Hill was one of seven cadets out of thirty in his unit selected to be a cadet corporal, the highest rank available to sophomores.

Returning to A&M the next year, he anticipated a happy reunion with his friends in Troop A. All was well until he learned that the corps was adding a chemical-warfare company and that cadets majoring in chemical engineering would be transferred to that new unit. Wanting to remain with his unit, Hill changed his major. When this did not change the decision to transfer him to the chemical-warfare company, he reverted to his original major. During the year he became frustrated with the changes, and his grades began to slip. By the time he went home for Christmas, his grades were dangerously low.

The young man decided to drop out of school. When he told his father, he found an understanding parent. Dr. Hill was making a trip to Hampden-Sydney, Virginia, the site of his own alma mater, which bore the same name as the town. The trip gave the two plenty of time to talk. On the way back to Texas, Dr. Hill mentioned that Tex might consider attending Austin College in Sherman, Texas, a private school with an enrollment of less than three hundred students a top-notch faculty, and high academic standards. Tex enrolled in the fall and was delighted to learn that most of his credits from Texas A&M would transfer and count toward a degree.[6]

Tex enjoyed his days at Austin College and excelled academically, but he had not given up his fun-loving activities. On one occasion

Hill as an aviation cadet at Pensacola Naval Air Station.
Courtesy Reagan Schaupp

before a football game against arch rival Trinity College, he traveled to Waxahachie, slipped up on the student-built bonfire (not yet burning), quietly tossed on a gallon of gasoline, and set it ablaze. He eluded the student guards and made a triumphant return to Sherman.[7]

During a visit home his senior year, Hill went to Randolph Field to take tests to become an aviation cadet in the Army Air Corps. A few weeks later the army informed him that he had failed to qualify, though no reason was given (and he never learned why). After graduating from Austin in 1938, he enlisted in the US Navy and was assigned to Opa-locka, Florida, to attend the Navy Flight Elimination Training Course. Of the twelve candidates to enter the three-week course, only

Hill's first carrier landing. *Official US Navy Photo*

ten completed the training. These graduates were then sent to Pensacola for thirteen months of instruction on flying all the primary aircraft types in the navy. The school also doubled as officers' training for the enlisted cadets, a routine Tex found easy after his years in military schools.

Hill almost "washed out" of flight training when he failed two check rides. One of his former instructors, Lt. Donald Frazier, volunteered to give Tex additional flying instruction, which helped him complete flight school. On November 1, 1939, the class graduated, and Hill received his commission as ensign and the coveted gold wings of a naval aviator. His first posting was to the USS *Saratoga*. The aircraft carrier was based in San Diego, California, and Tex was assigned to Torpedo Squadron 3 (VT-3), which flew the Douglas TBD-1 Devastator torpedo bomber. During Hill's first carrier landing, the arresting hook beneath his aircraft half-caught the cable and caused the plane to skid to the left, where it ended up hanging off the flight deck partway into one of the gun galleries. Following this near disaster, Hill made ninety-nine more landings without mishap. The *Saratoga* later joined the Pacific Fleet and participated in war games near Hawaii.[8]

In the fall of 1939 Hill was a member of one of six TBD crews selected to test a new concept for horizontal bombing. The group was assigned to the USS *Ranger*, at the time conducting Neutrality Patrol operations in the Atlantic. The carrier's primary duty was to join a merchant convoy out of Bermuda and escort it all the way to the Azores. But the crews never had a chance to test the new bombing concept as the war overtook the United States.

Hill was assigned to Bombing Squadron 4 (VB-4), which flew the SB2U Vindicator. The SB2U was an agile aircraft with considerably more speed, ceiling, and range than the clumsy TBD, allowing the pilot to quickly maneuver into position for a dive-bombing run. His squadron was broken into two scouting squadrons for the convoy-escort mission, flying reconnaissance missions looking for German submarines. On one patrol Tex spotted two enemy submarines and a submarine tender on the surface and called in British Navy units to attack them. On a later mission Hill's patrol sighted a Spanish vessel. Spain was neutral but sympathetic to Germany, and the Allies knew that Spanish ships were providing fuel to Axis submarines. The British were notified, and when the *Ranger* returned to Bermuda, the Spanish vessel was there, captured by the British. After its quota of escort missions was fulfilled, the *Ranger* returned to Norfolk for maintenance.[9]

After landing at the Norfolk Naval Air Station, the squadron's pilots walked into the operations office to see the operations officer talking to a man they did not recognize. The airmen were introduced to retired US Navy commander Rutledge Irvine, who was a recruiter for Claire Chennault, a former captain in the Army Air Corps who had resigned after ten years' service. In 1937 Chennault went to China to serve as Generalissimo Chiang Kai-shek's chief air strategist. Chiang later sent Chennault back to the United States to solicit support for China in its fight against Japan.[10]

Chennault toured the country, talking to politicians, newsmen, former air corps friends, and aircraft manufacturers. He was looking for aircraft and pilots to fly them. The chief of the Army Air Corps, Lt. Gen. H. H. "Hap" Arnold, was violently opposed to the idea of American planes, pilots, and crews going into combat in China. The chief of the navy's Bureau of Aeronautics, R. Adm. Jack Towers, also opposed the plan. While visiting the Curtiss-Wright factory in Buffalo, New York, Chennault learned that one hundred P-40B Tomahawks scheduled to go to England were just then rolling off the assembly lines. The British were persuaded to relinquish them to him and take delivery of a later-model fighter more suitable for combat against the Luftwaffe. Chennault now had his planes, but he still needed pilots and ground crews. The personnel problem was solved when Pres. Franklin D. Roosevelt signed an unpublished executive order on April 15, 1941, authorizing reserve officers and enlisted men from the Army Air Corps and the naval and marine air services to join Chennault's American Volunteer Group (AVG).

Recognizing that the United States was not at war with Japan, the US government could not deal openly with China. The Central Aircraft Manufacturing Company of China (CAMCO) was authorized to hire one hundred American pilots and several hundred ground crewmen to "operate, service and manufacture aircraft in China."[11]

Irvine explained the program to Tex, his close friend Ed Rector, and Bert Christman. Signing up with CAMCO would involve resigning from the navy and going to Burma to defend the vital Burma Road, China's supply line. The retired commander said that he and Chennault were looking for fighter pilots, but to get the AVG going they were accepting volunteers experienced with other types of aircraft. All three pilots indicated that they were interested in joining the group. Irvine left, saying that he would be in touch with them later. With the increased enemy submarine activity in the Atlantic, the *Ranger* put to sea and headed for the Azores. A month later when the carrier returned to Norfolk, Irving was waiting with contracts. The pay was considerably higher than an ensign's salary. Squadron leaders would receive $750 per month, flight leaders $650, and wingmen $600. He also told his recruits that although not in the contract, the Chinese government would pay a bonus of $500 for each Japanese plane destroyed in the air or on the ground. Eight men from the *Ranger* signed up for the AVG that day.[12]

Ultimately, more than 300 men volunteered to join—110 were pilots, the rest were aircraft mechanics, cooks, supply and finance clerks, radiomen, weathermen, photographers, and a chaplain. Most of the pilots were from the navy, six came from the marines, and fewer than

Flying Tiger P-40 fighter showing shark-teeth marking. *Official US Army Photo*

half were from the army. The volunteer group also included a dentist and three physicians.

The first group of forty ground crew left in early June aboard the S.S. *President Pierce* bound for Rangoon, Burma; a mixed group of 123 pilots and ground crew aboard the Dutch ship *Jaegersfontein* departed on July 10. Hill's group of twenty volunteers sailed on the Dutch ship *Bloemfontein* in late July. Two other Dutch vessels soon followed with the remaining volunteers. The men wore civilian clothes, and passenger manifests listed them as actors, musicians, salesmen, or teachers—anything but pilots.[13]

After arrival in Rangoon, the volunteers traveled 170 miles north to Toungoo, the site of a Royal Air Force (RAF) airfield. Chennault was eager to get the training program started, but the P-40s were still in crates in Rangoon. It was not until early August that a few planes were ferried to Toungoo. By the end of the month, twenty-two aircraft had been assembled, but all ninety-nine did not arrive until the end of November; unfortunately, one had been dropped into the harbor when the crate was being unloaded. Chennault instituted a program he called "kindergarten for the AVG." This consisted of seventy-two hours in the classroom and sixty hours in the air. Chennault was an excellent instructor, drawing on his years as a rural schoolteacher and director of an Army Air Corps flying school. He provided the basic, crucial knowledge that he had taken great pains to learn. Using captured Japanese flying manuals, Chennault instructed his men in the enemy's tactics. The volunteers spent five hours on familiarization of the P-40. The fighter was powered by an 1,150-horsepower liquid-cooled Allison engine, could reach a cruising speed of about 300 MPH, and had a ceiling of 32,000 feet. Its armament consisted of two .50-caliber and four .30-caliber machine guns.[14]

The volunteers were soon making training flights and engaging in mock dogfights. Three volunteers were killed during this early training. Chennault organized the men into three squadrons of eighteen aircraft each. The 1st Squadron took the name "Adams and Eves" and was made up of mostly Army Air Corps men. Tex was assigned to the 2nd Squadron, made up of mostly navy fliers and called the "Panda Bears." The 3rd Squadron, "Hell's Angels," was a combination of army and navy pilots plus three marines.[15]

On December 8, 1941, the volunteers were stunned to learn that the Japanese had attacked Pearl Harbor. The AVG went on full alert, with some concern that this would delay the proposed move to Kunming, China. On December 12 the 3rd Squadron was sent to Rangoon to support the British. Six days later the 1st and 2nd Squadrons relocated to Kunming. After landing, Hill noticed hundreds of Chinese workers crushing rock into gravel by hand to lay a two-foot runway foundation for a topping of asphalt.[16] (see map 6)

The facilities at Kunming were a vast improvement over Burma. The support buildings around the airfield were new. Hostel Number One, home of the 2nd Squadron, represented a quantum improvement over the rickety teak-wood barracks in Toungoo. The old stone building, formerly part of an agricultural college, featured clean rooms that could house two men each. There were also hot baths and room boys to look after bedding and clothing. The outstanding mess hall had delicious food and cooks familiar with American cooking. It also included a well-stocked bar.[17]

Hill missed the first combat action when he went to a nearby building for a coffee break. When the squadron was scrambled, a standby pilot took off in Tex's P-40, and he could only watch. Nine Japanese bombers were shot down in this first sortie. Tex was disappointed to have missed the first combat, but Chennault was pleased with the performance of his AVG. He called for a debriefing immediately, intending to use the opportunity to instruct the men while the action was fresh on their minds.[18]

Chennault decided to replace the 3rd Squadron in the Rangoon area because they were down to only eleven flyable planes following two Japanese raids that had destroyed or damaged several aircraft. Hill's squadron was sent to Rangoon on December 30 and initially quartered in an old, rickety barracks by the airfield at Mingaladon. As a result of the nightly air raids by one or two enemy bombers, the volunteers vacated the barracks and moved out to the surrounding area. Tex found a place a long way from the field in a *bashas*—a bamboo hut with a palm-leaf roof.

Hill's first taste of combat came in early January 1942. Intelligence reports indicated that Japanese aircraft were gathering at bases in Thailand within easy striking distance of Rangoon. Chennault decided that the AVG would go on the offensive and sent Tex, Rector, and two others to strafe Raheng, a small outlying field across the border. Hill shot down two enemy fighters but was nearly shot down himself.[19]

In late January Tex was sitting in the alert tent flipping through a magazine and watching some British Hurricane fighters, newly arrived from India, landing when the phone rang. A British officer told him that an enemy raid was incoming. He ran to one of the two P-40s on the strip that was ready to go. As he was taking off, he saw the RAF ground crews making a frenzied effort to refuel the Hurricanes. Hill and his wingman climbed to 12,000 feet, just below a small bank of clouds, and started looking for the enemy. Twenty-three Nakajima Type 97 "Nate" fighters were headed for the airfield, and Tex knew that if they made it through, the refueling Hurricanes would be torn up. The two P-40s arrowed into the top of the enemy formation, scattering the Japanese in all directions. Tex's first burst missed, but his second hit a Nate's tail and fuselage. The enemy pilot banked sharply, and the American's third burst peppered the cockpit, sending the Nate into a final spin. Hill's P-40 screamed out through the bottom of the Japanese formation, but his wingman was nowhere to be seen. Tex regained altitude and came around for a second pass, spotting a second Nate that did not seem to notice him. Lining up for a shot, he fired a medium-length burst. The P-40's tracers hit the enemy fighter, tearing a wing off and causing it to skid to the right before flipping over and fluttering earthward. As Hill dove from the action, 20-mm cannon shells slammed into the underside of his right wing. Low on ammunition, he pulled away from a handful of trailing fighters. His wingman had shot down four of the enemy.

By this time, three more AVG planes had arrived in the area and downed another Nate. This was enough for the Japanese, who fled. Several other AVG aircraft got airborne but did not participate in the action. When all aircraft were back at base, the ground crews prepared them for another sortie, believing that a second wave was on the way to bomb the airbase. When the air-raid warning went off, the squadron again scrambled along with the RAF Hurricanes. This time Tex remained on the ground because his plane was damaged. The combined force encountered thirty-one bombers and about as many Nates, with the Tigers shooting down five bombers and four Nates. Tex lost a close friend, Bert Christman, in this battle. After bailing out of his damaged plane, Christman was shot to death while descending in his parachute.[20]

On his next mission Tex had the opportunity to avenge his fallen comrade. Flying wingman to Bob Neale, he spotted seven twin-engine Ki-21 "Betty" bombers about 4,000 feet below them. The two of them pushed their fighters over and applied full power as the bombers continued to drone straight ahead. Then Tex saw a V-shaped flight of tiny, dark specks far behind the bombers. About that time they saw two RAF Buffalo fighters climbing toward the enemy bombers from another direction. The British pilots opened fire before the P-40s were in range. After several bursts, a Betty spouted flame from an engine, slowly rolled out of the formation and went down. The Buffaloes broke away to line up for another pass just as Tex fired at the lumbering rightmost bomber. As he flashed by he saw a wisp of white smoke coming from the engine he had hit. Neale's target was burning, in two pieces, as it began a fatal spin. The remaining bombers jettisoned some bombs and made shallow dives to gain speed. But they maintained a well-regimented formation while continuing toward their target, Mingaladon.

The airfield was coming into view when Hill and Neale charged in from the rear of the bomber formation. The British came at them from the other side. Tex opened fire with all his guns and watched debris tear out of a Betty's left engine. By now the enemy fighters had caught up to the bombers, but four other P-40s began diving into the formation of Nates. The enemy fighters peeled off to engage these new opponents and were soon in a swirling dogfight.

Hill focused on the right-hand bomber and fired all guns when within range. He watched as his tracers "walked" their way from the wing roots to an engine and then along the fuselage. Debris was flying

Tex Hill beside his P-51 fighter. *Official US Army Photo*

everywhere, and as Tex banked away, the bomber exploded. A piece of his victim hit his aircraft, punching a large hole in his left wing. While the damaged P-40 still flew tolerably well, it was time to get the ship down on the deck. But before he did, Tex noticed a lone Japanese fighter speeding into the conflict. He made a hard left-hand turn, hoping his right wing would hold up, lined up for a shot, and poured a salvo directly into the enemy's cockpit. Flames licked from the engine, and Tex guessed that the pilot was dead as the plane spun to earth.

Despite their losses, the Japanese continued their attacks on Mingaladon for the next six days. Hill scored his seventh victory during this period when he shot down another Nate. That date, January 29, marked the end of the Japanese effort to destroy the AVG in Rangoon.[21]

The Panda Bears made a raid of their own against a Japanese airfield at Chaing Mai, Thailand, where they caught forty enemy fighters on the ground, destroying three-quarters of the aircraft. During this action, the squadron commander, J. V. "Jack" Newkirk, was shot down by antiaircraft fire. When Chennault learned of the loss, he appointed Hill to take command of the squadron.

The battle-weary 2nd Squadron was transferred to Kunming (see map 6) in February. Chennault had been promised a "bomber AVG" from the States, but that plan was sidetracked long ago. Hill decided to make up for the lack of bombers by modifying some P-40s. He and the other former navy dive-bombing pilots designed bomb racks for the Tomahawk. The ingenuity of the ground crews resulted in bomb racks and release mechanisms for all of the fighters. Tex informed the AVG commander of the project and offered to demonstrate the effectiveness. Chennault nodded his approval, and they headed for the airfield, where a large circle had been marked on the ground. The demonstration aircraft, flown by ex-navy men familiar with dive bombing, carried dummy bombs. Chennault and the other spectators watched as all four aircraft put their bombs in the circle. Approvingly, he remarked: "That's great. I imagine it could come in handy sometime."[22]

With the fall of Rangoon to the Japanese in March 1942, British and Indian forces withdrew toward India and Chinese forces withdrew into China. All were vigorously pursued. The area of most interest to the Chinese was the Salween River on the Burma-China border, the last formidable barrier between the Japanese and Kunming. The river flows down from the Himalayas and carves a mile-deep gorge through the mountains of southern China. If the Japanese crossed the Salween and captured Kunming, China would be cut off from foreign aid and would have to surrender.

The Allied withdrawal was turning into a rout, and the Chinese Army in Northeast Burma fled in disorder. By May 5, Japanese forces were near the west bank of the Salween. Chennault knew that the AVG was the only force that could stop them; he also knew that an attack on the enemy column would mean the death of innocent refugees. He radioed Madame Chiang in Chungking and explained the situation. She responded by saying that the generalissimo instructed the AVG to attack the trucks, boats, and other enemy vehicles between the Salween and Lungling City.

The AVG had recently received a number of new-model P-40s, the Kittyhawk. Unlike the Tomahawk, these came equipped with bomb racks. Chennault decided to have four Kittyhawks bomb the armored column while four Tomahawks flew cover. Before takeoff, he spoke to the men who volunteered for the mission, telling them that if the Japanese were not stopped at the Salween, China would have to surrender. He also noted that this was the most important point in the war.

Hill led the first strike, accompanied by Rector and two others. The AVG armorers had adapted the Kittyhawks center-lines shackle, intended to hold a fuel tank, to accommodate a 350-pound Russian demolition bomb. The Tigers were to destroy the Burma Road by bombing it at a point where a landslide would result and make repairs on the road difficult. Approaching the Salween, they could see Japanese engineers unloading pontoons from trucks and hauling them to the river bank. Coming down the narrow road was a long column of tanks and trucks. To one side was a towering rock wall, on the other side a steep precipice. The enemy vehicles were trapped on the narrow road.

The four Kittyhawks dived and dropped their big demolition bombs, causing landslides that partially blocked the road. They then made another pass to drop their fragmentation bombs. Ammunition and fuel trucks exploded, tossing other vehicles into the gorge and ripping huge holes in the road. On the third pass, the six .50-caliber machine guns on the Kittyhawks raked the column, causing more destruction. When their ammunition was gone, the covering flight of four Tomahawks dived down and continued to strafe the trapped Japanese. Returning to base to rearm, Tex and other pilots were replaced with fresh men. After the AVG's second raid on the Japanese column, Chinese forces trapped on the west bank jumped out of their foxholes and attacked the panic-stricken survivors. During the next four days, Chennault attacked the Salween gorge with every plane he had, even borrowing a flight of Curtis Hawk dive bombers and a dozen old Russian twin-engine bombers from the Chinese Air Force.

By May 11 the Japanese had given up the drive into South China and prepared to attack the middle of that nation, particularly along the Hankow Railroad and up the Yangtze River. To meet this threat, Chennault deployed the AVG north to protect Kweilin and Chungking and began to dive-bomb airfields and shipping in Hankow and Canton. The Japanese stopped bombing cities and began to concentrate on AVG airfields. The Tigers went up to meet every one of these attacks, and their score of victories rose.[23]

Hill with Generalissimo Chiang Kai-shek. *Official US Army Photo*

With their one-year contract ending in July, there was an effort by the Army Air Corps to convince the volunteers to enlist in that service branch and remain in China as part of the newly arrived 23rd Fighter Squadron. After he learned that the AVG would receive no more support from the US Army if he refused induction, Chennault accepted the offer. He was commissioned a colonel and given command of the China Air Task Force (CATF), a part of the Tenth Air Force, composed of Army Air Forces fighter and bomber units in China. Shortly afterward, he was promoted to brigadier general. The army wanted the AVG disbanded on April 30, but Chennault knew it would take longer for the army to replace the unit. The date for disbanding the AVG later was pushed back to July 4, 1942.

Chennault believed that most of his men would accept induction if they were offered a thirty-day furlough home before returning to combat. On June 22 the induction board began visiting the various AVG bases. At Kweilin the pilots listened politely to the officials' plea to join the Army Air Force. Neale, who was the leading ace, was offered a commission as lieutenant colonel but turned down the offer. Other pilots were offered commissions as majors or captains, but no one accepted. The ground crews were assembled, and they all refused to enlist. The induction team had no better luck with the volunteers at other bases.[24]

On his return from ferrying replacement aircraft from India, Hill had a conversation with Chennault at the airbase in Peishiyi. The colonel related the meetings of the induction teams with AVG personnel and the dismal results. Tex said that he would stay around as long as he was needed. Chennault displayed his obvious relief with a rare smile, shaking Tex's hand and saying that was what he wanted to hear. He asked Hill to try to get some of the men to stay around for an additional two weeks to allow time to integrate the army replacement pilots. Tex returned to his squadron at Hengyang and talked to the men about extending their contract for two weeks. Most of them agreed. He then flew to the other bases to check with the remaining Tigers. Twenty-six pilots and fifty-seven ground crew agreed to stay the additional two weeks. Tex's friend Ed Rector and three other pilots agreed to stay and also to accept induction into the army. Twenty-two ground personnel also opted for induction.[25]

After the AVG units had moved to scattered airfields in East China, army personnel began trickling in by small groups, and a handful of Air Corps men had attached themselves to the AVG. On June 27 nine Air Corps P-40s of the 16th Fighter Squadron, 51st Fighter Group, arrived in Kunming, having been invited by Chennault from India to be attached for "training experience." They were not supposed to stay in China, but the colonel sent them on to Lingling and never returned them. These men proved to be capable combat pilots, and none complained about staying in China. The B-25 Mitchells of the 11th Bombardment Squadron arrived in Kunming by ones and twos until, by the middle of June, there were seven parked on the airfield. After several "warm up" raids, the B-25s were sent to Kweilin. Escorted by the AVG, they promptly began bombing raids on Hankow and Canton.[26]

In June Chennault was involved with a project by the Republic Film Studio to shoot an epic starring John Wayne. The movie, *Flying Tigers,* gave a wildly inaccurate impression of the AVG as a collection of former transport pilots who fought in China before the outbreak of the Pacific War, ending with Wayne and his sidekicks listening to news of the Pearl Harbor attack. The character Wayne played in the movie was based on Tex Hill. Meeting the actor years later, Hill told him that the movie was corny and the situation in China was not anything like that depicted in the picture. Wayne replied, "Well, it did all right, anyway, and I really enjoyed doing it." This was the beginning of a friendship that would last until the actor's death many years later.[27]

With the day rapidly approaching for the end of the AVG, it was difficult for Tex to watch his comrades preparing to depart. The three AVG squadrons would become the 74th, 75th, and 76th Fighter Squadrons of the 23rd Fighter Group. Frank Schiel would command the 74th in Kunming, Tex would command the 75th at Hengyang, and Ed Rector took the 76th at Kweilin. The 23rd Fighter Group was to be commanded by the newly arrived Col. Robert L. Scott Jr.

During the third week in June, Tex led a flight of P-40s in an early morning raid in East China. On the Yangtze River they found a Japanese gunboat escorting three transports downstream toward Hankow. The Tigers attacked the flotilla and sank all four vessels.

On July 3 Rector and six of his men raided Hankow and on the way home shot down five enemy fighters. Neale and three mates intercepted a dozen Nate fighters and shot down five. Spotting two more Nates, Neale gave chase and shot down one of them. The Flying Tigers had fought their last fight.

On July 4, 1942, the American Volunteer Group ceased to exist, having written a unique page in the annals of war. Only a dozen of their aircraft had been shot down; sixty-one had been lost on the ground to strafing, accidents, or by demolition at Loiwing to prevent their capture. The Flying Tigers were credited with downing 299 Japanese aircraft. They had, with the help of the RAF, kept the port of Rangoon open for two and a half months. At the Salween River, they had stopped the Japanese drive north that would have meant the end of China.[28]

The Japanese assumed that with the AVG gone, they would be facing green pilots and immediately launched heavy attacks on Hengyang. Hill and a few other veterans knocked down 30 planes in two days. The Japanese were determined to wipe out the CATF and continued to launch day and night raids against Hengyang and Kweilin. To accomplish this they gathered a force of 350–400 planes, including a new type of Zero fighter—the Oscar.[29]

In late July Tex left Hengyang alone in the early hours of the morning. Winging his way north, he followed a river to the mouth of the Yangtze and then proceeded northeast toward Hankow. Navigating by moonlight, he saw the glow of lights at the docks of Hankow. There enemy soldiers, under tung-oil lamps, were unloading supply ships. After surveying the scene, Hill went into a dive and dropped a 570-pound demolition bomb on a promising-looking building. He made another pass on the wharves and dropped two strings of fragmentation bombs. On a third pass he strafed a small boat, starting a fire aboard and causing considerable damage to the vessel.[30]

The strain of the countless combat missions was beginning to wear on Hill. He had an unidentified illness that had gradually worsened to a point that he could hardly function. Tex was finally persuaded to fly back to Chungking and visit a hospital, where he was diagnosed with malaria. He was flown to Chengtu, a town some 150 miles northwest of Chungking, to stay with a missionary family and recover his health. Taking to a bed in the missionaries' home, Hill was administered regular quinine treatments to battle the bacteria. The fever finally broke, and he slowly began to improve.

After nearly three weeks of recovery, a Chinese general visited the American and asked if he would like to fly a captured Japanese fighter. The Chinese had captured a nearly intact Nate that went down in their territory, and engineers had restored it completely. The general had flown the plane several times and showed Hill the details of the aircraft. Tex took off and once airborne found the Nate simple to fly. Putting the plane through its paces, he found that it could turn and loop with an agility that the P-40 could never approach. He had no problem with the landing and once on the ground thanked the general for the opportunity to fly the enemy fighter.

Within a few more days, Tex was ready to return to his squadron. The quinine treatments had worked, and his malaria was in remission. Thanking the missionary family for their care and hospitality, he left to rejoin his squadron.

The 75th Fighter Squadron, now stationed at Chanyi, had been on stand down for the lack of fuel and parts. On September 1 the unit flew east to the familiar base at Hengyang. The next day it joined up with the 23rd Fighter Group for a raid on Poyang Lake and Nanchang. When twenty-six junks were spotted on the lake, Tex's flight of eight

P-40s peeled off and made strafing passes on the rice-laden, Japanese-operated vessels. By the fourth pass the barge fleet was burning and capsizing.

The next day Japanese fighters in strength from Canton raided the American airfields at Hengyang, Lingling, and Kweilin. Wave after wave of Nates came through the area for hours. Tex was in the air several times during the six-hour running fight and shot down one raider. Following this period of intensive activity, Chennault withdrew the 23rd Fighter Group from the forward bases. Without sufficient supplies, the group could not continue the fight. It would be more than a month before the Americans could return.[31]

In early December Chennault held a farewell dinner for Hill and Rector prior to their departure for leave in the States. As a result of his fight with malaria, Tex was down to 147 pounds, and Rector showed signs of combat stress and extreme fatigue. Nevertheless, Hill told Chennault that he would like to return to the 75th when his leave was over.

Although anxious to get home, his orders directed him to immediately proceed to Washington, DC, to make a report on the China situation to the Joint Chiefs of Staff. After arriving stateside in January 1943, he gave a straightforward account, reporting on the outrageous supply situation and describing what could be accomplished if the CATF were given a higher priority on supply. After the briefing, there was a promotion ceremony in which Hill received the silver oak leaves of a lieutenant colonel. He was twenty-seven years old.

Returning to Texas, the aviator was embraced by his family. Tex made several hunting and fishing expeditions to the Hill Country with his father during his leave. Spending a great deal of time outdoors, his body gradually recovered from his long illness and combat fatigue. He began to put on weight and look more like himself. One of his longtime ambitions was to own his own place in the Hill Country. He had sent home most of his pay from the AVG and army to his father, who had put it in a savings account so that Tex had a nice nest egg to buy some land. He located a 1,600-acre ranch near Mountain Home, some fifty miles north of Kerrville. The down payment on the ranch was more than his savings, but an oilman friend of Dr. Hill's put up the additional money at a favorable interest rate. The young lieutenant colonel was now also a Texas rancher.[32]

This portrait of Col. David L. Hill hangs in the Pentagon.
Courtesy Reagan Schaupp

After his leave expired, Hill was given a temporary assignment at the Air Force Tactical Center in Orlando, Florida, which brought in pilots fresh from combat to pass on their experiences to pilots in training. While at the center, Tex was checked out in the latest fighter aircraft, equipment, and weapons. As his time there drew to a close, Hill received orders assigning him to the Proving Ground Group, where he would serve as the commander. His unit was a division of the army's Proving Command at Eglin Field, Florida, that had the mission to evaluate new projects that emerged from the laboratories at Wright-Patterson Field in Ohio. Tex's group focused on prototype aircraft and performance comparison between airframes.

Two weeks after taking command, Hill flew a P-40 to Victoria, Texas, where his father had come out of retirement to serve as interim pastor of the First Presbyterian Church. Tex's brother Sam, the church's pastor, had taken a leave of absence when he had joined the Army Air Corps. He was stationed nearby at Matagorda Island. Sam returned to the pulpit that Sunday, with his brother in the audience.

During the service, Tex spotted a beautiful young lady in a pew across from him. After dinner at the parsonage, he asked Sam about the girl, who his brother identified as Mazie Sale. "I have to meet that girl!" exclaimed Tex. That afternoon Sam made arrangements for both to visit Sale at her home. After the visit Tex said to his brother and family, "I'm going to marry that girl." He took every possible opportunity to return to Victoria to see Mazie. The whirlwind romance resulted in marriage in the First Presbyterian Church in Victoria on March 27, 1943. After a honeymoon in San Antonio, Texas, the officer took his bride to Florida, where they lived in base housing at Eglin.[33]

After several months on the job, Chennault, now a major general commanding the Fourteenth Air Force (formed from the CATF), requested Hill be returned to China. Tex's reaction was that if the general needed help, he was ready. On November 3 Hill arrived in Kunming after a flight that took him to Brazil, Africa, and India. Chennault informed him that he was to command the 23rd Fighter Group, with headquarters at Kweilin, part of the forward echelon of the Fourteenth Air Force. Arriving at his new post, he found that the group was gradually exchanging their P-40s for P-51 Mustangs that were trickling into China.

The supply situation in China was still a cause of great concern. There were more aircraft now, including the 308th Bombardment Group's B-24 Liberator heavy bombers, requiring more gasoline and spare parts. Even though the tonnage transported over the Himalaya Mountains had increased, there was rarely enough supplies to support full operations. China was still at the end of the world's longest supply line.

Tex's first order of business was to visit the group's three fighter squadrons. The 74th was based in Kunming to attack targets in Burma, the 75th was in Kweilin, and the 76th was split between Hengyang and Suichwan, a recently completed forward base less than a hundred miles southeast of Hengyang.

For Hill, a disadvantage to being group commander was that he had knowledge of strategic plans and future Allied moves. This made him, in the eyes of Chennault, too valuable to risk on every combat mission. Tex was the type of leader who preferred to lead missions himself but was ordered to be more selective about when and where he flew. He now would have to find some "reason" to justify leading the most dangerous missions.[34]

On November 25 Tex led a force of eight P-51s, ten B-25s, and twelve P-38 Lightnings in a strike on the Shinchiku Airdrome on the island of Formosa. Earlier reconnaissance had shown more than one hundred bombers on the field as well as 112 fighters. It was a secret operation because if the Japanese learned of the raid, it could result in the loss of the entire flight—only Tex knew the target. As the Americans approached the target, an enemy transport was coming down the coast; a P-38 was dispatched to go after it and shot it down. As the force approached the target, seven enemy fighters managed to get airborne but were immediately shot down. Several Japanese bombers were in a landing pattern and were also shot down. The B-25s pulled up to a thousand feet and dropped their bombs, causing considerable damage. This was followed by the fighters strafing the remaining aircraft on the ground, causing even more destruction. Low on fuel, Tex broke off the attack and led his planes back to their home bases. His personal score for the day was one Zero destroyed in the air, one bomber damaged on the ground, and one probable on the ground; his victory over the Japanese fighter made him the first pilot to shoot down a Zero in a P-51. All planes in the strike force returned safely to base. Shortly after the raid, a photoreconnaissance aircraft was sent to assess the damage. Its photos showed forty-three bombers burning on the runway. In addition, between the bombers landing and the fighters taking off, another fifteen enemy aircraft had been shot down.

Within a month after the Formosa raid, Tex was promoted again, making him at age twenty-eight one of the youngest full colonels in the Army Air Forces. In January 1944, when the forward echelon became the 68th Composite Wing, Tex became its vice commander while retaining command of the 23rd Fighter Group.[35]

There was little air activity to open 1944 because of foul weather. The only major mission for the 23rd was escorting B-25s to Hong Kong, where they bombed enemy shipping at the Kowloon docks. By April the Japanese high command decided that because of shipping losses in the South and East China Seas, they should create a land route of supply to Indochina in the south. To this end, 250,000 Japanese soldiers moved south from Hankow on May 26 and captured Changsha.

The victorious enemy army continued its drive toward Hengyang. The 23rd Group pounded the advancing force and inflicted severe losses. In June the Allies made plans to evacuate Hengyang. The 23rd continued to make offensive sweeps in the area to slow down Japanese forces. In August, after a valiant six-week defense by the Chinese against incredible odds, Hengyang fell. With its loss, the early warning net collapsed for Lingling and Kweilin. By the first week of September, the 23rd had evacuated to Liuchow, and the installation at Lingling was demolished.[36]

Hill received orders in early October to return to the States. His deputy, Lt. Col. Phil Loofbourrow, would take charge until the new commander, Ed Rector, arrived. Tex arrived at Washington's National Airport in late October and reported to his next assignment in Fighter Requirements at the new Pentagon. He was happy to escape the "red tape" of the bureaucracy when he received orders to assume command of a P-38 fighter group at Van Nuys, California. He had hardly settled in when he received orders to report to Bakersfield to assume command of the 412th Fighter Group. The 412th would be the first US command equipped with jet aircraft. In July 1945 the group relocated to Santa Marie Airfield, a hundred miles southwest of Bakersfield and by November moved again, this time to March Field, near the town of Riverside.

The 412th received experimental and prototype aircraft for evaluation, which were put through their paces and engaged in mock dogfights. The most promising of these was the P-39A, the prototype of the P-80 Shooting Star, which later became America's first combat jet, seeing extensive action during the Korean War. The group included a number of personnel who had served in China, including a surplus of colonels, among them fellow Aggie Jay Robbins. When the war ended in 1945, Hill was thinking about his ranch in Texas. Although he enjoyed his work with the 412th, he found that peacetime service did not bring him the same satisfaction.[37]

Hill left the service in 1946 and returned to Texas to visit family before moving to his Mountain Home ranch. While at his father's home, Tex met with three prominent citizens who asked him to consider running for governor. He thanked them for the honor and said he would have to talk to his wife and do some thinking. On April 11 Mazie gave birth to a daughter, Mazie Lee Hill, in San Antonio. Not long after the family drove to their ranch. Once there, Mazie saw the small house where she would live, and though less than pleased, she resolved to make the best of it. Tex bought small herds of cows, sheep, and goats. The three types of livestock were ideal for the Hill Country, for they ate different fodder. Tex spent much of his time on horseback tending to his stock, riding the fence line, or hunting game. At last, he was able to relax and before long he decided that he would not run for governor.[38]

Things took a drastic turn that winter with the coldest weather in over a century. The chickens froze on their roosts, and livestock dropped dead. His wife was despondent, and Tex knew that she had had enough of hard life on the ranch. He made up his mind that they had to move.

One morning as Maize was staring out the window, she saw a huddled figure in a long coat making his way up the driveway. They welcomed the stranger into their house and showed him to the fire. The man was Lt. Gen. Fred Walker, the adjutant general of Texas, who handed Hill a letter from Gov. Coke Stevenson offering him a position with the Texas Air National Guard. If he accepted, he would command the 58th Fighter Wing, headquartered at Ellington Field near Houston, and would be commissioned as a brigadier general. The job was not full time but would require his presence at Ellington on the weekends. Hill accepted the offer with Maize's wholehearted endorsement.

Continuing to live on the ranch, on weekends a guardsman from San Antonio would drive to Mountain Home to pick up the new general and drive him to the airport. A Beechcraft C-45 transport plane had been assigned to fly him to Ellington for his weekend duties. On a trip to the Pentagon, a general suggested that Hill take the examination for a regular commission in the soon-to-be-formed US Air Force. Anticipating his return to the regular service, Tex resigned from the National Guard.[39]

Hill moved his family to San Antonio, where they lived in several apartments before buying a house in Terrell Hills near Fort Sam Houston. One day after returning from Ellington Field, he received a letter from Merian Cooper, who had been Chennault's chief of staff with the CATC. Cooper, before the war a movie producer, was back to business in Hollywood. He was working on three pictures and wanted Tex to work for him; he agreed. Tex's first assignment was to go to Africa to capture a baby gorilla for use in the film *Mighty Joe Young*. His first stop was the Belgium Congo, but learning that gorillas were protected there and could not be taken, he moved on to French Cameroon to try to capture a lowland gorilla. With the help of a Greek veteran of many safaris into the bush, an expedition into gorilla country was organized. The safari eventually located a pack of the primates, and three young gorillas were captured. The next problem was getting one of the animals back to California. The Greek said that for a sufficient bribe, there would be no problem getting it out of the country. Yet there was a major problem getting the gorilla into the United States since primates were a protected species. Learning of the situation, Cooper said that he instead was sending a cameraman to shoot some film of gorillas in the wild.

Hill was anxious to get back to the States because Maize was due to give birth to their second child. But there was another reason, his US Air Force commission was approved, and he was required to report for duty by a certain date. He asked the air force for a thirty-day extension, which was granted, but he was informed that the new reporting date was firm; if he did not report, the commission would be withdrawn. When the African assignment dragged on into its third month, Tex realized that he could not make the extended report date either. His days of active military service were over.[40]

Tex returned to Victoria, where Mazie was staying with her parents awaiting the birth of their child. He arrived at the Sales's home just as his wife began having labor pains. They hurried to the hospital, where David Lee Hill Jr. was born on September 17, 1947.

After deciding that the movie business was not for him, Hill called Cooper and explained his position and why he could not complete his three-picture contract. The producer understood and told him to call if he changed his mind. Hill's next venture was the oil business. Teaming with two others, he formed Wildcats, Inc. and convinced several of his friends in the movie business, including John Wayne, to invest in the project. The first well hit oil but did not produce enough to be commercially viable.

The next well was near Coleman, a small town south of Abilene. It produced only salt water and the company had to fold. Tex remained in the oil business, though. He bought a lone well, Old Rodriquez, in

West Texas in the middle of nowhere. As a part of the deal, he also purchased a thousand acres surrounding it. He eventually put down thirty-seven wells in this field. After a few years of operating here, Tex became convinced that the field was near the end of its prime and sold out to another company. Later purchased by Texaco, the field continued to produce after new recovery techniques were employed.

Despite this mistake in judgment, Tex became a first-class field operator, buying up a low-production operation and determining what was needed to increase the yield or where new wells should be put down. When the production increased, he would sell the operation at a profit.

Near the end of the Korean War, Hill felt the urge to get back in the cockpit and do some flying. He was commissioned a colonel in the US Air Force Reserve and assumed command of the 8707th Flight Training Group at Brooks Air Force Base in San Antonio. The mission of the 8707th was to instruct any sudden influx of pilots in jet combat. Later the group's mission was changed, and the 8707th transitioned to C-119 Flying Boxcar transport. In early 1955 Tex transferred to command the 433rd Troop Carrier Group. This unit also flew the C-119 and later the C-5 Galaxy. Tex enjoyed the reserve duty and the opportunity to be back in the air behind the controls. In 1957 he bid farewell to the active reserves but would stay in the ready reserves until 1968.[41]

In the 1960s, Western firms found doing business in Southeast Asia a difficult prospect. Hill found himself in a particularly advantageous position because of his long association with many Chinese during World War II, having personal friends scattered throughout the region in high places, especially in Taiwan. When word got out about his connections, several companies approached him to help open commercial doors in the Far East. Tex was soon representing several companies and made several trips to the Asia in the 1960s and 1970s.

Tex always made time for the reunions of the AVG. By the end of 1950, the veterans held reunions every other year at a resort in Ojai Valley, California. Later reunions were held in places like New York, Taipei, San Diego, Mallorca, and San Antonio.[42]

Brig. Gen. David L. Hill's military decorations include the Distinguished Service Cross, Distinguished Service Medal, Silver Star, Legion of Merit, Distinguished Flying Cross with Three Oak Leaf Clusters, Air Medal with Oak Leaf Cluster, British Distinguished Flying Cross, Chinese Order of the Clouds and Banner (4th, 5th, and 6th Orders), and Chinese Air Force Order of the Star (Six Stars, Nine Stars).

Tex Hill died at the age of ninety-two on October 11, 2007, of congestive heart failure at his home in Terrell Hills. He was buried at Fort Sam Houston National Cemetery in San Antonio.

Gen. Michael Moseley (Texas A&M Class of 1971), US Air Force chief of staff said of Hill: "As a Flying Tiger legacy, his mentorship and leadership will forever be read about in history books. General Hill has forgotten more about leadership and what's important than most of us will ever know."[43]

★ 6 ★

Battlefield and Congressional Tiger

OLIN E. "TIGER" TEAGUE

CLASS OF 1932

Olin Earl Teague was born on April 6, 1910, on a wheat farm near Woodward, Oklahoma, to James Martin and Ida Sturgeon Teague. Woodward, located in northwestern Oklahoma, is the county seat of Woodward County and at the time had a population of about two thousand. Its main occupations were farming and ranching. Ten years after his birth, the family moved to Mena, Arkansas, where James Teague was engaged in the lumber business.

Mena, where Olin grew up, is a small town in southwestern Arkansas, located a few miles east of the Oklahoma border and fifty-six miles south of Fort Smith. It is the county seat of Polk County and had a population of about four thousand in the 1920s. Almost surrounded by the Ouachita Mountains, it advertises itself as the "Gateway to the Ouachita Mountains." Its main industries in the 1920s were agriculture, mining, and lumber; today it is tourism.

Teague attended school in Mena and participated in football and baseball, earning the nickname "Tiger" for his fierce play. During the summers between his high school years, he worked at various jobs in local lumber camps. In 1927, while in high school, he enlisted for three years in the Arkansas National Guard and was assigned to Howitzer Company, 153rd Infantry Regiment. After completing his enlistment, he was discharged in 1930.

In 1928 he applied for admission to Texas A&M and was accepted to major in agriculture education. He was assigned to Company G, Infantry, in the Corps of Cadets.[1]

During his sophomore year, his father suffered a heart attack, and Teague was left on his own financially to finish college. In order to stay in school, he worked at numerous jobs. At night he fed the show calves and shoveled the manure from their stalls for twenty-five cents an hour. Unable to afford the $28 room and board, he slept in the Animal Pavilion, where his friends brought him what food they could sneak out of the mess hall. When Kyle Field, the new football stadium, was being built, Teague worked for the contractor. He also had a job as a messenger for the post office. During the summer of his sophomore year, he stayed in College Station to earn money for the fall semester.

At the start of his junior year, he became a substitute clerk for the post office in addition to keeping his messenger job. He also worked the night shift at the train depot for the Missouri Pacific Railroad, meeting trains, selling tickets, and loading the mail. As if that was not enough to keep him busy, he was also the first sergeant of his cadet company and a member of the Ross Volunteers, an honor organization that serves as the honor guard for the governor of Texas.

When Teague did manage to live in a campus dormitory his junior and senior year, his roommate was Judson E. Loupot (class of 1932), who became an Aggie legend in his own right, known to students as "Ol' Army Lou." While a student, Loupot ran a business from his dormitory room buying and selling used text books. After leaving school, his student business was expanded into a successful bookstore operation off campus. Following his death in 1995, his family continued to operate the store until selling it to a national bookseller in 2010. Loupot's Bookstore closed its doors in 2012 due to bankruptcy. During his many years as a businessman in College Station, Loupot assisted numerous students with financial problems and was a great supporter of the Corps of Cadets.[2]

Teague continued to work at several jobs during his senior year. He was the cadet commander of Company G, Infantry, and remained active in the Ross Volunteers. But Teague did not have enough credits to graduate with his class in 1932 and enrolled in summer school. In August 1932 he accepted a full-time position as a clerk with the College Station Post Office. A few months later, on December 30, 1932, in Durant, Oklahoma, he married Freddie Dunman of Fort Worth. She had been a classmate in Mena and later attended Texas Christian University.[3]

Commissioned an infantry second lieutenant on September 29, 1933, Teague was promoted to first lieutenant in 1936. He volunteered for active duty with the Civilian Conservation Corps (CCC) that August. The CCC was created in 1935 as a result of a need to put young men to work during the Great Depression. Teague served as the welfare officer of CCC Company 3801 (C) at Camp SCS-5-C near Waco. The company was a segregated unit of black enrollees. The lieutenant was commended for his performance of duty during his eight months with the unit.[4]

Teague was ordered to active duty on October 5, 1940, and assigned to Camp Hulen, Palacios, Texas for duty as "police officer." From February 1 to March 28, 1942, he attended the Military Police School at Fort Meyer, Virginia. There he was ordered to report by April 5 to the Command and General Staff College, Fort Leavenworth, Kansas, to attend a course of instruction for officers being assigned to new divisions. The orders also assigned him to the 79th Infantry Division, serving as division provost marshal from May 5, 1942, to February 8, 1943. After his promotion to lieutenant colonel on October 20, Teague was ordered to Fort Benning, Georgia, to attend the Infantry Officer's Advanced Course. Upon returning to the division, he was assigned to the 1st Battalion, 314th Infantry, as executive officer. On April 11 he assumed command of the battalion.[5]

The 314th Infantry Regiment was organized on June 12, 1942, at Camp Pickett, Virginia, as one of three infantry regiments assigned to the 79th "Cross of Lorraine" Infantry Division; the other two regiments were the 313th and 315th. The initial cadre for the 79th was drawn from the 4th Infantry Division. Before departing overseas, the 79th in turn provided the cadre for the 86th Infantry Division.

During World War II, a US Army regiment was organized into a headquarters company, antitank company, and three infantry battalions. It had 3,068 officers and enlisted men and was commanded by a colonel. Each battalion contained a headquarters company, three rifle companies, and a heavy-weapons company. Commanded by a lieutenant colonel, it had 35 officers and 825 enlisted men. A rifle company contained three rifle platoons and a weapons platoon. It was commanded by a captain and had 6 officers and 187 enlisted men. Each rifle platoon had three squads of 12 men each and was led by a lieutenant.

During its initial training period, the division did its preliminary and basic training at Camp Pickett, Virginia, and later at Camp Blanding, Florida. This was followed by two months of rigorous field training in the Tennessee Maneuver Area. The 79th then moved to Camp Laguna, near Yuma, Arizona, for three months of desert maneuvers. In December 1943 the troops moved to Camp Phillips, Kansas, for field training under winter conditions. They departed Boston Port of Embarkation on April 7, 1944, and arrived in England nine days later.[6]

Allied forces landed on the Normandy beaches of France on June 6, 1944. Limited by the number of landing craft available, they could disembark only six divisions in the first seaborne lift, together with three airborne divisions that dropped inland from the beaches. The first footholds were soon expanded into a large beachhead eighty miles wide. The 79th, assigned to VII Corps, was a follow-on division and landed across Utah Beach on the fourteenth (see map 7). To this corps, consisting of the 4th, 9th, 79th, and 90th Infantry Divisions, went the assignment to seize the Carentan Peninsula. On June 19 the corps attacked toward Cherbourg with three divisions—the 4th on the right, the 79th in the center, and the 9th on the left—with the mission to drive across the base of the peninsula. Initially in reserve, the 314th Infantry Regiment was committed on June 20 against scattered resistance but soon ran into the outer belt of the enemy's prepared defenses around Cherbourg.

A major obstacle facing the troops was the infamous Normandy hedgerows, "centuries-old mounds of earth, stone, and underbrush bordering all cultivated fields, orchards, and roads." The hard-pressed German defenders cleverly incorporated the hedgerows into their defenses, which included "scores of strong points, emplacements, and concrete pillboxes. Each field was a miniature battlefield."

On June 22 the 314th began its attack, with Teague's 1st Battalion in the lead. The operation progressed until the Americans came upon a fortified position. Teague sent one company in a flanking movement to the left, where they encountered heavy German fire. That night the 3rd Battalion was ordered to seize a crossroad on the right flank, with the 1st Battalion to follow. Because of the situation, Teague could not break contact with the enemy until the following day. That morning, he moved his companies into positions to support the 3rd Battalion's advance. That afternoon both battalions continued the attack. The 3rd sustained heavy casualties and the 1st met less resistance, advancing well beyond its objective.

Teague's first Silver Star was awarded for actions on June 24–25, when he "made a personal reconnaissance of his battalion's objective, which took him deep into the enemy's lines." The next day "he personally led his battalion against the objective under heavy enemy artillery, mortar, and automatic-weapons fire." The lieutenant colonel was slightly wounded, but the battalion achieved its objective.

Fort du Roule, located at the northwest end of a high ridge commanding the city of Cherbourg, was the Germans' last major defensive position. The fort had been well supplied and armed to hold out indefinitely. After a furious fight part of the fort was captured by the 314th's 2nd Battalion. The next day the 1st and 3rd Battalions advanced through Cherbourg against stubborn resistance. The attacking force seized a row of pillboxes on the water's edge and advanced to the beach. That evening the guns in the unoccupied lower face of the fort opened fire. They were silenced after three hours of fighting. The fort was now in American hands.

On June 27 the 79th moved out of Cherbourg to relieve the 90th Division and to prepare for a drive south. The division began its operation on the morning of July 3. They soon made contact with the enemy, who put up a stiff resistance using the hedgerows as defensive positions. The division pushed down the west side of the peninsula, liberating towns and seizing objectives. The capture of the strongly fortified city of La Haye du Puits earned Teague's battalion a Presidential Unit Citation.

CITATION

> The First Battalion, 314th Infantry Regiment is cited for outstanding performance of duty in action during the period 7–8 July 1944 in France. This Battalion was assigned the important mission of as-

> saulting and capturing the strongly fortified city of La Haye du Puits. Located at the junction of two arterial highways, the city was a vital point in the breakout plans of Allied forces from Normandy to the south. Although the city was protected by a chain of well-built and carefully concealed machine-gun nests and other formidable defenses, the First Battalion advanced through a heavy concentration of artillery and mortar fire, and across dense mine fields to launch the attack. The Battalion suffered heavy losses, including many key leaders, but by nightfall it successfully occupied strategic positions along the outskirts of the town. On 8 July 1944, the First Battalion renewed its vigorous attack while again subjected to shelling and withering machine-gun fire. Displaying an indomitable fighting spirit and tenacious aggressiveness, the Battalion drove into the city and forced the defenders to abandon their positions. Although greatly weakened by severe losses, the Battalion, undaunted and with undiminished courage pursed the retreating enemy relentlessly, engaged them in vicious hand-to-hand fighting, and drove them from the city. The grim determination and courageous actions of the personnel of this battalion in pressing the vigorous attack against a stubborn enemy, secured a vital communications center for the subsequent advance of the Allies, and in so doing reflect great credit upon themselves and the military service.[7]

Teague's second Silver Star was awarded for actions on July 8, when after requesting armored support, he "proceeded to the forward elements of his command to reconnoiter the most effective route of attack for the tanks." Under heavy enemy fire, he positioned the tanks to aid the assault on a "stubbornly defended . . . series of enemy strongpoints." Despite numerous casualties and intense enemy fire, the objective was achieved, and a "strategic position gained and held."[8]

Continuing the advance to the south, on July 14 the attacking 313th and 314th Regiments reached the division objective on the Ay River. The 79th occupied defensive positions along the north bank of the Ay River while other divisions in VIII Corps continued their attack against the river front. For the next two weeks patrols were sent across the river. Meanwhile, higher headquarters were busy planning Operation Cobra, the great breakthrough that would drive the Germans out of France.

The 79th became part of VIII Corps, Third Army, during this time and initially played only a minor role in operations. Cobra kicked off on July 26, and the 79th followed the 28th Regiment (8th Division) across the Ay. For the next few days, the 79th pushed seven to eight miles against light resistance. On August 3 a new order placed the 79th in XV Corps to protect the left flank of Lt. Gen. George S. Patton's Third Army as it swung south and then east around the main enemy force. On the fifth the division was given the mission to "seize the important bridges over the Mayenne River in Laval." The Germans withdrew from the area first, though only after blowing the bridges. Teague's battalion crossed the river on rafts and any available boats, establishing a bridgehead and remaining in place until a replacement span could be constructed by the engineers.

The division's next objective was Le Mans, which it liberated on August 8 after overcoming only patchy resistance. By this time the Germans were fighting a rearguard action while their main force attempted to withdraw to the defenses along the German border. On the ninth new orders arrived for the division. The XV Corps was to make a 90-degree turn and drive north, with the 2nd French Armored Division on the left and the 5th US Armored Division on the right. The 90th would follow the French and the 79th would follow behind the 5th Armored. The 314th Regiment was motorized for this action while the others remained on foot.[9]

The German army was withdrawing to the east under heavy pressure. In their desperation to escape the Falaise pocket, they were moving during the day on roads dominated by Allied air power. The 78th Division made contact with enemy forces on August 14. Late that day the division was ordered to move east to Versailles and to the prize objective of all Allied forces—Paris. For the move, the division was motorized and would follow the 106th Cavalry Group.

But while planning for the push to Versailles, the division was given a new mission. Its new objective was to take the heights overlooking Mantes-Gassicourt, a town thirty miles northwest of Paris on the Seine River. Advancing against scattered resistance, at 11:30 a.m. on August 19, the 314th reached Mantes and reported the sector cleared. Teague's battalion crossed the river on rafts constructed by the division engineers and established a bridgehead on the east bank. He established his battalion command post on the third floor of a chateau overlooking the Seine, while one of his companies took over the wine cellar for its command post. When the chateau came under German artillery fire, Teague quickly moved his headquarters to the wine cellar.[10]

The Germans counterattacked the night of August 22 to eliminate the bridgehead. Some ground was gained, but they were stopped by heavy fighting. The next morning the Germans resumed their attacks and drove one company of the 314th from its position.

With the support of a company of tanks, the unit restored its position. The attacks continued while the beachhead was expanded. On August 24 the XV Corps and the 79th Division were shifted to the First Army. This was followed on the thirtieth with the 79th placed in the XIX Corps with a new mission. The division was to make a rapid advance to the vicinity of Saint-Amand, on the Franco-Belgium border, to arrive by midnight of September 2. The move to Belgium was led by the division cavalry squadron, which met only slight resistance. In seventy-two hours the division traveled 160 miles to an assembly area on the border.

The Germans were now in full retreat, and Patton's Third Army was racing across France. On September 9 the 79th moved to Reims, where it rejoined XV Corps, now with the Third Army. A new campaign against German positions around the Moselle River began on September 11, when the 314th attacked Charmes to establish a bridgehead on the east side of the river. The regiment arrived at the Moselle late that evening, bypassing defenders in several French towns who were left to be dealt with by following units. Early in the afternoon the next day, following significant street fighting, the 314th had secured Charmes.

Teague quickly ordered his troops to seize the bridge across the Moselle, only to have the Germans blow it up as they arrived. Reconnoitering the river, they found a ford about 300 yards north of the destroyed bridge. The troops attempting to cross, however, encountered very heavy resistance and were forced to withdraw.

The morning of the thirteenth, Teague's battalion, supported by tanks and tank destroyers, again attacked across the river at the ford. This time the attack was successful, and before 10:00 a.m. Teague's men had established a secure bridgehead on the east side of the Moselle. After crossing, the division resumed the attack on September 19 to the northeast in the direction of Luneville, with heavy fighting encountered along the Meurthe River. This was followed by stubborn resistance at Luneville the next day, when the town was liberated.[11]

The division's next mission was to clear the Parroy Forest, the same area where the 79th Division had fought during World War I. The attack was delayed several days due to poor weather that repeatedly postponed the planned intensive bombing of the forest. The bombing finally took place on September 28, following which the division jumped off, with the 313th and 315th Regiments leading. Initially in reserve, the 314th was committed to the battle on October 1. Their mission was to attack into the southwest corner of the forest and link up with the 315th Regiment. This was accomplished on October 3 after overcoming very stubborn resistance. The forest was finally cleared of enemy forces on the ninth. During the fighting, the 79th, as part of XV Corps, was transferred to Seventh Army.

The offensive was resumed on October 14, and for five days battle raged, with many German counterattacks. The division's objective, the high ground near Embermenil, was seized on October 22. Afterward the troops were relieved by the 44th Division and moved to a rest camp near Luneville. The stand down gave the troops time to get cleaned up, maintain their equipment, sleep in beds, write letters home, and take care of personal matters. The new replacements were assigned to units and given intensive training. After sixteen days in the rest area, the division was ordered to begin the advance to the Rhine River.[12]

The division's mission was to press through the Vosges Mountains and drive the Germans out of Alsace (see map 9). On November 9 the 314th and the 315th moved to seize a ridge just north of Harbouey. The Germans withdrew from Harbouey under cover of heavy fire and occupied prepared positions farther east. The Allied attack continued through several small French towns and villages before, on November 23, the French 2nd Armored Division captured Strasbourg. Following closely behind the French, the 79th Division received orders to attack north to seize the important enemy supply depot at Haguenau. As this occurred, on December 4 the division passed from XV Corps to VI Corps, which was preparing to strike northwest and breach the Siegfried Line. The plan was for VI Corps "to attack with the 79th Division on the right flank, the 103rd Division in the center, and the 45th Division on the left. The 14th Armored Division served as a ready reserve to exploit the gains made as they happened."

The 79th was to attack "on the axis from Bischwiller to Seltz, destroy the Rhine bridges in its zone, and protect the corps's right flank. It was also to seize the town of Haguenau and be ready to clear the nearby forest." The division attacked in the morning of December 9 with its three regiments abreast. The 314th met stiff resistance but reached the southwest outskirts of Haguenau that evening. The following day "the regiment stormed into town only to find a few snipers, the main body of the enemy having fled north."[13]

After capturing Haguenau, the division continued the attack to the northeast against a determined enemy. They reached the Lauter River on December 15. The river served as the boundary between France and Germany. The division entered Germany on December 17 with the 313th driving northeast of Lauterborg and the 314th attacking in the same direction from Scheibenhardt. After initial gains the attack was slowed as the Americans neared the Siegfried Line, where they were met by heavy enemy fire. The area was filled with pillboxes about forty yards apart and tied in with minefields and wire defenses. There was also a formidable antitank ditch in front of the pillboxes.

On December 13, in preparation for the renewed assault, Teague "made a personal reconnaissance deep into enemy territory and then, although under enemy artillery and mortar fire, returned to lead both assault companies and each supporting tank destroyer into position. Feeling that the battalion observation post did not offer an adequate observation of the entire sector, Teague was making his way forward when he was caught in a heavy enemy artillery concentration." He took shelter behind a tree, but his left foot and leg remained exposed and he was seriously wounded. As Teague crawled from the area, he was hit twice in the backside by shell fragments. Although suffering intense pain by the time aid reached him, the lieutenant colonel refused evacuation until he had left detailed instructions for the continuance of the attack. His foot and ankle were intact, but the shell fragment had taken three inches out of his lower leg bones.

Teague's 1st Battalion and the 79th Infantry Division had to withdraw to defensive positions on the Lauter River as a result of the major German offense in the Ardennes that came to be known as the Battle of the Buldge. On December 31, 1944, the Germans launched a counteroffensive, Operation North Wind, in the lower Vosges Mountains to seize Strasbourg and the Severne Gap. The 79th helped stem the enemy tide and, after the front was stabilized, the Germans withdrew to the Siegfried Line. The division was then shifted north and participated

McCloskey Military Hospital, where Teague recuperated after being seriously wounded in France. *Public domain* (postcard from authors personal collection)

in the Rhine crossing in the Ruhr Valley. The end of the war on May 9, 1945, found the 79th along the Ruhr River.[14]

On December 30, 1944, Freddie Teague received a Western Union telegram from the War Department: "REGRET TO INFORM YOU YOUR HUSBAND WAS SERIOUSLY WOUNDED IN ACTION IN GERMANY EIGHTEEN DECEMBER UNTIL NEW ADDRESS IS RECEIVED ADDRESS MAIL FOR HIM QUOTE LIEUTENANT COLONEL OLIN E TEAGUE SERIAL NUMBER (HOSPITALIZED) CENTRAL POSTAL DIRECTORY APO 640 C/O POSTMASTER NEW YORK NEW YORK UNQUOTE YOU WILL BE ADVISED AS REPORTS OF CONDITION ARE RECEIVED—DUNLOP ACTING THE ADJUTANT GENERAL."[15]

Six months and four days after wading ashore at Utah Beach, "Tiger" Teague's war was over. From his battalion aid station, he was evacuated through medical channels and eventually to the 43rd General Hospital. He was transferred from there on February 14, 1945, and arrived in the States on March 4. The officer was admitted as a patient at McCloskey General Hospital, Temple, Texas, on the eighth. After arriving at McCloskey, his wife moved the family to Temple to be near Teague. The family remained in town until his release.[16]

Colonel Teague after the war. *Courtesy Jack Teague*

As a patient at McCloskey, Teague volunteered to perform duty as assistant liaison officer and later as personal-affairs officer. In addition to these duties, he served on the Army Retirement Board and as summary court officer. He was promoted to colonel on February 27, 1946, while still in the hospital.[17]

During his hospitalization in Temple, Brooks Army Medical Center in San Antonio, and Walter Reed General Hospital in Washington, DC, Teague underwent almost two dozen operations. His ankle was irreparably shattered, but doctors managed to connect his foot and leg with medal pins that enabled him to walk with the aid of a specially built fourteen-pound shoe. The colonel was medically retired on November 5, 1946, and returned with his family to College Station.[18]

There are various reasons ascribed to Teague's desire after the war to run for public office. According to J. E. Loupot, a college roommate and longtime friend, Teague was "fed-up" with doctors and lawyers getting disability benefits for spurious claims while he was in a veteran's hospital being treated for battle injuries. "Lawyers and doctors were getting 50 and 60 percent disability with these back and head pains," Loupot said. "The doctors didn't know whether they were crazy or had back pains or not. Soldiers like Teague who had had a foot, arm, or leg shot off were only getting 10 or 20 percent, just because they didn't know what to do. It just wasn't right." So according to Loupot, Teague took fifty files on men he thought should be getting increased disability payments to Washington. "Look at these files and do what's right," he challenged. That brief encounter with federal bureaucracy was enough to prompt him to consider a political career.

When the incumbent of the Texas Sixth Congressional District, Rep. Luther Johnson, announced that he would not seek reelection, Teague decided to enter the race. The Sixth District stretched from Brazos County to the south part of Dallas. He faced two local politicians in a special election and received enough votes to be matched against Tom Tyson in a runoff election.

Compared to the radio and television blitzes of today, the Teague organization's campaign strategy was simple. The colonel's friends from Bryan and College Station put together weekly car caravans draped in banners reading "Tiger Teague for Congress" and toured the towns in the district. Teague and usually one friend took walking tours in the district to meet with residents face to face. They also distributed a brochure with comments from men the colonel had served with during World War II. The primary campaign was a success, but Teague's effort took its toll. He wound up in the hospital with another leg infection just before the runoff election. But Tyson withdrew from the campaign, ensuring Teague his first term in Congress. He went on to serve thirty-two years in the US House of Representatives.[19]

Courage was no stranger to Teague. His aggressive playing on the sports fields of Mena had earned him the nickname "Tiger," while his military decorations attest to his bravery in battle. He continued to exhibit that courage in Congress. As a member of the House of Representatives, he was not afraid to challenge his party's leadership when

Teague with General Eisenhower and Col. Bill Becker at Aggie Muster in Kyle Field in 1946. *Courtesy Jack Teague*

---

he thought they were wrong. In 1966 he blasted Pres. Lyndon Johnson and other national leaders for the "increasing violence" in the United States. Following a speech at the East Dallas Chamber of Commerce, he was quoted as saying: "I think we've had very poor leadership from the top. It's hard to have a Texan in the presidency who you would like to make the best record possible. But in this field, I think they both [President Johnson and Vice President Hubert Humphrey] are wrong. And in my opinion the only correction will come from the bottom."[20]

In 1967 Teague accused Sen. Edward M. Kennedy of giving aid and comfort to the enemy through his criticism of US military operations in Vietnam. As chairman of the House Veterans Affairs Committee, he ripped into the Massachusetts senator for his claim that the bloody and bitter battle over "Hamburger Hill" was "senseless and irresponsible." In a statement Teague said, "The senator's disgraceful damaging comments, obviously based on news reports and without any effort to seek out the facts, were not only untimely, but worse, comforting to

US Rep. Olin E. Teague. *Courtesy Jack Teague*

---

an enemy whose only hope for success in aggression is to weaken the will of the United States at home."[21]

In 1977 Teague gave an interview from his bed at Bethesda Naval Hospital that blasted Pres. Jimmy Carter's blanket pardon to draft evaders. He said: "An army survey showed that only 14 percent of those processed under the amnesty program [of President Ford] were motivated by objection to the war. Personal problems and concern for their own safety were most often mentioned." He also stated:

> While presidential pardons are provided for in our constitution, a blanket pardon is tantamount to a mass burial of due process of law. Judicial findings in light of individual circumstances are circumvented, and while our judicial system is not perfect, no American should expect more, nor settle for less, than his fair day in court. More than most, I know full well that wars are fought by boys, suf-

> fered by women, and started by men old enough to know better. But—and here is the crucial "but"—while we hate war we, as a free nation, should never desist in our support for those who are called upon to fight.
>
> History will judge what wars are "just" ones, [but] without a firm and recognized obligation of its citizens to serve when asked, our nation's history could be short-lived, for no free nation can survive unless its peoples are willing to accept the huge obligations of their freedom.[22]

When Teague received his discharge from the army, he probably thought he had seen the last of war. That was not to be case. In October 1947, as a member of a five-member subcommittee of the House Foreign Affairs Committee, he made a trip to Greece. At the time that nation was involved in a civil war with communist forces. While visiting Greek army positions in the north near the borders with Bulgaria and Yugoslavia, the group came under mortar fire, with several shells falling near the congressmen. The group spent almost a week in the rugged mountains of Macedonia. They studied the civil war at close quarters and came to the conclusion that the situation had deteriorated and would not improve until the Greek army went on the offensive. The congressmen were able to talk to several captured or surrendered guerrillas, giving the Americans a low opinion of the opposition. Teague stated: "They call themselves the Democratic Army of Greece, but they are neither democratic nor civil. The outrages they are committing in the villages, where they loot, rape, recruit people forcibly, and burn their houses, cry to heaven. Those whom we met we found to be mostly the scum of the earth, poor, illiterate, and the gangster type."[23]

As a member of the Veterans Affairs Committee, Teague had a look at his third war when he visited Korea in January 1952, spending a week touring frontline units. Upon his return to the United States, he proposed dropping atomic bombs on North Korea and threatening destruction of some of China's coastal cities to force an armistice. One immediate result of his trip was to get the troops proper footwear for winter conditions on the peninsula.[24]

Teague visited Vietnam three times during that war. In November 1966 he went where most congressmen would not go, traveling mainly by helicopter, often over areas held by the Vietcong, to areas where American control and security was tenuous at best. In Saigon he visited with his friend Gen. William C. Westmoreland, having served on the US Military Academy Board of Visitors when Westmoreland was superintendent.[25]

The trip to Vietnam in February 1966 was at the request of the Johnson administration to meet with South Vietnamese leaders to help them establish a veteran's program patterned after the US model. Visiting the 25th Division, Teague was shown tunnels used by the Vietcong. He then went to see the 1st Division, which was headquartered at a rubber plantation. At the 1st Cavalry Division, he was reunited with an Aggie friend, Col. William Becker. One night during his stay, the cavalry's camp received heavy mortar fire. Visiting wounded troops in the hospital, he took the names of many and upon his return to Washington sent letters to their parents.[26]

His last visit to Vietnam in May 1967 was at the request of President Johnson, who wanted a frank appraisal of the situation. During the two-week trip, Teague again visited with Westmoreland and with Aggie friends, including Brig. Gen. James Hollingsworth of the 1st Division and Maj. Gen. Bruno Hochmuth, who commanded the 3rd Marine Division. The congressman was accompanied by William Driver, head of the Veterans Administration (VA). Part of their mission was to look into veteran matters and get a program going that would provide information to troops returning home for discharge on what was available to them in the way of veteran benefits. In his report to the president, Teague urged the mining of Haiphong Harbor and taking other military action in North Vietnam to quickly bring an end to the conflict. He also recommended the bombing of all power plants and water works as well as other prime targets.[27]

During his years of service in Congress, Teague authored more than two hundred bills, primarily in the areas of veterans' affairs and the space program. He was chairman of the House Veterans Affairs Committee from the 84th Congress until the 93rd Congress, when he left Veterans Affairs to accept the chairmanship of the Space and Astronautics Committee. He was also the chairman of the subcommittee of manned space flight throughout the moon-landing program and of the subcommittee on legislative oversight, which investigated the deaths of three astronauts.

In 1949 Teague had fought against the Truman administration's proposed single, universal, comprehensive health-insurance plan.

He received an avalanche of letters from doctors, insurance executives, hospitals, lawyers, and various associations opposing the plan, thought of by many as "socialized medicine." The congressman was particularly bothered by the compulsory part of the proposal. This effort by the federal government to administer the medical community was soon ended.[28]

The following year Teague supported an initiative by a citizens committee to locate the proposed US Air Force Academy in the Brazos Valley. The effort was spearheaded by Travis B. Bryan, a prominent banker in Bryan and a civic leader in the area. A study commissioned by the committee mentioned the promise of support by Texas A&M, including use of facilities and faculty in the early years of the new military school. But in 1954 Colorado Springs, Colorado, was selected as the site for the Air Force Academy.[29]

The GI Bill of Rights passed in 1944 provided government subsidies for veterans who were unemployed until they found a job and gave them long-term benefits to attend college or a trade school. It also provided for low-interest loans for buying a home or farm. Unfortunately, some veterans took advantage of the programs to make money or applied for benefits they did not deserve. Teague believed that such actions were threatening the whole concept of veterans' benefits. As a result, he introduced legislation restricting certain heavily abused activities and initiated a select committee to carry out a limited investigation of the GI Bill programs. The Texan prepared a new GI Bill for returning Korea veterans that preserved the intent of the 1944 measure but eliminated many of the abuses that had occurred; it passed in 1952.

Teague continued his support of veterans when he confronted the Eisenhower administration about cuts in the VA budget. A revised budget was passed after a number of compromises were accepted. Although it was not entirely acceptable to Teague and other veterans advocates, it was recognized as better than the original proposal. He also prevented the VA direct-loan program from being phased out under Eisenhower. Teague discovered through hearings that loan applications for veterans were being slowed down by having to apply through the Voluntary Home Mortgage Credit Program first. As a result, he threatened to write a bill that would phase out that organization, which would clear the path for veterans loans. Procedures were soon changed to improve the application process.[30]

McCloskey General Hospital, where Teague spent so much time as a patient, was transferred in 1946 to the VA for use as a general medical and surgical hospital. In 1949 a domiciliary unit was added, and the hospital became a full VA Center. In 1979 it was renamed in honor of Teague as a champion of veterans for thirty-six years.

The first serious reelection challenge he experienced came in 1960, when longtime Texas state representative William T. Moore announced his run for the office. Moore was a powerful politician who later became a state senator and was known as the "Bull of the Brazos." Teague won reelection by a landslide.

After he retired in 1978, the Sixth District seat was taken by Texas A&M economics professor Phil Gramm. Gramm later served in the US Senate. Teague remained in the Washington area, where he had a home in Bethesda, Maryland. He donated his papers to Texas A&M, where they are housed in the university archives.[31]

Rep. Olin E. Teague's military decorations include the Silver Star with Two Oak Leaf Clusters, Bronze Star, Army Commendation Medal, Purple Heart with Two Oak Leaf Clusters, and French Croix de Guerre with Palm.

In 1977 Teague's left foot was amputated at Bethesda Naval Hospital. In September 1978 he suffered a mild stroke. Tiger Teague died from kidney and heart failure on January 23, 1981, at Bethesda, Maryland. He was laid to rest with full military honors among other warriors at Arlington National Cemetery.

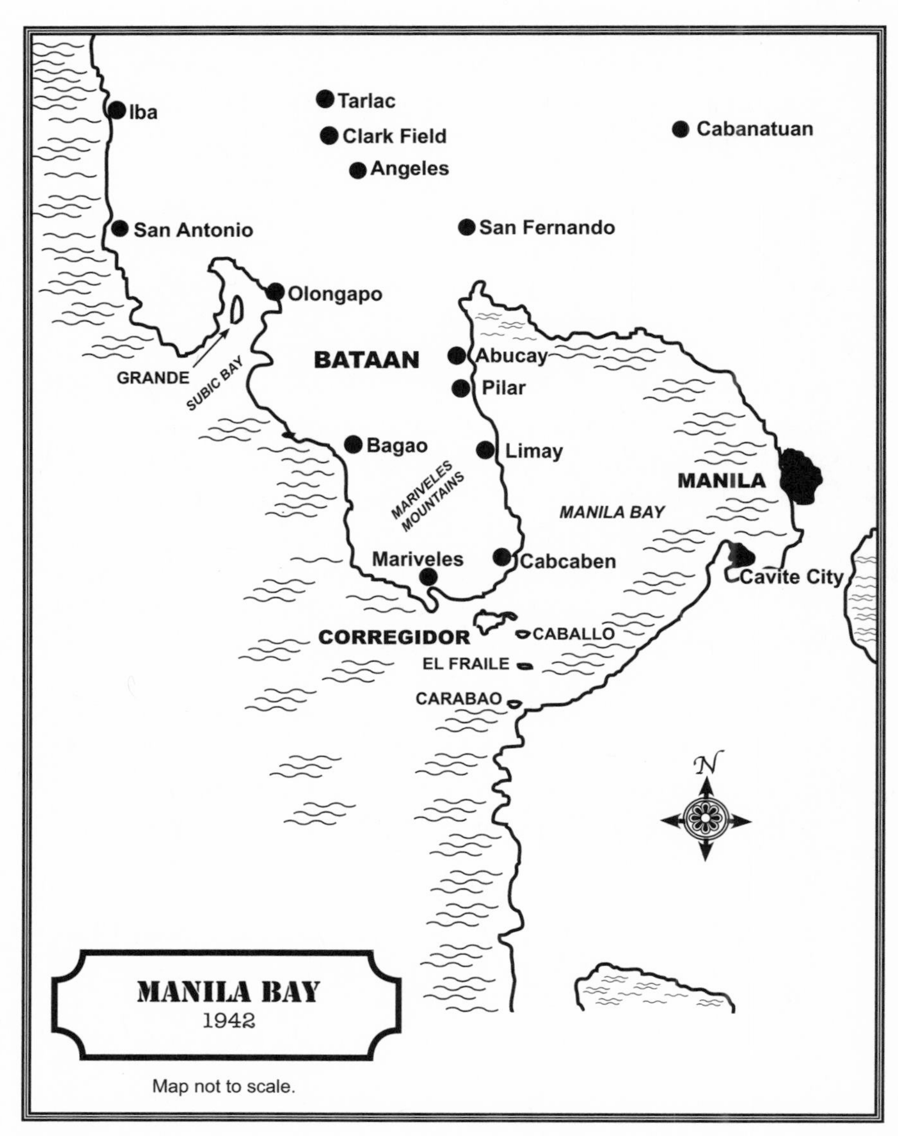
Iba
Tarlac
Clark Field
Angeles
Cabanatuan
San Antonio
San Fernando
Olongapo
BATAAN
Abucay
Pilar
GRANDE
SUBIC BAY
Bagao
Limay
MARIVELES MOUNTAINS
MANILA
MANILA BAY
Mariveles
Cabcaben
Cavite City
CORREGIDOR
CABALLO
EL FRAILE
CARABAO
N
MANILA BAY
1942
Map not to scale.

Map 1

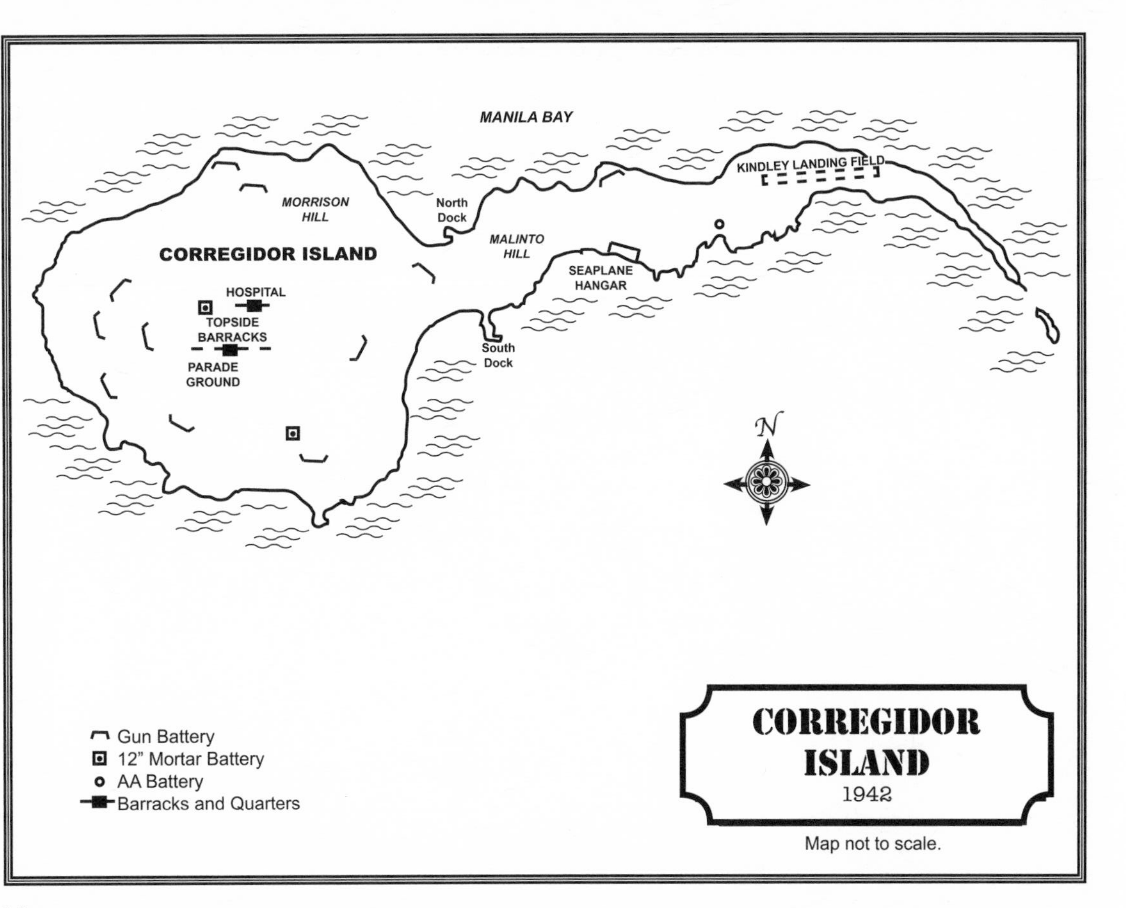
MANILA BAY
KINDLEY LANDING FIELD
MORRISON HILL
North Dock
MALINTO HILL
CORREGIDOR ISLAND
SEAPLANE HANGAR
HOSPITAL
TOPSIDE BARRACKS
South Dock
PARADE GROUND
N
Gun Battery
12” Mortar Battery
AA Battery
Barracks and Quarters
CORREGIDOR ISLAND
1942
Map not to scale.

Map 2

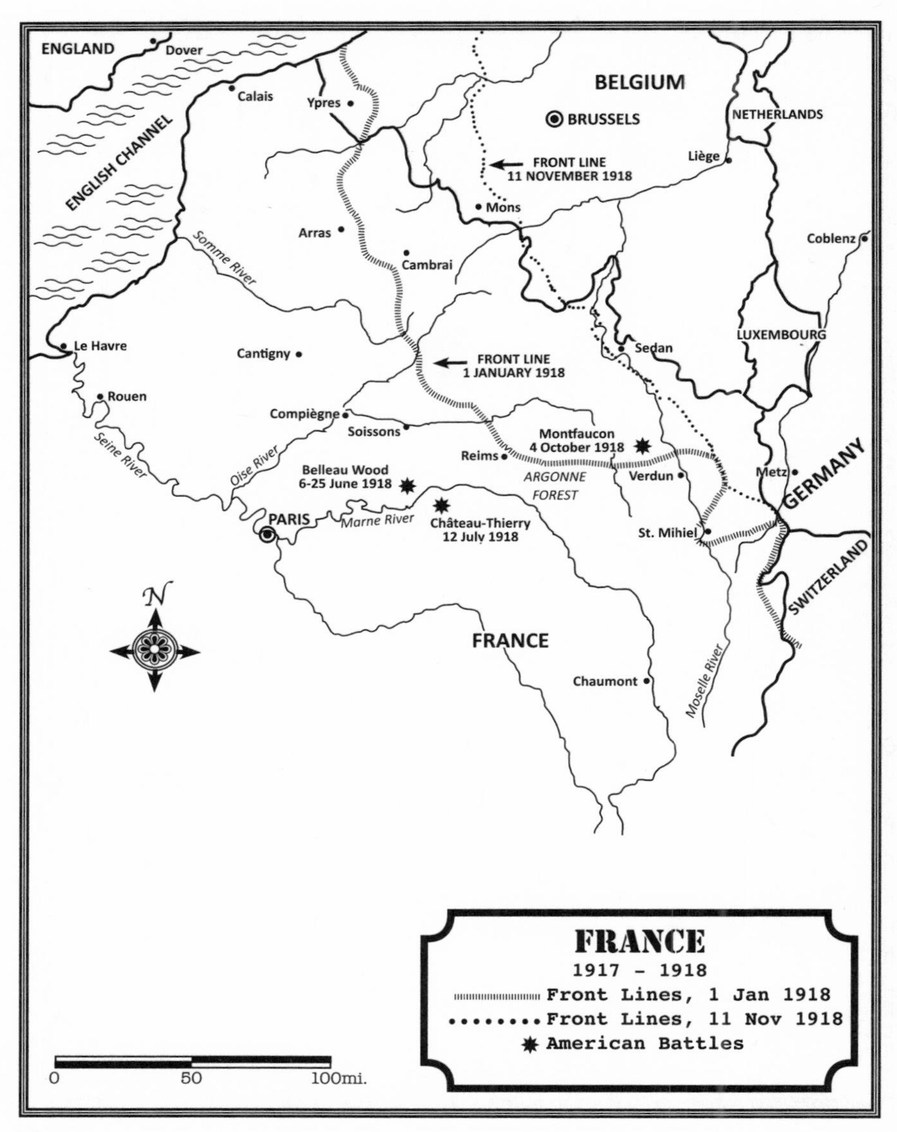
ENGLAND
Dover
Calais
Ypres
BELGIUM
BRUSSELS
NETHERLANDS
ENGLISH CHANNEL
FRONT LINE
11 NOVEMBER 1918
Liège
Mons
Arras
Cambrai
Coblenz
Somme River
Le Havre
Cantigny
Sedan
LUXEMBOURG
FRONT LINE
1 JANUARY 1918
Rouen
Compiègne
Soissons
Montfaucon
4 October 1918
Reims
ARGONNE
FOREST
Verdun
Metz
GERMANY
Seine River
Oise River
Belleau Wood
6-25 June 1918
PARIS
Marne River
Château-Thierry
12 July 1918
St. Mihiel
SWITZERLAND
N
FRANCE
Chaumont
Moselle River
FRANCE
1917 - 1918
Front Lines, 1 Jan 1918
Front Lines, 11 Nov 1918
American Battles
0
50
100mi.

Map 3

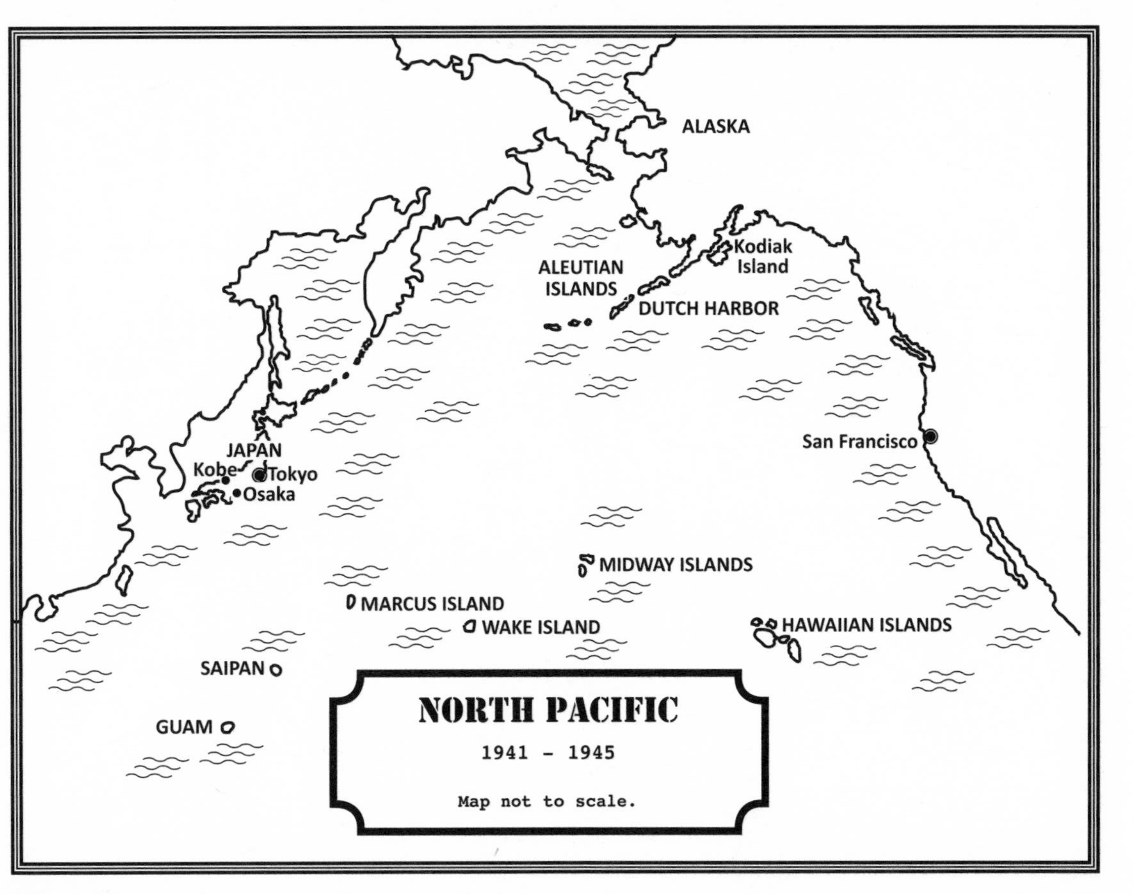
ALASKA
ALEUTIAN
ISLANDS
Kodiak
Island
DUTCH HARBOR
San Francisco
JAPAN
Kobe
Tokyo
Osaka
MIDWAY ISLANDS
MARCUS ISLAND
WAKE ISLAND
HAWAIIAN ISLANDS
SAIPAN
GUAM
NORTH PACIFIC
1941 - 1945
Map not to scale.

Map 4

CHINA
Tumen River
Chongjin
CHOSIN
RESERVOIR
Yudam-ni
Yalu River
Koti-ri
An-Tung
Sinuiju
Hamnung
Hungnam
NORTH KOREA
EAST SEA
(SEA OF JAPAN)
Wonsan
Pyongyang
Kaesong
Panmunjom
Kangnung
Inshon
Seoul
SOUTH KOREA
YELLOW SEA
Taegu
Kwangju
Pusan
Mokpo
N
KOREA
Map not to scale.

Map 5

N
Lanchow
CHINA
Sian
Chenchow
Nanking
Shanghai
Chengtu
Chungking
Salween River
Yeching
Kunming
Hengyang
Lingling
Kweilin
Liuchow
Canton
Nanning
FORMOSA
BURMA
Hanoi
Hong Kong
SOUTH CHINA SEA
LAOS
Rangoon
THAILAND
PHILIPPINE ISLANDS
Bangkok
FRENCH INDO CHINA
SOUTHEAST CHINA
1941 - 1944
Map not to scale.

Map 6

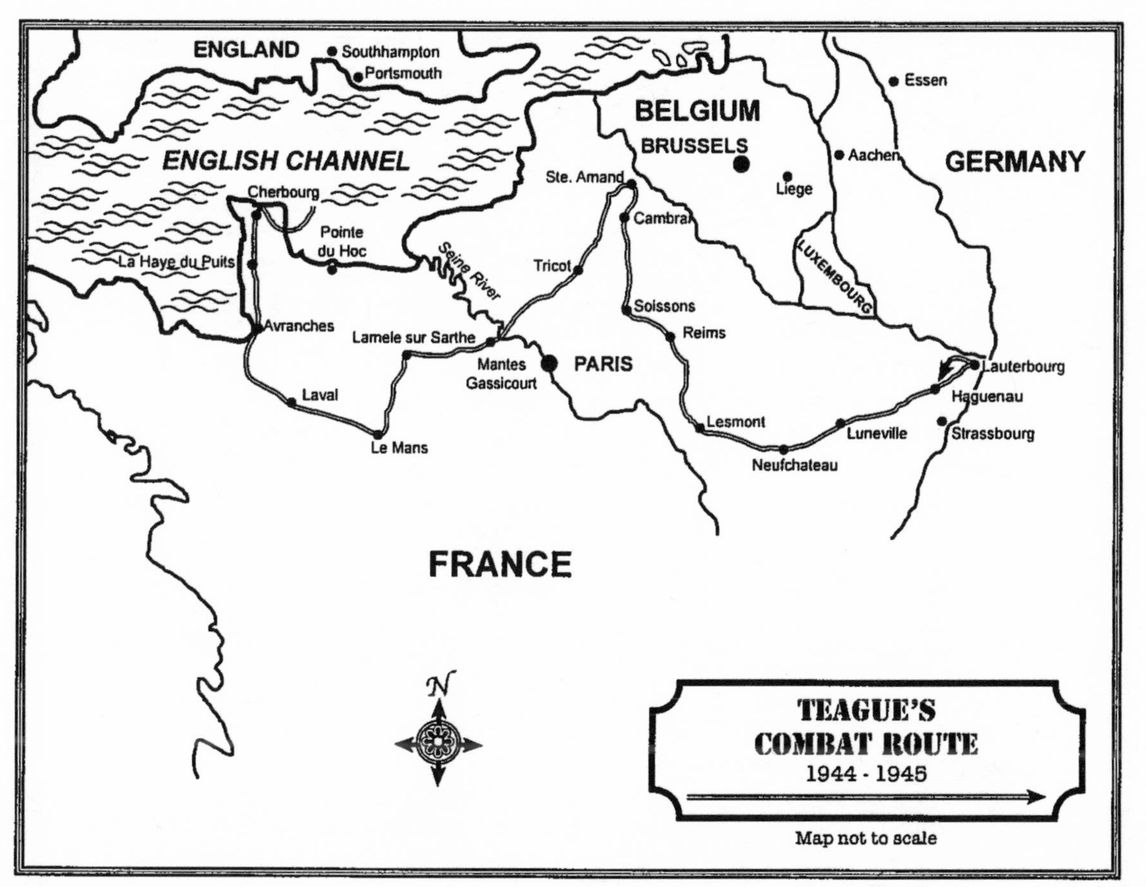
ENGLAND
Southhampton
Portsmouth
ENGLISH CHANNEL
Cherbourg
Pointe du Hoc
La Haye du Puits
Avranches
Laval
Le Mans
Lamele sur Sarthe
Seine River
Mantes Gassicourt
PARIS
Tricot
Ste. Amand
Cambrai
Soissons
Reims
Lesmont
Neufchateau
Luneville
Haguenau
Strassbourg
Lauterbourg
BELGIUM
BRUSSELS
Liege
Aachen
Essen
LUXEMBOURG
GERMANY
FRANCE
N
TEAGUE'S
COMBAT ROUTE
1944 - 1945
Map not to scale

Map 7

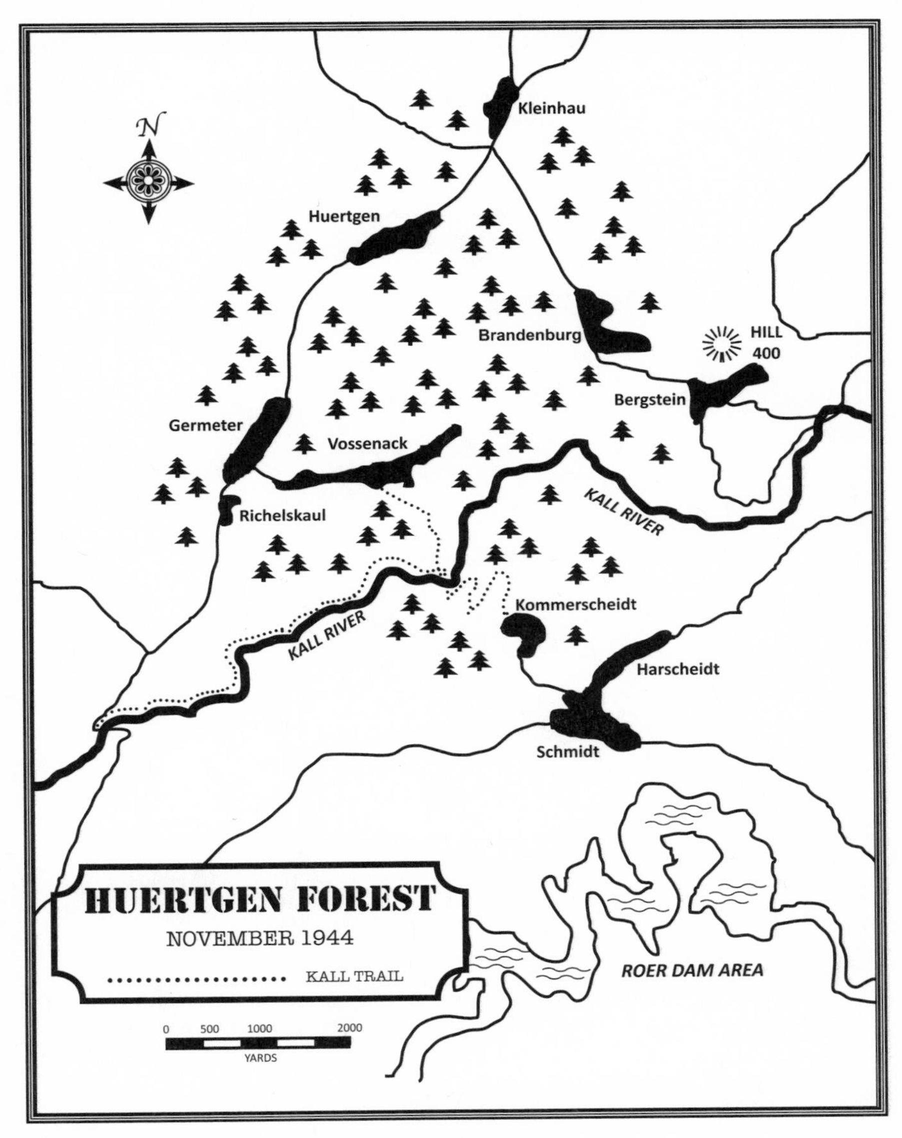
N
Kleinhau
Huertgen
Brandenburg
HILL
400
Bergstein
Germeter
Vossenack
Richelskaul
KALL RIVER
Kommerscheidt
KALL RIVER
Harscheidt
Schmidt
HUERTGEN FOREST
NOVEMBER 1944
KALL TRAIL
ROER DAM AREA
0
500
1000
2000
YARDS

Map 8

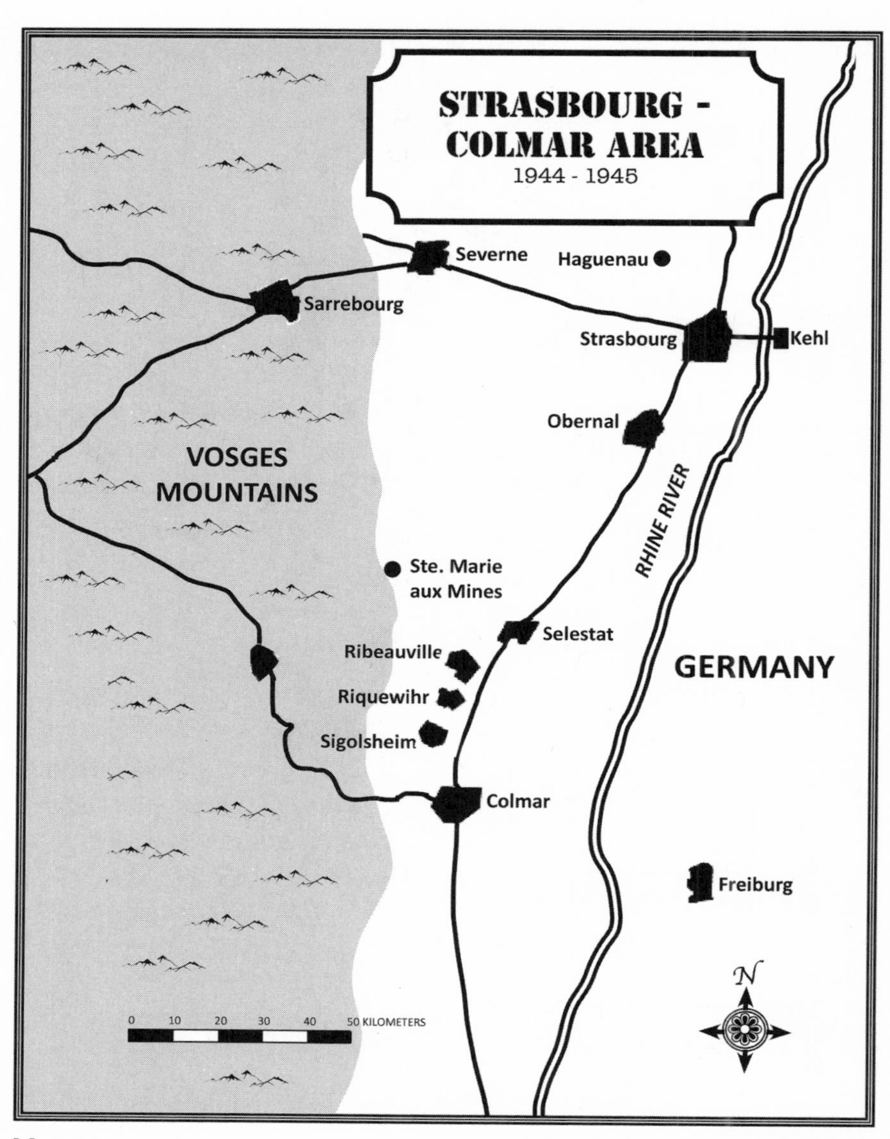
STRASBOURG -
COLMAR AREA
1944 - 1945
Severne
Haguenau
Sarrebourg
Strasbourg
Kehl
Obernal
VOSGES
MOUNTAINS
RHINE RIVER
Ste. Marie
aux Mines
Selestat
Ribeauville
GERMANY
Riquewihr
Sigolsheim
Colmar
Freiburg
N
0 10 20 30 40 50 KILOMETERS

Map 9

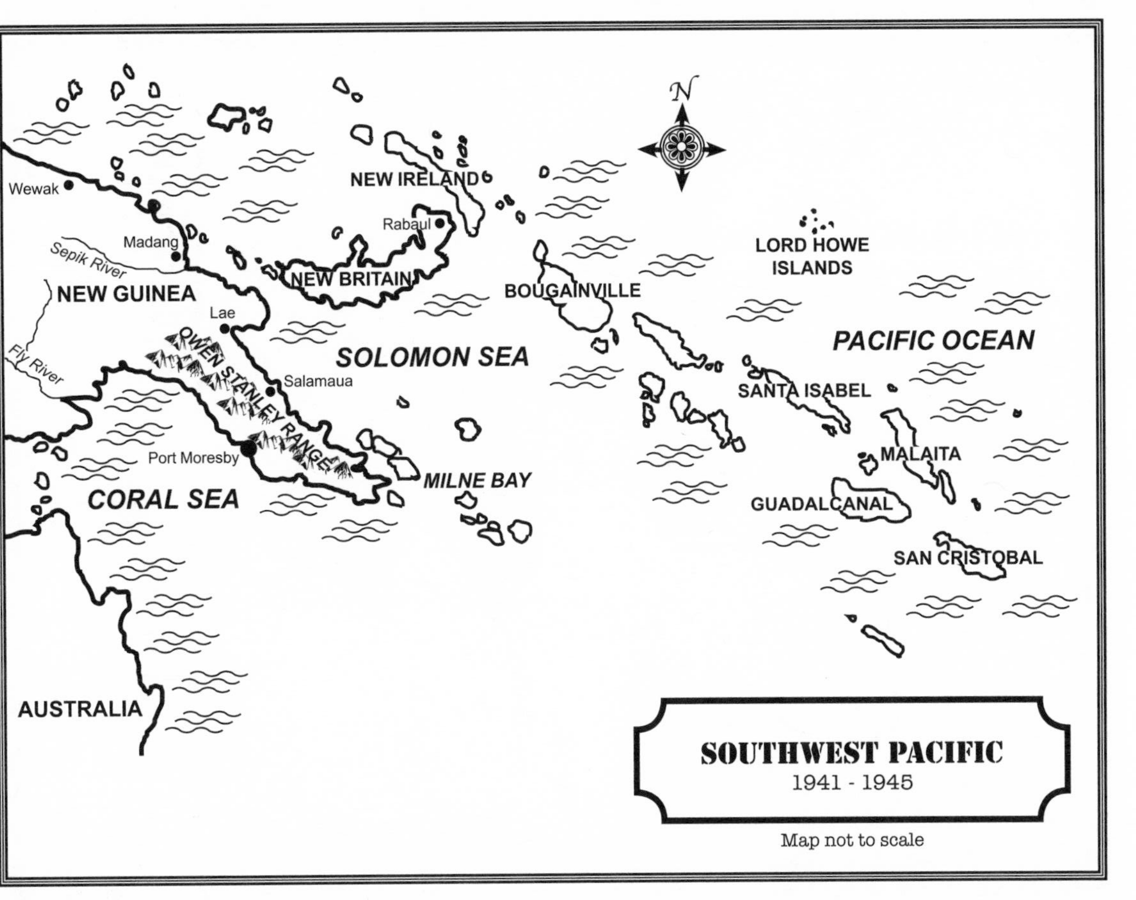
N
NEW IRELAND
Rabaul
NEW BRITAIN
Wewak
Madang
Sepik River
NEW GUINEA
Lae
Fly River
OWEN STANLEY RANGE
Salamaua
Port Moresby
SOLOMON SEA
MILNE BAY
CORAL SEA
AUSTRALIA
BOUGAINVILLE
LORD HOWE
ISLANDS
PACIFIC OCEAN
SANTA ISABEL
MALAITA
GUADALCANAL
SAN CRISTOBAL
SOUTHWEST PACIFIC
1941 - 1945
Map not to scale

Map 10

CHINA
HANOI
LAOS
GULF OF
TONKIN
DMZ
Khe Sanh
Hué
Phu Bai
Da Nang
MR1
THAILAND
Mang Buk
Kontum
Pleiku
Duc Co
An Khe
Cheo Reo
Tuy Hoa
CAMBODIA
MR2
Nha Trang
Loc Ninh
An Loc
MR3
Bien Hoa
SAIGON
CAM RANH
BAY
SOUTH
CHINA SEA
Can Tho
MEKONG
DELTA
Soc Trang
MR4
GULF OF
THAILAND
N
SOUTH VIETNAM
1955 - 1975
Military Regions (MR)
National Boundaries
0 100 200km
0 100 200mi

Map 11

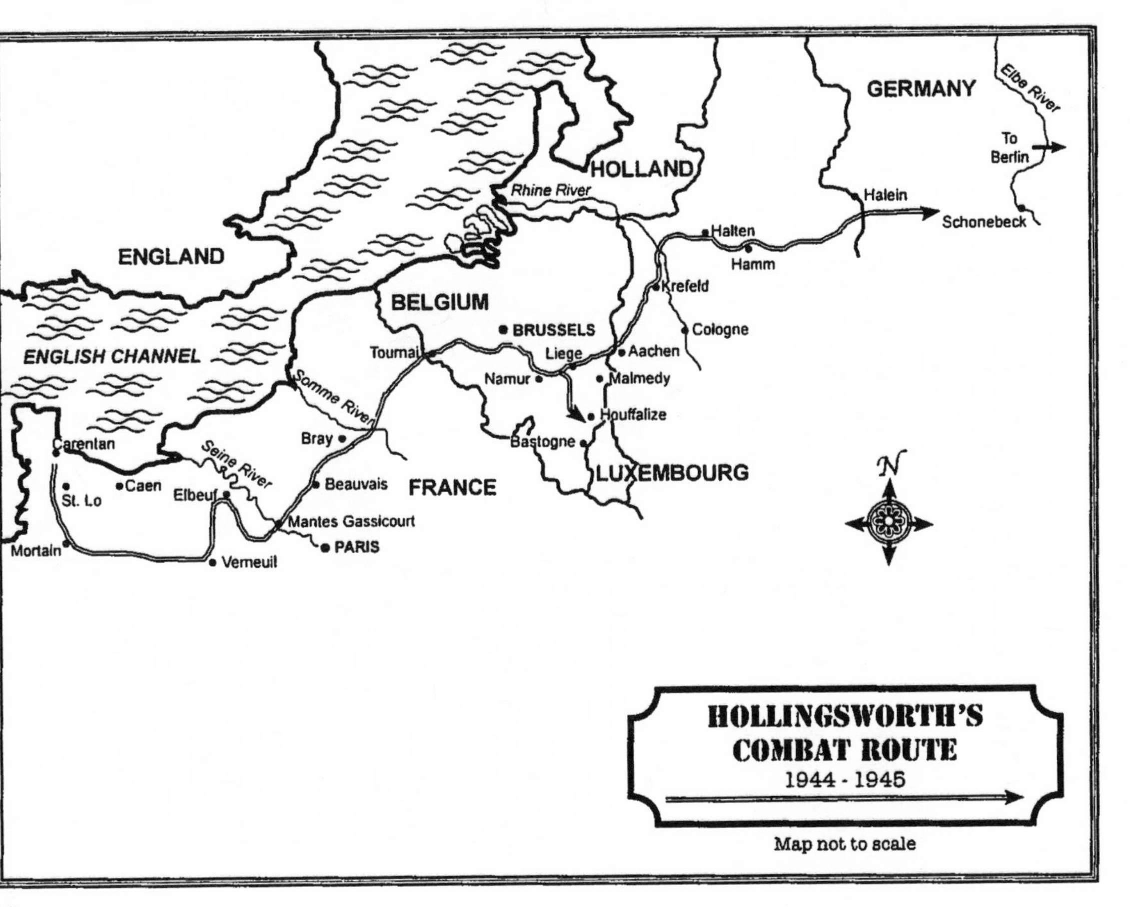
HOLLINGSWORTH'S
COMBAT ROUTE
1944 - 1945
Map not to scale
N
GERMANY
Elbe River
To
Berlin
Halein
Schonebeck
HOLLAND
Rhine River
Halten
Hamm
Krefeld
Cologne
ENGLAND
BELGIUM
BRUSSELS
ENGLISH CHANNEL
Tournai
Liege
Aachen
Namur
Malmedy
Houffalize
Bastogne
LUXEMBOURG
Somme River
Bray
Carentan
Seine River
St. Lo
Caen
Elbeuf
Beauvais
FRANCE
Mantes Gassicourt
PARIS
Mortain
Verneuil

Map 12

★ 7 ★

Highpockets, One Tough Marine

RAYMOND L. MURRAY

CLASS OF 1935

Raymond Leroy Murray was born on January 30, 1913, in Los Angeles, California, the son of Thomas F. and Alice Rogers Murray. He was their first child and was followed by two brothers and three sisters. His father was a Boy Scout administrator, which led to a vagabond life for the family. They moved to Phoenix, Arizona, in 1920; Galveston, Texas, in 1921; and then back to California (Redondo Beach). The next assignment involved a return to Galveston in 1927, and from there back to Alhambra, California, where young Murray attended two years of high school. In 1928 the family moved to Mercedes, Texas. Attending Harlingen High School, Murray played football and was captain of the basketball team. In the school's 1929 yearbook, his football coach said of him: "This big end from California was always down the field on punts and was also a consistent tackler. He was good at snatching passes and when one came his way it usually landed in his big, long

Murray lettered three years on the varsity football team and was an All-Southwest Conference end. *Courtesy Texas A&M University Yearbook*

arms." Murray was president of his class during his senior year. Graduating in the spring of 1930, he enrolled in Texas A&M that fall.

In his application for admission Murray stated that he wanted to major in agricultural administration but enrolled in landscape architecture instead. He requested the infantry as his first choice for his required military science and was assigned to Company B, Infantry, in the Corps of Cadets. During his first year at A&M, he played on the freshman football team, then played end on the varsity team for three years, earning All–Southwest Conference recognition and being named most valuable player in 1933. Murray also played on the varsity basketball team. Dropping out of college the spring of 1932 to earn money, he returned to school in September 1932, changing his major to English but continuing to play football and basketball. During his fifth year at A&M, Murray served as the infantry regimental commander in the Corps of Cadets, with the rank of cadet lieutenant colonel.

Having completed his athletic eligibility, he became an assistant coach for the freshman football team and in the spring was a coach on the track team. Murray was selected to the Hall of Fame (equivalent to today's Who's Who) in the *1935 Longhorn* with the accompanying statement: "We honor Raymond L. Murray because of his ability as an athlete and a good friend to everyone." He received his bachelor of arts degree on May 31, 1935.[1]

About a month before graduation, an Army ROTC instructor had called Murray to his office and asked if he would like to join the marines. The colonel explained that the Marine Corps was expanding and needed one hundred new officers. At the time Murray's best prospect for a job after graduation was as a teacher-coach earning about $90 a month for nine months. The Marine Corps would pay him $125 a month for the year. He was selected for the corps along with two other Texas A&M cadets—Bruno Hockmuth and Joe McHaney.[2]

On July 9, 1935, he was commissioned a second lieutenant and ordered to the Philadelphia Navy Yard to attend the Marine Corps Basic School, a nine-month course that all new officers had to attend. After completing this training, Murray was assigned to the 1st Battalion, 6th Marine Regiment (6th Marines in Marine Corps parlance), in San Diego, California. On a blind date he met Evelyn Roseman, the daughter of a retired naval officer. They were married on August 20, 1937, and only had nine days together before he boarded the cruiser USS *Marblehead* bound for Shanghai, China.

Embarking with the 2nd Marine Brigade in September, Murray served for a short time with the 2nd Anti-Aircraft Battalion in Shanghai. The brigade's mission was to protect Americans and foreigners living in a designated housing area known as the International Settlement. In January 1938 he joined the marine detachment at the US Embassy in Peiping (Beijing) and was promoted to first lieutenant in August. His wife joined him in Peiping, where they rented a house in the USSR Embassy compound. They had a "number one" servant, a cook, a cook's assistant, a wash "amah" for the washing, and a private rickshaw; the monthly expense was only thirty dollars. Their first son, Bill, was born in China. During this time, Murray learned to speak Chinese. In July 1940 the family returned to the States aboard the liner *President Coolidge*. Upon arriving in San Diego in September, Murray again saw duty with the 1st Brigade, stationed at Camp Elliot, California. On February 1, 1941, the brigade was redesignated as the 2nd Marine Division comprising three infantry regiments—2nd, 6th, and 8th Marines—plus artillery, armored, and other supporting units.[3]

Promoted to captain in March 1941, Murray was assigned to the 6th Marines, serving as a company commander. The regiment was then detached from the 2nd Marine Division and assigned to the 1st Marine Brigade (Provisional), then being formed in Charleston, South Carolina. The 6th Marines departed San Diego in an atmosphere of wartime secrecy on May 31. Most of the marines thought their destination was the Caribbean, some officers even packing their summer-service uniforms and dress whites. Another rumor was that the unit was going to Martinique, and yet another held the Azores as their new station. Unknown to the deploying marines, Prime Minister Winston S. Churchill had requested that Pres. Franklin D. Roosevelt send troops to Iceland to replace that island's British garrison, which was desperately needed elsewhere.

The little convoy of three transports and four destroyers passed through the Panama Canal and arrived in Charleston on June 17. The 1st Marine Brigade (Provisional), commanded by Brig. Gen. John Marston, was formed about the time of the arrival of the 6th Marines. Consisting of 4,095 marines, the new brigade departed Charleston five days later in a convoy of twenty-five vessels, including two battleships and two cruisers. The ships moved into Placentia Bay, Newfoundland, on the night of June 27. The transports weighed anchors just before midnight on July 1 and headed for Iceland. Located on the edge of the Arctic Circle, it was a large volcanic island strategically important to protect the "life line" between North America and the British Isles.

Early on July 7, the American convoy approached Reykjavik, Iceland's capital. Once ashore the marines occupied former British army camps, some as far as fifteen miles away. The marines found the camps laid out in a haphazard arrangement, whereas they were accustomed to uniform camp designs. The haphazard arrangement was by design so enemy reconnaissance could not identify unit areas.

Norway was within range of Iceland and was occupied by German forces. During the long summer days, enemy reconnaissance planes flew over the island on photo missions. To prevent the Germans from learning they were in Iceland, the marines did not fly the American flag. Another reason was that the United States was not at war. The brigade's mission was to serve as a "mobile force" to support the remaining British division in defense of the island.

It was on Iceland that Murray picked up the nickname "Highpockets." Standing six feet, three inches tall, his pockets were somewhere near the chest level of most of the men in his command. He believed that the name came from his unit's communication section, but it was never spoken to his face. One of the communications men, Leon Uris, who was an aspiring writer, had a way of identifying each marine with a name suitable to his physical appearance or mannerisms. Uris later became the bestselling author of *Battle Cry, Exodus,* and other popular books. *Battle Cry* was made into a movie of the same name, in which the commander was called "Highpockets."

In August the first US Army contingents arrived, and the British units began preparations to return to England for redeployment to North Africa. As elements of the army's 5th Infantry Division arrived, the marines were busy repairing and expanding their own camps and building new ones for the arriving troops.

On December 7, 1941, Japanese aircraft bombed US naval forces at Pearl Harbor in the Hawaiian Islands and conducted aerial raids on army and air corps installations elsewhere on the island of Oahu. America was now officially at war, but the marines on Iceland were already on a war footing and ready to fight the Germans or the Japanese.

In January 1942 the brigade received orders to prepare to leave for the States. The first unit to depart, the 3rd Battalion, sailed on January 31. The last units departed Reykjavik on March 9. After a thirty-day home leave, Murray returned to San Diego in April 1942. The following month he was promoted to major and appointed battalion executive officer.[4]

While the 6th Marines was in Iceland, the 8th Marines was sent to American Samoa and the 2nd Marines attached to the 1st Marine Division for the Solomon Islands operation.

In March 1942 Adm. Ernest J. King, chief of naval operations, proposed an offensive that would secure the Solomons and thus deprive the Japanese of land bases from which to strike the vital supply line between Hawaii and Australia. The ground forces would consist of the 1st Marine Division, commanded by Maj. Gen. Alexander Vandegrift; the 1st Marine Raider Battalion; the 1st Marine Paratroop Battalion; and from the 2nd Marine Division, the attached 2nd Marines. On July 22 the invasion fleet left Wellington, New Zealand.[5]

The Americans approached the islands undetected by the Japanese. Their principal objective was the island of Guadalcanal (see map 10).

Lying northwest to southwest, the "Canal" is ninety miles long and twenty-five miles across the belly, which is where the 1st Marine Division hit, midway from tip to tip on the island's north shore. Vandegrift's staff, lacking detailed intelligence of the island, planned to land "where the enemy was not"—east of the Ilu River about 8,000 yards from an airstrip then under construction and nearing completion.

The transports on the morning of August 7 (D-Day) offloaded the landing force, which went ashore unopposed. The islands of Florida, Guvatu, and Tulagi, located twenty miles north of Guadalcanal, also were assaulted by the 1st Raider Battalion and 1st Paratroop Battalion, reinforced by the 2nd Marines. Aware that he controlled three-quarters of America's carrier strength in the Pacific and that any carrier sunk could not be replaced for months, R. Adm. Frank J. Fletcher, in overall tactical command, decided that he could only support the landings for two days. Despite protests from Vandegrift and R. Adm. Richmond Turner, commander of the amphibious force, Fletcher was determined to get his carriers out of harm's way as quickly as possible.

Japanese reaction to the landings came quickly, with air raids on the beachhead and raids by strong naval forces that not only shelled positions onshore but also administered the US Navy a defeat at the Battle of Savo Island (August 9). This disaster forced the withdrawal of the transports and cargo ships, though only half of the needed supplies had been offloaded.[6]

By the third day (D+2), the marines had neutralized the key small islands adjacent to Florida and secured a toehold on Guadalcanal centered around the now-captured airfield. The Japanese took advantage of their dusk-to-dawn control of the waters around the main island and landed reinforcements and supplies at night. On August 15, destroyer transports brought in a small complement of Marine Corps air-operations personnel and bombs, ammunition, gasoline, and aircraft spare parts. The airfield, named Henderson Field in honor of a marine dive-bomber pilot killed at Midway two months earlier, now was ready to receive planes. Five days later an escort carrier brought in a marine squadron of twelve dive-bombers and nineteen fighter planes.[7]

After the defeat at Savo Island, in the Battle of Eastern Solomons on August 24, the navy repulsed a powerful Japanese naval force north of the island chain. This victory temporarily dissuaded enemy transports within range of American planes from Henderson. But the Japanese continued to sneak in reinforcements by night in destroyers, cruisers, and even barges. On October 11 a Japanese naval force was detected moving down on Cape Esperance, the northern tip of Guadalcanal. About midnight between Cape Esperance and Savo Island, US cruisers met the enemy. The ensuing battle was short, sharp, and resulted in a clear-cut American victory.[8]

Fighting off a major ground attack against Henderson Field, the marines could do little more than hang on to their perimeter while waiting for reinforcements. That help came in the form of the 7th Marine Regiment, which was released from garrison duty in Samoa. Both sides on Guadalcanal were racing to bring in reinforcements, and to this point the Japanese were winning. The arrival of the US Army's 164th Regimental Combat Team gave Vandegrift a total of 23,000 troops on Guadalcanal and an additional 4,500 men on Tulagi Island.

Forces on Guadalcanal were reinforced with the arrival of the 2nd Marine Division and the army's Americal Division. The 25th Infantry Division was sent directly from Hawaii to relieve the ragged, weary 1st Marine Division at the end of December. In all the fighting, the 1st Marine Division had lost 774 men killed and 1,962 wounded; in addition, more than 5,400 marines had been stricken with malaria.

With the withdrawal of the 1st Marine Division, Maj. Gen. Alexander Patch, the commander of the Americal Division, replaced Vandegrift as commander of the expanding ground force on the island. Patch became commander of the US Army XIV Corps, which in early January 1943 fielded 50,666 men.[9]

On New Year's Day, 1943, the 6th Marines, to include Murray's 2nd Battalion, arrived on Guadalcanal. General Patch was anxious to launch the long-awaited drive to Cape Esperance. The 6th Marines passed through the 2nd and 8th Marines and attacked up the north coast. The 25th Division attacked inland to prevent the Japanese from retreating into the hills. It was during this period that Murray was awarded his first Silver Star.

Mop-up operations began on February 2, and the island was declared secure on the ninth. Of the estimated 36,000 Japanese who fought on the island, more than 14,000 were killed and another 9,000 perished from disease. American ground forces suffered approximately 1,600 men killed and 4,300 wounded. The navy was battered in a half-dozen battles and lost about 4,900 men at sea but carried out its main task of supplying and protecting the ground troops.

The 2nd Marine Division, commanded by Major General Marston, departed for New Zealand. The 6th Marines had been the last to arrive on Guadalcanal and now were the last to leave. By March 1 the entire division was reassembled in Wellington. In the six months of the campaign in the Solomons, the division had lost 263 men killed, 15 missing, and 912 wounded.[10]

Murray's battalion was stationed at McKay's Crossing, about two miles from Wellington. The accommodations were New Zealand–made huts and conical tents heated by coal or oil stoves. The marines were welcomed by the residents, and hundreds of them married New Zealand sweethearts. After a few weeks of rest and relaxation, the units started a training program, in part to help acclimate replacements who had arrived into units decimated by battle losses and sickness. Battle training was augmented by an extensive sports program. During this time, on May 1, Marston yielded division command to Maj. Gen. Julian C. Smith.[11]

The most exposed portion of the Japanese defensive ring was the Gilbert Islands. Adm. Chester Nimitz, commander of the Pacific Fleet, decided to seize several islands in that chain for bases, with the Tarawa Atoll as the primary objective. Betio (pronounced Bayshio), a generally east–west oriented island in the atoll, is the one nearest to the break in the reef sheltering the entrance to the lagoon. The 350-acre landmass is surrounded by reefs located eight hundred to a thousand yards offshore.

The attacking force was divided into two wings, a northern one to seize Makin Island with 7,000 troops of the 27th Infantry Division, and a southern one to take Tarawa with the 2nd Marine Division of 18,000 men. Held in reserve was the 6th Marines. This assault would be the first attempt to storm a heavily defended beach since the 1915 British tragedy at Gallipoli, Turkey.[12]

Amphibious tractors called amtracs, officially known as LVTs (for Landing Vehicle, Tracked), made up the first invasion wave, hitting the beach at 9:10 a.m., as well as the following two landings. Successive waves, though, were made up of Higgins boats (LCVPs), which were unable to cross the reef, forcing their passenger troops to wade several hundred yards to the shore, all the time under intense machine-gun and artillery fire. Losses among these men were heavy. Some 1,500 marines became pinned down on the beach against a barrier wall, one of them sending a message stating, "the mission is in doubt." Additional troops were pushed ashore, but by the evening of the first day, the marines' position ashore remained precarious. About 5,000 men had been involved in these landings, but one of every three of them now was dead or wounded.[13]

A message reached General Smith the following day that Japanese troops were trying to cross the sandbar to Bairiki, the next island in the atoll east of Betio. Murray's battalion was ordered to Bairiki, a tiny pile of coral and sand just three and a half miles southeast of Betio, to prevent the enemy from landing there. Hurriedly on the second day, Murray and his men went ashore on Bairiki two hours before nightfall. Although the marines did not expect opposition, they soon came under long-range machine-gun fire. Murray called in navy planes to knock out the guns, located in a pillbox in the center of the island. The pilot of a Hellcat fighter spotted the position, strafing it and scoring a lucky hit that eliminated the strongpoint. On Thanksgiving Day, November 25, the marines began moving along the atoll's string of islands, accompanied all day by a crowd of Gilbertese natives who wanted to help carry their gear, show them the best places to ford, and generally be as helpful as possible.

"The first day's march did not uncover any Japanese. By midafternoon the following day, the marines had reached Burariki, the last island of the atoll, where any surviving Japanese had to be unless they had somehow been evacuated. Murray sent a company to reconnoiter, and the men encountered an enemy patrol at sunset. Murray and his men dug in for a possible night attack. The next day the Japanese were everywhere, in thick jungle reminiscent of Guadalcanal." Murray had a close call when one soldier with a knife broke out of the bushes and attacked him. Although cut on the arm, he grappled with the assailant, knocking him down and then hitting him in the head with the butt of his pistol. By nightfall the battle was over, the last pocket of Japanese resistance on Tarawa obliterated and the atoll secured. The 2nd Battalion, 6th Marines, suffered ninety-one casualties, while 175 Japanese lay dead in the jungle. Murray was awarded his second Silver Star.

"The Japanese lost 4,690 men on Tarawa; only 17 were captured along with 129 Korean laborers. US casualties were 948 killed, 2,162 wounded, and 88 missing in action. Of the 125 amtracs in the assault, 35 sank at sea, 26 sank on the reef, 9 burned on the beach, and 2 were blown up by mines. Only 53 vehicles reached the beach."[14]

The battle was over in seventy-six hours, and the 6th Marines were assigned the cleanup. On January 8, 1944, the liberty ship *Prince George* was in the harbor embarking troops; Murray, suffering from dengue fever, was carried aboard on a stretcher. The 2nd Marine Division was bound for a new station, Camp Tarawa, located on the Parker Ranch on the island of Hawaii. The cold climate of the mountains was beneficial to men still haunted by malaria contracted on Guadalcanal. The Parker ranges also provided excellent training terrain to rebuild the division.

Murray had been receiving letters from his wife about health problems with their baby Michael, who had been born on April 11, 1943. Shortly after arriving in Hawaii, he received a call from his wife that the baby had died. The marine flew back to the States for the funeral of a son he had never known.[15]

The next few months on Hawaii were spent in intensive training in amphibious exercises, jungle warfare, and weapons training. The plan for the major Pacific operation, the invasion of the Marianas Islands, came down to the division on April 10 and outlined an assault on Saipan for mid-June. The units designated for this landing were the 2nd Marine Division, now commanded by Maj. Gen. Thomas Watson; the 4th Marine Division; and the army's 27th Infantry Division in reserve.[16]

Saipan is a small island, less than fifteen miles long and seven miles across at its widest point. High cliffs dominate its eastern and northern sides, while the western part is a low-lying plain. The center of the island is dominated by a 1,500-foot mountain and two smaller hills. The eastern coast is mostly devoid of coral reefs, whereas the western side is almost completely ringed by reefs.

The 2nd Marine Division departed Pearl Harbor on transports on May 25, and on June 14 the blacked-out ships moved around the northern tip of Saipan and down its western shore. As part of the invasion plan, the 6th Marines and 8th Marines would land in the first wave on the left portion of the beach while the 4th Marine Division splashed ashore on the right. The landing was preceded by airstrikes and intensive naval bombardment. Despite this bombardment, Japanese defenses remained intact and met the marines with devastating fire.

At 8:45 a.m. on June 15, the assault units went ashore in amtracs. Murray's battalion moved about a hundred yards beyond the coastal road and was caught in a murderous crossfire. While searching for a place to put his command post, a mortar shell landed right behind him, killing two lieutenants and wounding fourteen other marines. Murray was seriously wounded and was knocked out for a few minutes. When he regained consciousness, his first thought was that he must be dead. Then he began to feel better and decided to cross the road and seek cover so his wounds could be treated. He was wounded again when a bullet ricocheted and hit him in the hip. Navy corpsmen treated his wounds as best they could. Murray continued to command the battalion, crawling from place to place. When the regimental commander arrived, though, he ordered the major evacuated and the battalion executive officer to take over. The new commander was hit by mortar fire less than two hours later, and a lieutenant colonel attached as an observer took command for a short period until another major from the 6th Marines arrived. Murray was put on a hospital ship back to Hawaii. After treatment there, he was flown to San Francisco on a Boeing clipper. For his heroism on Saipan, Murray was awarded the Navy Cross.

Meanwhile, back on Saipan the fighting continued, and the 27th Division was committed ashore. The island was declared secure on July 9, but the dangerous task of discovering individual Japanese hidden in the ravines and caves continued. The two marine divisions were pulled out of combat on July 13 to prepare for the Tinian landings. Saipan had exacted a high toll on the American troops, the three divisions having lost 3,229 men killed and 10,992 wounded or missing. The Japanese lost almost their entire garrison of more than 20,000 men.[17]

Arriving in San Francisco, Murray requested to be sent to San Diego. Instead, he was given fifteen days' leave and ordered to report afterward to Quantico, Virginia, for duty as an instructor. Still wearing many bandages, Murray drove his family to Quantico and upon arrival checked into the hospital. After returning to duty, his teaching activities were interrupted when, after Franklin Roosevelt died, he was assigned to command the honor guard for the president's funeral.

A second son, James, was born on August 21, 1946. Shortly after the birth, Murray was ordered to Hawaii as the deputy chief of staff to Garrison Forces in the Pacific. His job was to visit all the island posts and meet with the commands to help them better organize. Meanwhile, another son, Daniel Walker, was born on June 23, 1948. The following month Murray was ordered to Quantico for temporary duty on the Marine Corps Board at the Basic School. In January 1949 he returned to Camp Pendleton, where he served consecutively as assistant chief of staff, G-4; commanding officer, 3rd Marines; and executive officer, 5th Marines.[18]

In the predawn hours of June 25, 1950, more than 100,000 North Korean People's Army (NKPA) troops crossed the 38th Parallel to invade South Korea. The ill-prepared and underequipped South Korean Army was quickly routed, and the capital city of Seoul fell three days later. The United States rushed in army forces from Japan to delay the North Koreans, but these troops were pushed back to the Naktong River in the southernmost part of the Korean Peninsula. A defensive position, known as the Pusan Perimeter, was established and over time reinforced piecemeal with units arriving from Japan and the States. The newly authorized United Nations command held the perimeter with the US 24th and 25th Infantry Divisions, US 1st Cavalry Division, and the Republic of Korea (ROK) 1st, 3rd, 6th, 8th, and Capital Divisions.[19]

The 1st Marine Division was alerted to organize a brigade for deployment to the Far East. Although Murray was a lieutenant colonel and the command of a marine regiment was typically a colonel's position, he was selected to head the 5th Marines. He sailed with the regiment on July 11 and arrived at Pusan on August 2 (see map 5).

Four days later the 5th Marines became heavily engaged against the North Koreans and suffered their first causalities in the Korean War. Murray's regiment was called upon for two major offensives against the NKPA to blunt penetrations of the perimeter, and he earned his third Silver Star during these actions. On September 5 the 5th Marines left the front lines to prepare for embarkation and a surprise amphibious operation.[20]

The landing at Inchon was Gen. Douglas MacArthur's audacious plan to land behind the NKPA and cut their supply lines to North Korea. Additionally, he aimed to recapture nearby Seoul. It was a risky venture as the invasion force would have to navigate a channel during high tide with just four hours to complete the landing. With no chance to rehearse and little time to plan, Murray took advantage of the three days at sea to prepare the attack; conduct what training he could, such

Murray meets with General MacArthur after the Inchon landing.
Official US Army Photo

---

as training with ladders to scale the seawall; and integrate replacements into his units. His plan called for one battalion to hit Wolmi-do, on an island causeway, just before dawn on September 15. The other two battalions would land on the evening tide and climb the thirty-foot seawall using ladders and ropes. Murray went ashore with the men and established his command post in trenches built by the North Korean defenders. He soon began receiving reports of the capture of many of the initial objectives. By 11:00 p.m. his units were meeting very little resistance and another regiment, the 7th Marines, had come ashore.

The next day the marines moved out toward Ascom City and Kimpo Airfield. The following day the North Koreans attacked with six tanks and two hundred men, but were quickly defeated. General MacArthur arrived at this moment and turned to his aide and said, “Get this man’s name; I’m going to give him a Silver Star.” Murray thus received his fourth Silver Star, his second from the US Army. He also earned another Purple Heart when an exploding mortar shell sent fragments into his cheek and nose.[21]

Fighting their way through the hills west of Seoul, Murray’s marines reached the Han River about eight miles from the capital. The major sent a swimming party of fourteen men, mostly from the Reconnaissance Company, across the river on the evening of September 19. Reaching the other side, they signaled for the rest of the company to cross, but when the amtracs entered the water, they were met with mortar and machine-gun fire and returned to the south bank. The regiment began an assault crossing at 6:45 the next morning and suffered heavy casualties. After seven days of intense fighting, the 5th Marines entered the city. By September 27 the regiment had reached the capital building; in a ceremony at the Government House, MacArthur announced the liberation of Seoul. But house-to-house fighting continued in order to clear the city of the enemy. For their success during this period, the 1st Provisional Marine Brigade was awarded a Presidential Unit Citation.

CITATION

For extraordinary heroism in action against enemy aggressor forces in Korea from 7 August to 7 September 1950. Functioning as a mobile, self-contained, air-ground team, the FIRST Provisional Marine Brigade, Reinforced, rendered invaluable service during the fierce struggle to maintain the foothold established by friendly forces in the Pusan area during the early stages of the Korean conflict. Quickly moving into action as numerically superior enemy forces neared the Naktong River on the central front and penetrated to within thirty-five miles of Pusan in the southern sector, threatening the integrity of the entire defensive perimeter, this hard-hitting, indomitable team counterattacked serious enemy penetrations at three different points in rapid succession. Undeterred by road-blocks, heavy hostile automatic-weapons and highly effective artillery fire, extremely difficult terrain and intense heat, the Brigade met the invaders with relentless determination and, on each crucial occasion,

> hurled them back in disorderly retreat. By combining sheer resolution and esprit de corps with sound infantry tactics and splendid close air support, the Brigade was largely instrumental in restoring the line of defense, in inflicting thousands of casualties upon the enemy and in seizing large amounts of ammunition, equipment and other supplies. The brilliant record achieved by the unit during the critical early days of the Korean conflict attests to the individual valor and competence of the officers and men and reflects the highest credit upon the FIRST Provisional Marine Brigade, Reinforced, and the United States Naval Service.[22]

Following the battle in Seoul, Murray's regiment withdrew to Inchon after being replaced by army units. There they boarded LSTs (Landing Ship, Tanks) for transport to Wonsan on the eastern coast to make an amphibious assault. They departed Inchon on October 17 and moved into the Yellow Sea and made the voyage around the tip of Korea into the Sea of Japan. After arriving in the Wonsan area, the amphibious assault was cancelled since South Korean troops had captured the port. The landing force had to wait while the channel was cleared of mines. They went ashore on October 27.

The 1st Marine Division, along with the US Army 3rd and 7th Divisions and ROK 3rd and Capital Divisions, were a part of the US Army X Corps commanded by Maj. Gen. Edward M. Almond. The boundary between Eighth Army and X Corps was the Taebaek Mountains. The Taebaeks divided the Korean Peninsula and were an area of high peaks with steep slopes and narrow, twisting valleys. In places the peaks reached 6,000 feet or more. During the winter the temperature could reach 20–30 degrees below zero.

The marines were unaware of the situation in the Eighth Army on the other side of the peninsula. Hundreds of thousands of Chinese Communist Force troops had crossed the Yalu the night of October 15 and onward. The Chinese units were hiding in the North Korean mountains. They were not detected by the UN Command until several days later when they attacked a few Eighth Army units. By the end of October there were reports of the Chinese intervention.

Clearing the area around the Wonsan was the marines' first task. Then they pushed north to Hamhung and Hungnam, an important commercial and industrial center on the eastern coast. The division continued north toward Yudam-ni. The village was about halfway to the reservoir and was the end of a seventy-eight-mile-long main supply route (MSR) along a one-lane road.

While the 1st Marine Division and elements of the 7th Division moved north, part of the 7th Division reached the Yalu River. Larger ROK forces, operating independently, also reached the Yalu. The marines provided security for the MSR on the way north.

"The 5th and 7th had been assigned parallel tracks along either shore of the reservoir. Unable to support each other across the wide stretch of intervening water, the two regiments were on roads leading essentially nowhere, though both were bound vaguely for the Yalu."[23]

"An eighty-mile-wide corridor separated X Corps from Eighth Army, and the inland flanks were totally exposed." In western Korea the Chinese soon had the Eighth Army in full retreat, though no word of this reached X Corps. Instead it continued heading north, unaware that there were 120,000 Chinese infantrymen concealed in the mountains around the reservoir waiting for the advancing marine and army troops to enter their trap.

Winter struck early in the Chosin region that year, arriving with violent force and subzero temperatures on November 10, the day the marines reached the Koto-ri plateau. The Americans were freezing in their summer uniforms, inadequate blankets, and sleeping bags. Parkas and other warm clothing were soon on the way, though not before many troops suffered cold-weather injuries.[24]

On November 26 the 5th Marines turned over the east side of the reservoir to the 1st Battalion, 32nd Infantry Regiment, 7th Infantry Division. After the relief the marines were to take the road leading westward from Yudam-ni into the vastness of the Taebaek Mountains to link up with the Eighth Army. The 1st Marine Division hoped "to concentrate the bulk of the division around the vital road junction at Hagaru, sixty-four miles from the sea and fourteen miles south and east of Yudam-ni." At the same time, the Chinese were "preparing a special fate for the marines. Massed infantry formations were slated to isolate, segment, and destroy the 1st Marine Division and the 1st Battalion. The blow fell on the night of November 27," when CCF infantry streamed across the frozen reservoir headed for the 5th Marine's headquarters, which was only a makeshift tent. There was fighting in every direction until the Chinese suddenly broke and ran. Another assault later was beaten back. The Chinese continued to attack during the night, but at dawn they disappeared.[25]

The 5th and 7th Marines established a defensive perimeter in Yudam-ni, and the two regimental commanders issued a combined order for the breakout to the south. The wounded were loaded on any available vehicle, sometimes on stretchers tied to trailers, and the frozen dead were stacked like cordwood on trucks. Orders from X Corps directed the 7th Marines, commanded by Col. Homer L. Litzenberg Jr., to attack south from Yudam-ni to clear and secure the main supply route to Hagaru-ri. The 7th was replaced by Murray and his marines and assumed responsibility for Yudam-ni. Late on November 30, Murray was told that his regiment should begin moving south to Hagaru-ri. The division had organized provisional companies and platoons from headquarters, service, and artillery units. The provisional units would provide flank security for the vehicle column. Prior to the move, an enormous amount of equipment and supplies was destroyed and in some cases abandoned.[26]

The marines had something the Chinese did not—close air support. The troops understood its value and had a special relationship with the navy and marine pilots. Supporting the breakout by bombing and strafing the surrounding hills, these aerial assaults proved very effective, especially when using napalm.

For five days and five nights of unspeakable horror, the two regiments fought without rest through masses of CCF infantry and dozens of roadblocks. Fending off the Chinese and still taking casualties, the head of the column reached the Hagaru-ri defenses the night of December 3. Marines continued to arrive throughout the night and most of the next day. These units were assigned defensive positions in the perimeter as they came in.[27]

On December 4 General Almond flew in and decorated Smith, Litzenberg, and Murray with the Distinguished Service Cross. That same day Murray was ordered to take over the defense of Hagaru-ri while Litzenberg marched south with his 7th Marines. All excess supplies and equipment were put on a bonfire. Casualties were flown out and two days' rations were issued to each of the remaining men. The plan was for the marines to fight their way from Hagaru-ri for twenty-one miles to Chinhung-ni, where the 3rd Infantry Division had established a forward defensive line. On December 6 at a meeting with his officers,

Maj. Gen. Raymond L. Murray's last assignment was in Vietnam.
Official US Marine Corps Photo

Murray made a remark now enshrined in Marine Corps history: "We're going to take our dead, wounded and equipment when we leave. We're coming out I tell you as marines or not at all."[28]

The division column moved out and, fighting all the way, reached the perimeter at Koto-ri on December 7. Continuing their march the next day, it was again a constant effort of fighting, clearing hills on the flanks, and breaking through road blocks. The lead elements of the 7th Marines reached Chinhung-ni on December 10; by the next evening most of the other marine units were in the Hamhung-Hungnam area.[29]

Murray and the others expected to defend a sector of the Hamhung-Hungnam "enclave," but by that time a new X Corps plan ordered the evacuation of all forces from the area to the Eighth Army on the east coast. The marines marched straight down to the docks, and over December 11–14 they boarded twenty-eight ships. In total the 1st Marine Division had suffered about 10,500 casualties since landing at Wonsan. The entire division was accorded a rare honor, a Presidential Unit Citation, an award usually reserved to commend smaller units for outstanding performance under fire. Lieutenant Colonel Murray was awarded a second Navy Cross in addition to the Army Distinguished Service Cross.

The 3rd Infantry Division was the last to leave the area. Hamhung, Yonpo Airfield, rail facilities and rolling stock, bridges, tunnels, supplies, and all military equipment that could not be removed were demolished. Finally, the docks and port of Hamhung were destroyed in one gigantic explosion. Nothing of value was left behind for the CCF. The evacuation was completed just before Christmas Day, 1950.[30]

The 1st Marine Division was lifted by troop transport and LSTs to Masan, South Korea, for rest and refitting. They docked at Pusan on December 15 and moved to Masan, where a tent city awaited. From there the marines moved up the east coast to Pohang-dong, where they commenced a system of extensive reconnaissance patrolling in the guerrilla-infested mountains. North Korean insurgents operating in the Eighth Army's rear areas were whittled away by surrounding them band by band, pounding them with mortars and artillery, and then moving in to eliminate any survivors. On March 11 Murray was relieved of command and ordered to Washington, DC, to attend the National War College. Before leaving Korea, he was promoted to colonel.[31]

Traveling from the West Coast with his family, Murray stopped at College Station, Texas. This was the first time he had been back to Texas A&M, and he wanted to show the family where he went to college. His wife and three boys enjoyed the beautiful campus and were delighted to see where he had played football. Arriving in Washington, the colonel was assigned a temporary job commanding the Headquarters Battalion at Marine Corps headquarters. He started course work at the National College in the fall and graduated in June 1952 with orders to report to Quantico as commanding officer of the Marine Corps Basic School.

It was during the tour at Quantico that his twin daughters, Sherry and Terry, were born on September 6, 1953. Serving two years in Virginia, his next assignment was at Camp Pendleton, California, serving first as commanding officer, 1st Infantry Training Regiment, until February 1955, then as chief of staff for the base until July 1957. During his final year at Pendleton, he was assigned to the 1st Marine Division, serving as division inspector general, chief of staff, and assistant chief of staff, successively. In June 1959 Murray was promoted to brigadier general and ordered to Okinawa.[32]

In July 1959 he moved his family to San Diego and in August reported for duty in Okinawa as assistant commander of the 3rd Marine Division. During his tour in Okinawa, his wife became ill, but he was not aware of the seriousness of her condition until he received a call from a good friend, Maj. Gen. Victor H. Krulak, telling him to request an emergency leave as soon as possible. His wife died on June 6, 1960.

With two daughters and two sons at home, Murray had to decide what to do with them since he had to return to Okinawa for three more months. His solution was to farm the kids out to relatives in Southern California. He asked Gen. David Shoup, commandant of the Marine Corps, to be placed somewhere where there were stewards (enlisted aides) for general officers. Ordered back to Camp Pendleton as assistant base commander, Murray was assigned a steward, James Harris, who did the cooking, housework, and, on his own, went beyond the call of duty to help the children get ready for school, seeing that they were well fed and disciplining them when necessary.

A few months after returning to California, he met an attractive widow, Helen Longshore, who helped him with social functions. They started dating and were soon married. In July 1962 Murray received orders to Parris Island, South Carolina, as commander of the Recruit Depot. He packed his family in the car and headed for the East Coast. They moved into Quarters One on the base, an historic two-story house with twenty-seven rooms and seven fireplaces. His steward, Harris, was also transferred to Parris Island and continued his duties with the family. Promotion to major general came for Murray on February 1, 1963.[33]

Transferred to Marine Corps headquarters in June 1964, he was assigned as inspector general of the corps. After living in temporary quarters, Murray found a beautiful Georgian home in Alexandria, Virginia, in the vicinity of Mount Vernon. Since he was no longer authorized a steward, his wife had a friend from California come and live with them and do the cooking. As inspector general he would travel extensively and be away from home most of the time. His role was to be the eyes of the commandant and to report to him the state of affairs on all commands worldwide.

After twenty-six months as inspector general, Murray assumed the duties of assistant chief of staff, G-3 (operations and training.) With the Vietnam War ongoing, the commandant asked him to give particular attention to the recruiting program. Murray visited colleges and universities to get qualified educated men interested in becoming marines. He attended the commissioning exercise at the University of Texas in June 1966 and at the Marine Military Academy in Harlingen, Texas. On April 21, 1967, he was the speaker at the annual Aggie Muster on the campus of Texas A&M.[34]

In September 1967 Murray was detached from headquarters and the following month assumed duties as deputy commander, III Marine Amphibious Force (III MAF), in Vietnam (see map 11). The III MAF, with headquarters in Da Nang, was commanded by Lt. Gen. Robert E. Cushman and consisted of the 1st and 3rd Marine Divisions, a marine air wing, and supporting units. Murray was given responsibility for the community-action platoons that were part of the civic-actions program. These units were stationed in Vietnamese villages with the mission of helping the residents and protecting them from the communist enemy.

While Murray was with the III MAF, there was a major battle at Khe Sanh and fierce fighting during the Tet Offensive, when the enemy captured the historic city of Hue. The III MAF was reinforced by US and Army of South Vietnam divisions to regain control of the northern portion of South Vietnam.

While in Vietnam, Murray began having medical problems in February 1968, in particular having trouble with his balance. He thought it might be another bout of malaria or his gallbladder issues that would go away, but it got worse. Murray knew he had to tell Cushman about it. The general had noticed that something was wrong with his deputy and ordered his return to the States for medical attention. Murray was flown to the US Naval Hospital in Bethesda, Maryland, where his condition worsened. After extensive testing it was determined that the problem was a viral infection in the inner ear. He remained in the hospital until his retirement on August 1, 1968.[35]

Returning to Oceanside, California, Murray bought a house and began a new life in retirement. He tried selling real estate but found that it was not for him. Some approached the retired general about a run for political office, but he had no interest in that. Murray instead found that he liked to work with the youth in the community and with veterans. Joining the Rotary Club, he served a year as its president. All the while he managed to play golf three times a week, despite continuing bouts of vertigo.

His daughter Terry became ill and was diagnosed as having non-Hodgkin's lymphoma. She died July 9, 1997, at the age of forty-three. During this period, Helen was also having medical problems; she died March 23, 2000.

A year and a half after the loss of his second wife, Murray was asked to judge a youth forum by a local lady, a longtime acquaintance of Helen's, Zona Deckelman. They had dinner a few months later and then began dating. The couple married on September 29, 2001, and spent their honeymoon first in Quebec, Canada, then in New York for a few days. In August 2002 they flew to San Antonio to attend a Chosin Few Reunion. Murray took advantage of the trip by visiting College Station again, this time to show Zona and a grandson around the A&M campus. This proved to be the last time he would visit his beloved alma mater.

Maj. Gen. Raymond L. Murray's military awards include the Navy Cross with Gold Star, Army Distinguished Service Cross, Silver Star with Gold Star and Two Army Oak Leaf Clusters, Legion of Merit with Combat "V" and Gold Star, Purple Heart with Gold Star, and Republic of Korea Ulchi Medal with Gold Star.

Murray's health began to deteriorate in October 2002, when he contracted a staph infection during a short stay in a local hospital. By February 2003 he was walking with a cane but in March broke his ankle. In October he was back in the hospital, and on Veteran's Day, November 11, 2004, the tough marine passed away. He was buried at the All Saints Cemetery in San Luis Rey, California.[36]

★ 8 ★

Sole Survivor of Torpedo Squadron 8

GEORGE H. GAY JR.

CLASS OF 1940

The early months of 1942 were dark days for America. The US Pacific Fleet had suffered devastating losses at Pearl Harbor on December 7, 1941, and that same month Guam and Wake Island had fallen to the Japanese. US and Filipino forces on Bataan surrendered in April 1942, and Corregidor fell in May. The only bright spot during those depressing months was the raid on Tokyo by sixteen B-25s led by Lt. Col. James H. Doolittle. Americans needed a victory and a hero. Adm. Chester Nimitz, commander of the Pacific Fleet, provided that victory at the Battle of Midway, and US Navy ensign George Henry Gay Jr. became the hero.

Gay was born on March 8, 1917, in Waco, Texas, the son of George Henry and Sudie Halsey Gay. In 1921 the family moved to Dallas, where young George attended Our Lady of Good Counsel Academy, later attending Oak Cliff High School for two years. At Oak Cliff he was a member of the school band and the all-city honor band. He had taken piano lessons for years, but in order to march in the band, he learned to play the trumpet. He also participated in the Reserve Officers Training Corps (ROTC) and attended ROTC summer camp at Camp Dallas, located near Mineral Wells. This month-long military-training camp was sponsored by the Dallas School System for high school ROTC cadets from Dallas and Fort Worth.

His father was a title man who worked for various mortgage and oil companies. When oil activities became centered in Houston, the family moved there. After the oil company he worked for was sold, the elder Gay opened his own title office. Because of this move, young George transferred to San Jacinto High School, where he joined the school band and orchestra. He also was a member of Houston's all-city band, a drum major for both bands, and participated in his school's ROTC unit, serving as a cadet officer. His junior year he joined the Texas National Guard and attended summer camp at Camp Sterling near Houston.

With the Great Depression in full swing and coming from a family of modest means, Gay worked after school and during summer vacation to save money for college and to assist his family. He was an assistant truck driver, a roustabout in the oil fields, a helper in an A&P grocery store, and also delivered newspapers. Gay planned to work while in college to pay his own way. During the summer following his high school graduation, he worked in a galvanizing plant in Houston.

His mother insisted that he learn to swim at an early age, a skill that would prove invaluable later in life. Gay's first airplane flight was a memorable experience. The Texas State Fair in Dallas one year included an attraction offering rides in a Ford Tri-Motor plane. Gay asked his father to take him up, but he would not. He then asked his mother, who also declined. Then his grandmother said, "Come on son, I came here in a covered wagon and I'm not afraid of that thing."

Gay could have graduated from high school in 1935 but elected to remain in school and accumulate extra credits; besides, he did not have enough money to attend college. That year he only went to school for half-days and earned money by grading geometry papers for one of the teachers and by working nights in a gas station. He graduated in 1936 and received his discharge from the National Guard.

In his application for admission to Texas A&M, Gay stated that he chose the university because of the reputation of its engineering curriculum, the military training he would receive, and the general spirit of the school. The five-foot-eleven, 140-pound freshman entered A&M

in September 1936 and selected mechanical engineering as his academic major. He chose coast artillery for his required military-science training and was assigned to A Battery, Coast Artillery.

Gay attended A&M for five semesters and two summer sessions before withdrawing in the spring of 1939. His declared reason, like that of so many other students during the Great Depression, was the lack of funds.

He wanted to join the Army Air Corps, taking a physical at Randolph Field in San Antonio, but was turned down. After working on his uncle's farm in Beeville, Gay took a job in Victoria with an engineering company working on a Rural Electrification Administration project that provided electricity to rural areas of Texas. But after the field work was done, he found himself sitting in an office, just the type of job he did not want. He then moved to Corpus Christi and took a job as a field engineer. He later worked in construction on a project to build a bridge out into the bay to an oil-well foundation.[1]

With the war in Europe getting worse by the day, the young Texan decided to go to Canada and join the Royal Canadian Air Force. He also considered going to England to join the Royal Air Force. One day a friend told him that there was a navy medical team in town looking for people interested in flying in the US Navy. After calling the telephone number his friend provided, Gay was told to make himself available for exam the next morning. He met with the navy representative, took a thorough physical, and was accepted for flight training. His first duty station was the naval base at Opa-locka, Florida, just north of Miami, where he was given quarters and issued uniforms. As a member of the V-5 program for aspiring aviators, he was given the enlisted rank of seaman second class.

After completing basic flight training, Gay was discharged on April 2, 1941; appointed an aviation cadet; and assigned to Class 4-A-41-J at Jacksonville Naval Air Station. From there he was transferred back to Opa-locka to the advanced carrier base for more training. On September 6 he was commissioned an ensign in the US Naval Reserve and ordered to the Advanced Carrier Training Group, Norfolk Naval Air Station, Virginia. He was assigned to Torpedo Squadron 8 (VT-8), commanded by Lt. Cmdr. John C. Waldron.

The squadron commander was known as a "hard-driving" leader. He instituted a training program that consisted of unit runs around the deck and group calisthenics. Aviators from other squadrons, lounging

TBD-1 torpedo bomber flown by Gay during the Battle of Midway.
Courtesy National Archives

on the deck during these activities, hooted at Waldron's men. This only brought the group closer together. They also noticed that their commander pressed relentlessly for the extra equipment his command needed. His men griped a lot, but they believed in Waldron completely.[2]

The squadron was equipped with the TBD-1 Devastator, a fine torpedo plane in its time, but in 1942 an out-of-date machine. When first introduced, the Devastator was the pride of the US Navy. It was the first all-metal, low-wing, folding-wing aircraft in the fleet, weighing 9,000 pounds and powered by a single Pratt-Whitney nine-cylinder R-1830 engine. The attack bomber's speed was supposed to be 206 miles per hour, but its actual speed was much less, especially when carrying ordnance. The torpedo it carried was a World War I–vintage Mark 13 Bliss-Leavitt. The 2,000-pound, fourteen-foot-long monstrous (and most often dud) weapon cut the Devastator's speed and range drastically.

After months of intensive training, VT-8 departed Norfolk on March 7, 1942, aboard the aircraft carrier USS *Hornet* bound for the Pacific. Prior to sailing, the squadron was divided into two groups. Those going on the *Hornet* would take the old Devastators; the other group, under the squadron's executive officer, Lt. Harold "Swede" Larsen, would remain behind to await the issue of the Grumman TBF Avenger. Twenty-one new Avengers arrived in March, but there was not enough time to change over to the new aircraft prior to the carrier's departure.[3]

Passing through the Panama Canal, the *Hornet* arrived at San Diego on March 20. The ship then sailed to San Francisco Bay, where tugs towed it to Alameda Air Station. Once docked, the *Hornet*'s navy aircraft were stored in the hanger and US Army Air Force B-25s were brought aboard and filled the flight deck. The carrier departed on April 2, and once at sea, Lieutenant Colonel Doolittle, commander of the 1st Special Aviation Project (the Doolittle Raiders), first read telegrams of good wishes from Lt. Gen. Henry H. "Hap" Arnold, Gen. George C. Marshall, Adm. Ernest J. King, and President Roosevelt, then told his crews that their target was Japan.

Doolittle's plan was to launch his sixteen B-25s when about 350 miles from Japan. This would give the pilots enough fuel to reach China after hitting their targets. Unfortunately, the task force was detected 650 miles from Japan, a fishing boat managing to send a signal before the cruiser *Nashville* blew it out of the water. As a result, V. Adm. William F. "Bull" Halsey Jr., the task-force commander, ordered the bombers launched immediately. The carrier turned into the wind, and Gay and his squadron mates watched as the B-25s lifted off the flight deck on their way to strike the Japanese homeland. After the last craft was airborne, the *Hornet* and its accompanying ships turned and proceeded southeast to Pearl Harbor (see map 4).[4]

After a short stay in Hawaii, the *Hornet* sailed on May 1 headed for the Coral Sea but arrived in the area just after the naval battle there had been fought. On May 26 the carrier returned to Hawaii. Meanwhile, US naval intelligence had indications of a major Japanese move eastward toward Midway Island. Japanese war planners, particularly Adm. Isoroku Yamamoto, chief of the Combined Fleet, viewed an attack on Midway as a means to achieve the dual goals of extending their defensive perimeter eastward and drawing the American carriers into a decisive naval battle. The threat to Midway, located 1,135 miles west of Hawaii, would compel the US Navy to come out and fight.[5]

Lt. George H. Gay Jr. in flight suit.
Official US Navy Photo

The massive Japanese task forces assigned to this ambitious operation, together totaling more than two hundred ships, departed home waters May 26–28. The Northern Area Task Force headed to the Aleutians to invade the islands of Kiska and Attu. The Midway Occupation Force was bound for Midway, with transport ships carrying 5,000 soldiers to invade the island. The Main Body and the 1st Carrier Striking Force, with four aircraft carriers, had the mission of destroying the American fleet if it came out to fight. A fourth fleet, the Advance Expeditionary Force, containing a light cruiser and sixteen submarines, was to establish submarine patrols between Hawaii and Midway prior to the attack. Japanese forces were under the overall command of Admiral Yamamoto aboard the huge battleship *Yamato*.[6]

The Americans countered first with Task Force 16, commanded by R. Adm. Raymond A. Spruance, which departed Pearl Harbor on May 28 with the aircraft carriers *Hornet* and *Enterprise*, six cruisers, and eleven destroyers. Two days later Task Force 17, commanded by R. Adm. Frank J. Fletcher, departed with the carrier *Yorktown*, two cruisers, and five destroyers. Fletcher, being the senior officer, was also in command of the combined US forces.[7]

At 3:30 a.m. on June 4, general quarters sounded on the *Hornet*. The crews of VT-8 gathered in the ready room, where all eyes were on the illuminated three-by-three-foot reflector screen above the teletype machine. Projected on the screen was the last message that had been received, stating that four seaplanes had made torpedo attacks on enemy ships southwest of Midway. When it became obvious that the squadron would not launch at dawn, everyone in the ready room relaxed and settled into the big leather desk chairs. Some tried to read with no success. At 8:00 a.m. many of the officers went to the wardroom for breakfast. Just as they broke from their meals, the clang of the ship's bell, the shrill of the boson's pipe, and a hollow voice over the squawk box told all that the time of action had come.

"General quarters!" "Flight quarters!"

"All pilots report to your ready rooms!"

The screen in the ready room read, "MIDWAY BEING ATTACKED BY JAPANESE AIRCRAFT!" The pilots quickly took down last-minute information and then raced to their aircraft. Gay wrapped up his last assignment. As the squadron's navigation officer, one of his duties was to make sure that every pilot had a mimeographed copy of the charts covering the expected area of operations.

The fighters were the first to launch, followed by the scouts, and then the dive bombers. VT-8 was the last squadron airborne and was flying without the fighter escort that Waldron had requested on several occasions. Under these conditions, the commander reasoned that their best chance was to fly just above the water so enemy fighters could not attack them from below.

VT-8 launched a little before 9:00 a.m. Only six of the squadron's planes were on the flight deck initially, the other nine waiting below. As soon as the elevators were cleared, these TBDs were brought up as well. Once all planes were airborne, the squadron assembled and began its flight into history.[8]

As VT-8 approached the enemy carriers, defending Zero fighters swarmed all around them. Waldron signaled the squadron to close up for mutual protection. He then broke radio silence and said: "We will go in. We won't turn back. Former strategy cannot be used. We will attack. Good luck." Soon the first Devastator went down and was followed by others. Machine-gun bullets hit Gay's aircraft several times; Japanese fighters were coming at the Americans from all directions. Waldron's plane was shot down very early in the action. Gay saw his squadron commander's TBD burst into flames; Waldron stood up to get out of the fire just as his plane hit the water, and he disappeared.

As Gay pressed in on his torpedo run, his rear gunner, Bob Huntington, suddenly exclaimed, "They got me." Gay looked back and saw him slumped down almost out of sight. "Can you move?" he asked. There was no reply and no movement. Being right on the water at full throttle, the Texan no longer had to fly straight and level to accommodate his gunner's return fire, so he started evasive maneuvers. He pulled up a few times to take some shots at Zeros as they would go by. Then something hit his left arm. He felt a lump there, and when he squeezed it, a bullet popped out.

The carrier that was Gay's target began to turn to starboard as he bore down on its forward port quarter. He aimed about one-quarter of the ships' length ahead of the bow and prepared to attack. Flight speed was supposed to be about eighty knots when launching the torpedo, so he had to slow down. Just as he reached for the throttle, he was hit in his left hand and so pulled the throttle back with his thumb, then punched the torpedo-release button. Nothing happened, so he reached across to pull the cable with his right hand. The cable release came out of the instrument panel, and he almost lost control of his plane. Gay was not sure if the torpedo was dropped, though it felt like it had. By this time he was about 850 yards from the enemy carrier; he slammed the throttle forward and flew over his target. Gay looked at the bridge and saw a Japanese officer with a pair of binoculars in one hand and a samurai sword in the other.

Flying as low as he could, he went between two carriers and out past a destroyer, all the time being fired upon by the ships he passed. Gay was then attacked again by the Zeros, and a 20-mm cannon slug hit his left pedal and blew it apart, knocking a hole in the firewall. This set the engine on fire, which burned his left leg through the hole. The control wire to the ailerons and rudder went out with the pedal's destruction, so the only control left to him was the elevators, which allowed him to pull the nose up. Gay was able to hold the nose up and slow down to almost a decent ditching speed as he descended. His right wing hit first, and the plane slammed into the water in a cartwheel fashion that banged the canopy shut. With the nose of the plane going under and water rising in the cockpit, Gay burst his way out to find Zeros diving and shooting at him. The pilot swam back to the sinking plane to recover Huntington, even though he was almost positive the gunner was dead. He got to the plane just as it was going down and was unable to retrieve his crewman. When Gay returned to the surface, the Zeros were still strafing. He jerked off his helmet and goggles to keep them from flashing in the sun, grabbed a cushion floating nearby, and put it over his head. He then noticed that the fighters had stopped strafing the area and saw that the Japanese ships were steaming right down on him.[9]

Torpedo Squadron 8's attack was followed by VT-6's fourteen torpedo bombers from the *Enterprise* and VT-3's twelve torpedo bombers from the *Yorktown*. Of the forty-one warplanes in these attacks, thirty-seven were shot down and four ditched because of damage or empty gas tanks. No damage was done to the Japanese fleet by the Devastators. Shortly afterward, though, the American dive bombers arrived and caught the enemy carriers with their flight decks full of recovered aircraft. Three carriers, *Akagi, Kaga,* and *Soryu,* were sunk by the dive bombers, which returned later and sank the fourth Japanese carrier, *Hiryu.*[10]

The enemy fleet steamed past Gay, and one cruiser nearly ran him down. Some of the sailors on it saw him and started pointing, but no effort was made to pick him up. Gay's cushion was about twenty inches long, a foot wide, and an inch thick. He bent it over his head in an inverted V, and when another enemy ship came past, he turned the flat part toward it. Several times while peeking past the edge, he saw enemy sailors looking in his direction with field glasses.

Gay later managed to recover his life raft, a big, four-man affair, but did not inflate it since it would give away his position. Instead, he rode it like an underwater horse to keep it out of sight. He did not inflate his life jacket either. When darkness fell, he inflated the raft and discovered that three of its four air compartments had leaks, but the one good compartment kept it afloat.

During the night he watched as enemy ships picked up survivors from the burning carriers. By the next morning the Japanese had departed the area, and the Texan was alone in the middle of the Pacific Ocean. At about 6:30 a.m. he heard the sound of an approaching aircraft that turned out to be a PBY Catalina seaplane. Gay was spotted, and the pilot rocked the PBY's wings to acknowledge the sighting. The seaplane then continued on in search of the enemy fleet.

At daylight he opened his survival kit, containing such items as a safety knife, a metal signaling mirror, patches for the raft, dye markers for turning the sea around him a fluorescent lemon, a survival book, a prayer book, a sea anchor, concentrated candy, and some K rations. Floating alone, he took time to repair the raft. Late that afternoon, after thirty hours in the water, he heard the sound of an aircraft approaching from the west—the same PBY that had spotted him that morning. The seaplane passed over his head and then began a turn back toward the raft into the wind. It touched down nearby and taxied slow enough to pick up Gay. The big bubble on the port side was open, and a sailor leaned out and yelled, "Seen any Jap planes lately?" Gay replied, "I haven't seen a thing since you came by this morning." "Good," he said. "Let's get the hell out of here!"[11]

The rescuers took him to Midway, where he received medical attention, and early the next morning, June 6, he was flown 1,100 miles to Pearl Harbor. Gay was placed in the hospital to treat burns, wounds, and dehydration. Shortly afterward, the young pilot was visited by the commander in chief of the Pacific Fleet, Admiral Nimitz, and a group of staff officers. Nimitz listened as Gay recounted his experiences during the battle. When the admiral asked if he had notified his parents that he was all right, Gay replied that he had not because he could not send messages from the war zone. Nimitz had him dictate a message to a staff officer, who then sent it on to the Texan's home. During his stay in Hawaii, Gay was awarded the Navy Cross.

He returned to the States on June 24 aboard the troop-carrying cruise ship *Lurline*. Given a thirty-day leave, the officer went home to Houston. One morning after being at home two weeks, his father came into his room with a newspaper whose headline read, "ENS. GAY SOLE SURVIVOR OF TORPEDO SQUADRON EIGHT AT MIDWAY." His father asked, "What's this all about?" Gay replied that it was a secret and he was not supposed to talk about it without permission from the navy.

He later told his mother about his experiences. She listened quietly and then said, "I knew it was bad, but I didn't know it was that bad." After his leave ended, Gay reported to his next duty station in San Diego, where he joined the just-activated Torpedo Squadron 11 (VT-11).

He found a room in the area where the squadron was eventually to be quartered. There was a desk, chair, telephone, and one sailor. He was a mechanic and said that he and another sailor were all the crew for the squadron so far. As the only officer, Gay found himself in charge. Shortly after arriving, he received a phone call from navy public-relations staff wanting to know if he could go to Los Angeles. Thus began a lifetime of appearances, bond tours, and speeches.

In Hollywood Gay did a series of interviews with *Life* magazine and was surprised when the story came out on August 31, 1942, his picture on the cover. Twentieth-Century Fox made an offer to make a movie about his exploits at Midway, but after several weeks of haggling, the deal fell through. During this time, though, he had the run of the studio and met many movie stars, including Tyrone Power and Ann Baxter.[12]

Gay shuttled between San Diego and Hollywood as the new squadron's crews were filled out. Five new TBF Avenger torpedo bombers arrived along with several enlisted men and one ensign. The Avenger was the navy's newest torpedo bomber, with greater speed, armament, and range than the old TBD-1 Devastator.

After the squadron was fully manned and additional aircraft arrived, a full training program commenced. Following completion of this, VT-11 was transferred to Hawaii for more training before traveling to the Fiji Islands aboard a jeep carrier. From the Fijis the squadron flew to Guadalcanal on Easter Sunday, 1943, and its new base at Henderson Field. The crews were soon flying combat missions.[13] (see map 10)

Guadalcanal had been invaded by US Marines on August 7, 1942, and by April 1943 the struggle for the island was over. Flying from Henderson Field, the torpedo bombers of VT-11 were out every night—skip bombing, mine laying, or attacking enemy airfields and installations. Every day there were air strikes conducted in the area north of Guadalcanal known as "The Slot." Gay, who by this time had been promoted to lieutenant (junior grade), was awarded an Air Medal for the period April 26–July 17. The recommendation for the decoration stated that he had completed twenty-one combat missions during that time.[14]

Suddenly and unexpectedly, VT-11 was told that it was relieved of all flying and would be going to Sydney, Australia, for some rest and relaxation. The squadron members were divided into three groups, with one group leaving each night aboard a DC-3. Gay was in the second contingent and was about to get aboard the transport when the group commander asked if he could take the lieutenant's place to attend to something in Sydney as soon as possible. Gay thus left on the third flight, learning upon his arrival in Sydney that the second plane had crashed and everyone aboard was lost. Since his name was still on the manifest, he initially was reported as killed in the accident.

While in Australia the men were surprised to receive orders transferring their squadron to the West Coast via Hawaii. From Pearl Harbor, they returned to the States aboard the *Lurline*, which by now was undergoing a valiant effort by its crew to convert the ship back to its usual configuration as a cruise ship. Arriving in San Francisco, the squadron members were quartered in the Francis Drake Hotel, where they would await individual orders for their next duty stations. Gay received orders to report to Jacksonville, Florida, to be an operational-training instructor, with a delay en route to go to Hollywood to sell the navy, the war, and war bonds. There he made speeches at war-bond rallies, lunches, and dinners along with radio shows and stage appearances.[15]

Because of official demands for his time to make personal appearances at various events, Gay was a month overdue in reporting to his unit in Jacksonville. His new commanding officer was not exactly overjoyed and took a dim view of his situation. Gay realized that he would have to stay on his toes. Not long after his arrival, his unit moved to Opa-locka for additional training. Gay's duty was as an instructor to teach brand-new ensigns all about torpedo planes and tactics. Despite his training responsibilities, he was continually sent on public tours. This led to ongoing clashes with his commander until that officer was reassigned and a new man arrived.

Now promoted to lieutenant, Gay was reassigned in April 1945 to Quonset Point Naval Air Station, Rhode Island, to form his own squadron and go to war for a third time. But as the pilots and planes began to arrive, there was still time for public-relations activity. The young officer was in New York about as often as he was at Quonset Point. After the fighting ended in Europe on May 7, 1945, Gay began to consider what he wanted to do after the war was over.

Gay with cadets during a 1942 visit to Texas A&M. *Courtesy Cushing Memorial Library and Archives, Texas A&M University*

During the Battle of Midway, Gay had been wounded but had never received the Purple Heart. On May 18 he wrote to Admiral Nimitz, who ordered an investigation to determine why he had not received the medal. In a letter to the lieutenant dated June 4, 1945, Nimitz stated that the oversight was probably due to the excitement after Midway, that a citation now had been signed, and the Purple Heart was being sent to Gay's commanding officer for presentation.

Even though he liked the navy, the Texan decided to look at opportunities in commercial aviation. By August 14, 1945, VJ Day, he had talked to representatives of some of the airline companies and had nearly decided which one he wanted to join. When a notice came out that holders of the Navy Cross could be discharged immediately, he took one of the squadron's aircraft and flew to Boston to be separated from the service. He was out of the navy before the end of the day.[16]

At the time of his discharge, Gay made what he later considered the biggest, most costly error of judgment that he ever made. Instead of joining an airline immediately, he took time off to unwind. Had he hired on first and then taken a leave of absence, he would have been about 250 numbers higher on the company's seniority list.

Once he did take a job with an airline, he began to feel secure enough to get serious about a girl he had met at his going-away party at Opalocka. Her name was Esther "Tess" Huffman Bevacqua, and they were married on May 14, 1946. Esther brought two children from a previous marriage into the union. Gay was now a pilot with Trans World Airlines and eventually became a captain, flying to locations around the world.

In 1975 Gay heard rumors a movie was being made about Midway. This was confirmed when he received a call from Booker McClay of Universal Studios, who had been looking for the veteran and had just gotten his number. McClay told him about the movie then in production and wanted Gay and his wife to come to California to watch the filming of the scene of his rescue after the battle, which was being shot at a naval station south of Los Angeles. Another spectator who had been at Midway, Capt. Joseph Rochefort, USN (Ret.), was there too. Rochefort had been the intelligence officer who broke the Japanese code and enabled US naval forces to ambush the Japanese fleet. The actor who played the captain in the movie, Hal Holbrook, was also there. Others on the scene were Henry Fonda, Robert Wagner, Eddie Albert, and Charlton Heston.

The technical advisor on the film asked Gay if flyers would have been wearing big kapok life jackets like the ones the actors had on. The veteran replied: "Definitely not. Those are strictly for ships. Aircraft crews use only the flat, inflatable types." The director blew his top, and everything came to a halt while the prop men obtained suitable life jackets. After the scene was filmed, Gay realized that it had been thirty-three years to the day that he had been plucked from the Pacific.

When *Midway* was released in 1976, he and Tess joined the promotional tour in the Dallas–Fort Worth area and went on to Houston, Miami, Atlanta, Philadelphia, Boston, and Detroit. In Washington they joined Fonda, Heston, and others. The couple went on to spend five days in New York, three in Chicago, and a week in Hollywood before the opening.[17]

During his thirty-year career as a pilot with Trans World Airlines, Gay continued to make public appearances at conventions, universities, civic organizations, corporate groups, and other organizations. During this time he lived in Naples, Florida, but later moved to Marietta, Georgia.

Lt. George H. Gay's military decorations include the Navy Cross, Air Medal, and Purple Heart.

Gay died of a heart attack in Marietta on October 21, 1994. Prior to his death, he had requested that his cremated ashes be flown to the spot in the Central Pacific where Commander Waldron and the rest of his squadron mates had gone down while attacking the Japanese fleet. There his ashes were scattered in the wind, and George H. Gay Jr., Class of 1940, rejoined his comrades of Torpedo Squadron 8.[18]

★ 9 ★

Danger 79er

JAMES FRANCIS HOLLINGSWORTH

CLASS OF 1940

James Francis Hollingsworth was born on his family's farm seven miles northwest of the small town of Sanger, Texas, on March 24, 1918, the first son of James Newton Hollingsworth and Mamie Ella Hollingsworth. Sanger is twenty-five miles north of Denton and was founded in 1886 as a stop on the Santa Fe Railroad. The company named the town in honor of one of its customers, the Sanger family, who owned stores in Dallas and Waco. It became a trade center for that part of Denton County and boasted a flourmill and cotton gin. The main agricultural products of the surrounding area were wheat, oats, maize, and cotton as well as cattle and other livestock.

Hollingsworth attended the Union Hill School, which consisted of three teachers and three rooms, through the ninth grade. From an early age he was assigned chores around the farm. At ten years old he was given responsibility for twenty-five to thirty fieldworkers during the harvest. Hollingsworth entered tenth grade at Sanger High School, seven miles from his home, which he walked or rode on horseback each day. Joining the Future Farmers of America (FFA) chapter, he served as chapter secretary his first year and later served as vice president and president. He also was involved in many FFA projects and won several awards. High school sports were also important to him, and he lettered in football, basketball, and track.

After graduating from Sanger High School in 1935, Hollingsworth enrolled at North Texas Agricultural College (NTAC), now the University of Texas at Arlington. At that time NTAC was part of the Texas A&M System. With the help of his high school superintendent, he secured a job in the college dairy to help pay expenses. Since he had done well in high school chemistry, Hollingsworth became the laboratory technician at the dairy. He had to be up at 4:00 a.m. to start sampling the milk that came from local dairies so the farmer could see his bacterial count and fat content on the spot. Following a day of classes, he returned to the dairy to work until about 8:30 p.m. After a year at NTAC, he applied for admission to Texas A&M and was accepted to study dairy husbandry and vocational agriculture.[1]

Based on his experience at the NTAC dairy, Hollingsworth was offered a job in the A&M dairy, where he worked long hours to help pay his expenses. Hollingsworth selected infantry for his required military-science course and was assigned to Headquarters Company, 1st Infantry Battalion, in the Corps of Cadets. He was a corporal his sophomore year and a sergeant his junior year. During his senior year, Hollingsworth served as a cadet captain on the 2nd Infantry Battalion's staff. In addition to his job at the dairy, he found time to participate in corps and college activities.[2]

Following graduation in May 1940, he worked for Hughes Tool Company in Houston until called to active duty in July as a second lieutenant. Assigned to the 2nd Armored Division at Fort Benning, Georgia, Hollingsworth reported to the 3rd Battalion, 68th Armored Regiment. There were four other officers in his unit, a major commanding and three first lieutenants, who were company commanders. Hollingsworth was initially given the duties of battalion executive officer, personnel officer, supply officer, and operations officer. The deputy division commander was Col. George S. Patton Jr., who became division commander following his promotion to brigadier general. Hollingsworth was eventually given command of Company I,

2nd Armored Division tanks at Fort Benning, Georgia, in 1940. *Public domain*

in which he served until sent to an automotive course at Fort Knox, Kentucky. Returning to Fort Benning, the lieutenant was temporarily assigned to the 5th Armored Division for six months to conduct tests in the desert to determine whether tanks should use gasoline or diesel engines. From there he was sent on a classified mission to Belem, Brazil, to investigate reports of German submarines putting agents ashore in that country. In his oral history Hollingsworth implies that he was working with the FBI. This assignment lasted until December 1942, when he rejoined the 2nd Armored Division in North Africa shortly after its landing in Morocco.

Taking command of a tank company (three platoons of five tanks each plus two tanks assigned to company headquarters), Hollingsworth saw his first combat near Kasserine Pass, where the German Afrika Korps had previously defeated the Americans. An enemy force of ten tanks was heading for his battalion's position, with four of the German tanks towing 88-mm antitank guns. Nearing the Americans, the antitank guns were dropped off and set up in concealed positions. Hollingsworth suspected such a ruse, which had been used against British forces during the desert campaigns. The Germans pressed forward, and the lieutenant's tanks took them under fire. When the enemy started to withdraw, Hollingsworth ordered his tanks forward but placed some of them in a position to cover them. When the anti-tank guns opened up, these tanks returned fire and destroyed all four enemy guns.

Company I was in combat almost every day until the campaign in North Africa was over. Its next operation was the invasion of Sicily on July 10, 1943. Prior to the campaign, Hollingsworth was given command of the regimental maintenance company. After twelve days of combat in Sicily, the division entered a period of duty as occupation forces. The tankers played an active part in the installation of a military government on the island. This was a testing ground for the governing of formerly hostile territories, with procedures worked out that were later employed in Germany.

In October 1943 US armored divisions were reorganized according to the latest table of organization and equipment, becoming "light" divisions. For some unknown reason, perhaps because of influential armor leaders such as Patton and others who were in England, Eisenhower amended the order to permit the 2nd and 3rd Armored Divisions to retain their regimental structures. So while the division did undergo some reorganization, it was internal. The 2nd Armored disbanded the 68th Armored Regiment and sent a company of light tanks from the 68th to each battalion in the 66th and 67th Regiments. These battalions now consisted of two medium-tank companies and one light-tank company. The 41st Armored Infantry Regiment was not affected. Tactical headquarters were Combat Command A and Combat Command B, which had tank and infantry units attached according to the tactical situation.

In November 1943 the 2nd Armored Division left most of their vehicles in Sicily and boarded transport ships for the voyage to England; the ships docked at Liverpool on Thanksgiving Day. Tidsworth Barracks, the division's new home, was a former British cavalry post located on the Salisbury Plain. It was a huge military reservation, with permanent barracks made of red brick and stone. Once quartered, the division was issued new equipment.

Training began in earnest, starting with individual and crew drills and continuing on to driver instruction. After crew and squad training, the units progressed to platoon and company exercises. The next phase involved weapons firing and tactical training. The tanks and

M-4 medium tank lands on Normandy beach. *Official US Army Photo*

---

artillery were sent to firing ranges for additional practice and instruction. Lessons learned from North Africa and Sicily were integrated into all training.

The 2nd Armored moved from Tidsworth Barracks on June 6–7, 1944, to the marshaling areas of Portsmouth and Southampton. The major part of the division loaded aboard ships and started for France that night. The first elements landed on Normandy Beach on the ninth, and by July 2 all divisional units were in France. Once ashore, the initial units were heavily bombed by the Luftwaffe and bombarded by enemy artillery (see map 7).[3]

With the landing of the 2nd Armored Division, the first phase of the invasion was completed. The division's tank, infantry, and reconnaissance units sent out patrols to make contact with the enemy. While in the reserve role, the division had the tactical mission to repulse any counterattacks. On several occasions the 2nd Armored sent units to support the 29th Infantry and the 101st Airborne Divisions.

Moving out from the beaches, advancing tanks struggled with the hedgerows in Normandy until Sgt. Curtis G. Culin of the 102nd Reconnaissance Squadron designed and tested a hedgerow cutter. The device consisted of heavy steel prongs, salvaged from dismantled German beach obstacles, welded to the front of the tanks. The cutter allowed the vehicles to force their way through the numerous hedgerows.

On July 26, after fighting through the hedgerows and hitting the open country, the 2nd Armored attacked as part of Operation COBRA, the plan to break out of the beachhead. The 2nd and 3rd Armored Divisions opened a gap in the German lines that allowed General Patton's Third Army to pour through in pursuit of the retreating enemy. Following the passage of the Third Army, the 2nd Armored swung east and engaged scattered enemy forces. It often bypassed German strongpoints, leaving them to be reduced by the following infantry divisions.[4]

On July 29 Hollingsworth was in command of the service trains of Combat Command B, approximately forty vehicles loaded with gasoline and oil, which were dispersed in the woods near Notre Dame-de-Centilly. The site was attacked by German bombers, and one of the gasoline trucks was set afire. The vehicle ultimately exploded, spraying fuel all around it. Hollingsworth got in a nearby truck and drove it to a safer location, returning twice to remove other endangered trucks while the enemy continued to bomb the area.

During the advance through France, Hollingsworth repeatedly directed the removal of wrecked vehicles from the front of advancing columns while subjected to enemy small-arms and artillery fire. The 2nd Armored Division fought its way east, passing north of Paris; crossing the Seine, Somme, and Meuse Rivers; and pushing its way across Belgium to the Siegfried Line in Germany.[5]

On October 1, 1944, Hollingsworth took command of the 2nd Tank Battalion, 67th Regiment, which was then at the Wurm River in Germany. The fighting to penetrate the Siegfried Line was ferocious, with a murderous crossfire from dug-in machine guns, antitank guns, and artillery. Once through these defenses, the 2nd Armored Division continued its attack north of Aachen toward the Rhine River. The drive ended in December 1944 when the Germans launched their massive counteroffensive against the Allies through the Ardennes Forest in Belgium and northern Luxembourg. The attack was designed to split the Allied forces and capture the vital supply port of Antwerp. Caught off guard in this lightly defended area, the Allies fell back while sustaining heavy losses.[6]

The 2nd Armored was on the north flank of what became known as the Battle of the Bulge as part of the US Ninth Army. On December 21 the division was ordered to move seventy miles to the west to an assembly area. Its three thousand vehicles stretched one hundred miles and moved under blackout restrictions over narrow, icy roads. The movement began at 11:30 p.m. and by midnight the next day had arrived at the assigned assembly area west of Huy, Belgium.[7]

The division was transferred to the First Army and joined VII Corps under Maj. Gen. J. Lawton "Lighting Joe" Collins. It was held in reserve awaiting the opportunity to strike the advancing enemy force in the flank. The division attacked on January 3, 1945, with five task forces, one of which was led by Major Hollingsworth. On January 9 his task force was held up by stiff resistance and was ordered to reassemble about halfway to its objective. The assault-company commander also was having radio and engine trouble with his vehicle. Hollingsworth sent his own command tank to assist this captain and mounted another tank to direct his force.

The major acted as ammunition loader on this tank because the crew was one man short. "After two attacks had failed, the enemy launched another counterattack. During the process of beating off this attack, the 75-mm gun recoiled against Hollingsworth's arm. In extreme pain from a possibly fractured arm and the loss of his thumb and forefinger, he continued to load the gun and would not let himself be evacuated after being ordered by the combat commander." After the battle Hollingsworth was evacuated to Paris and then to England, where he spent about three weeks in the hospital. Anxious to get back to his unit, he went AWOL from the hospital and hitchhiked to Paris, where he requested transportation back to the front. He rode to Liege, Belgium, with a truck company and then called division headquarters for transportation. His battalion sent a jeep, and the Texan was soon back in the fight.

The 2nd Armored's attack blunted the spearhead of the German offensive and prevented the enemy from reaching the Meuse River in Belgium. In the fighting the division's tanks destroyed the 2nd Panzer Division. On January 16 in a field just west of Houffalize, Belgium, the division's reconnaissance battalion met up with the advance forces of Patton's Third Army, attacking from the south. The Allied pincers had closed, and the Battle of the Bulge was over.[8]

Afterward, the division continued its drive toward the Rhine. The town of Krefeld was captured, and Major Hollingsworth's battalion soon after crossed the Rhine on March 24, using a bridge built by the division's 17th Engineer Battalion. His unit was the lead element and advance guard for the division. They stumbled into a German tank-training camp and found themselves surrounded by hostile tanks. While these were relics with the engines removed, their guns remained in place for use by recruits. As Hollingsworth later described it, "All hell broke loose as everyone opened up." The Germans immediately opened fire and his tank quickly replied, knocking out one tank at 1,500 yards and another only 75 yards away. Minutes after the battle ended, a truck loaded with German soldiers came down the road toward the Americans. Hollingsworth ordered his troops to hold their fire. When the truck was about 75 yards away he gave the order to fire, and the tanks opened fire. The truck was riddled with machine gun bullets and turned over. Many of the occupants were dead when they hit the ground, but a few were still alive and were screaming. When Hollingsworth went forward to examine the scene, he found that the truck was loaded with German female soldiers.[9]

After crossing the Rhine River and surrounding the Ruhr industrial area, Allied forces began the race to the Elbe River—and beyond that, Berlin. Capturing small cities, some of which surrendered without a fight, while others offered resistance, often by old men and young boys, the attack continued. On one occasion where the enemy occupied prepared positions, "Hollingsworth lined up thirty-four tanks and gave a command rarely heard in modern warfare: "Charge!" Guns roaring, the American tanks raced toward the enemy position, and the Germans broke and ran."

On April 8, after reaching their first-phase objective line, the division paused to perform much-needed maintenance and resupply. The crews hoped for at least forty-eight hours before continuing the attack, but they were ordered to push on the next day.

Hollingsworth's battalion met no resistance as they moved rapidly through undefended towns until they came to Osterwieck, where a Home Guard regiment stopped them. The Home Guard was composed of elderly Germans and young boys. Many of the Germans seemed ready to surrender but, according to a prisoner, a group of SS soldiers were forcing them to fight. When Hollingsworth heard this he called for his jeep and, taking a sergeant and two other enlisted men with him, went looking for what were believed to be eleven SS soldiers.

He circled the town before entering along a cow path. Hollingsworth, wearing two Colt automatics "strapped low on his hips, Western style" and carrying a Thompson submachine gun, grabbed a passing civilian and demanded to know the location of the SS soldiers. The German was terrified and quickly disclosed the location. They were in a nearby large house with a barn. The house and barn were surrounded by a high fence. Approaching the house, they spotted a doorway in the fence. They leaped out of the jeep and raced to the door, which they smashed in with their shoulders. As they entered the yard an SS soldier rushed toward them with a raised submachine gun. Hollingsworth cut him down with his Thompson. The three other men raced to the house and threw several hand grenades through the windows. About this time, Hollingsworth saw another SS man in the open hayloft door and shot him with his .45 automatic. Upon entering the house they found six dead SS soldiers, killed by the grenades, and three other SS soldiers who quickly surrendered. Their work done, they rushed back to the column. [10]

Three hours later his battalion reached the high ground overlooking Schoenebeck and Bad Salzelmen. Beyond these towns, in the early evening light, Hollingsworth could see the Elbe. Through his binoculars he could see that the highway bridge over the river was intact. The road from the south contained a column of German tanks, horse-drawn artillery, headquarters vehicles, and personnel carriers filled with troops headed to the bridge to escape east. The major's plan to capture the bridge was to have a tank company move to the south to block the road, then have another company join the tail of the German column crossing the river. If this deception worked, they could seize the bridge once across.

The Americans trying to follow the Germans were soon spotted and taken under fire. Moving into Schoenebeck, Hollingsworth's tanks fired into the rear of the retreating German tanks in turn. Squeezing by the burning vehicles, the American tanks charged through the town. Reaching the town center, they encountered enemy fire coming from all directions. Many of the buildings were on fire, brightly illuminating the area even though it was 11:00 p.m. Reaching the approach to the bridge, the major found the way blocked by irregularly placed stone walls. Hollingsworth was on foot guiding his lead vehicle when an antitank shell exploded fifteen yards ahead. Cobblestone fragments flew through the air, some hitting him in the face and cutting his lip and forehead. Working his way through the stone walls, Hollingsworth was shot in the knee. When Hollingsworth's commander arrived on the scene, he found the major "unable to walk and bleeding all over the place." Hollingsworth was evacuated to the 4th Station Hospital, but after a short time he managed to talk his way out of there and returned to his battalion. Before the Americans could reach the bridge, the Germans destroyed it. Hollingsworth believed that if he could have crossed the Elbe that night, he could have been in Berlin in only eleven hours.

Earlier, though, Eisenhower had declared that the Elbe River would be the dividing line between the Allies and the Russians, information that had not yet reached his forward units. Some elements of the 2nd Armored crossed the Elbe but were ordered back to the west bank to comply with the general's decision. Soon after, the division was withdrawn from the Elbe line and assigned to conduct mopping-up operations in the rear areas. With the end of the war, the 2nd Division's primary duty as an occupying force was security in its area of responsibility. Its units assumed their roles in a military government with few rules, but their experience as an occupying force in Sicily provided some guidance. On May 12 the division was relieved of its occupation duties and moved to a staging area for troops destined for Berlin.

On July 1 the advance party departed for Berlin, with the main body following two days later. The division had the honor of being the first combat unit to enter the German capital.[11]

In September 1945 the division commander was assigned to Fort Riley, Kansas, as the commandant of the Cavalry School. He selected Hollingsworth to command the School Troops Regiment, later becoming chief of combined-arms tactics.

Leaving Fort Riley after four years, he returned to Germany as commanding officer, Special Troops, US Constabulary. The constabulary was an elite force of about 35,000 men organized into twenty-seven squadrons designed to exercise broad police powers over civilians and US military personnel in the American Zone of Occupation. It also operated 126 posts for border protection, especially on the Soviet Zone boundary and the Czechoslovakian border.[12]

Hollingsworth was transferred in May 1950 to Seventh Army Headquarters in Heidelberg, where he served as chief of the operations branch. After the start of the Korean War the following month, a decision was made in Washington to build up the American commitment to NATO. US forces in Europe thus were increased from 55,000 to 225,000 men, and Hollingsworth's role was to house those forces in West Germany as cheaply as possible by using old Wehrmacht facilities. He left Europe in August 1951 to attend the Command and Staff College at Fort Leavenworth, Kansas.[13]

Completing the nine-month course and graduating in the top 10 percent, his next assignment was at the US Military Academy at West Point, New York, where he served as a combined-arms instructor. Norman Schwarzkopf, then a plebe at West Point and later a four-star general and leader of Coalition forces during the Gulf War, was impressed with Hollingsworth. He remembers the Texan as a colorful and profane character, who in the classroom would "digress from the lesson plan and . . . be off in North Africa or charging across Europe in a tank column." The cadets thoroughly enjoyed such occasions as Hollingsworth "described glorious scenes of victory." Once on the firing range, Schwarzkopf was training with a 3.5-inch rocket launcher, shooting at tank-silhouette targets, when his dummy round scored a hit. Hollingsworth, walking up and down behind the firing line, patted him on the back and said: "That's great, Mister! You're just the kind of killer we want to have in our Army!"[14]

In December 1953 Hollingsworth received a call from the Department of the Army ordering him to report to Gen. Matthew B. Ridgeway, who had been appointed chief of staff. But Hollingsworth did not want to leave West Point because he loved working with the cadets. He instructed tactics and leadership, taught handball, and was responsible for hunting and fishing on the academy's reservation.[15]

Reporting to the Pentagon, he was assigned as executive officer in the Office of Legislative Liaison for the secretary of the army. At that time the army was in a struggle with the Eisenhower administration over proposals to greatly increase US reliance on strategic air power at the expense of army force structure and modernization. The military budget proposed cuts that would result in a drastic reduction in troop strength and cut the army from twenty divisions to fourteen. Known as the "New Look," this policy "relied on strategic nuclear weapons, improved local defense capabilities of allies, and the belief that no future war would be fought solely with conventional forces."

During this period, members of the army staff were debating a response to the New Look in their Pentagon offices and afterhours in private homes and government quarters around Washington. Hollingsworth joined them and was responsible for contacts with members of Congress. The officers leaked position papers and other documents to congressmen and friendly journalists to gain support for the army position. In January 1956 this informal collection of officers became known as the Coordination Group. During the interservice squabbles, the national press became aware of the group and dubbed their actions as the "Colonels' Revolt." Once exposed, the staff officers were threatened with courts-martial, with Hollingsworth accused of passing classified documents to Congress, specifically to members of the House Armed Services Committee, House Appropriations Committee, Senate Foreign Relations Committee, and the House Foreign Affairs Committee. But since all members had high-security clearances, the investigation was terminated and no charges were filed.

On May 21 at a Pentagon press conference, an agitated Secretary of Defense Charles Wilson, joined by his uncomfortable military chiefs, assured reporters that accounts of interservice rivalry and dissent due to White House defense policies were all grossly exaggerated. The press noted that a series of leaks came from colonels on the army staff attacking other services, criticizing President Eisenhower's defense strategies, and advancing budget proposals at odds with the priorities of the nation's civilian leadership. Army chief of staff Maxwell D. Taylor replied that he did not know who "these colonels" were, even though the revolt had been reported in front-page newspaper articles all week. Meanwhile, the secretary of the General Staff, Brig. Gen. William C. Westmoreland, was busy preparing reassignment orders for the members of the Coordination Group. These sent the affected officers to career-enhancing positions such as unit command or senior service schools, and within days they were gone. Hollingsworth received orders to report to the Army War College at Carlisle Barracks, Pennsylvania.

In the end the Colonels' Revolt did make a difference in the military. The resulting debate reversed the trend toward the diminution of the army and tactical air force and turned the services from dependence on strategic nuclear weapons to a sense of balance between nuclear and conventional to defend the country and its interests. The army also began receiving the helicopters needed for modern troop mobility.[16]

Hollingsworth was promoted to colonel in July 1956 and reported to the Army War College in August. During his studies there, he chaired several committees, one of which was of particular interest—to study the Iran–Pakistan–Black Sea region. Hollingsworth believed that this led to his next assignment as chief, US Army Element, Military Assistance Advisory Group (Pakistan), where he served from August 1957 to June 1959.

During this tour of duty, the colonel gained the confidence of Pakistani general Ayab Khan. Hollingsworth's mission was to train five or six divisions of the Pakistan Army and equip them with American equipment. One afternoon Khan's aide called and said the general wanted to meet with Hollingsworth at his quarters. During the meeting, Khan asked if the American colonel had ever thought about taking over a country. Hollingsworth replied that he had studied all of the principles involved and what must be done. After hearing a detailed description of the actions needed, Khan said that he was going to take over Pakistan following such principles. Hollingsworth quickly informed the Central Intelligence Agency, Military Assistance Advisory Group chief, and US ambassador of the pending coup, but apparently no one believed it would happen. Yet on October 6, 1958, the Pakistani army led by General Khan seized control of the government, following to the letter the plan Hollingsworth had laid out. It was almost a bloodless coup, with only one person killed and the prime minister and his family exiled to England.[17]

When his Pakistani tour ended in the summer of 1959, Hollingsworth moved to Fort Hood, Texas, where he became deputy commander of Combat Command A, a part of the 1st Armored Division. From July 1960 to July 1961, he served as chief of staff, 2nd Armored Division, also at Fort Hood. The division was engaged in training in preparation for deployment to Europe in case of an emergency.[18]

Leaving Fort Hood in July 1961, the colonel reported for duty in the Pentagon as deputy director (later director) of the Reserve Affairs Division, Office of the Assistant Secretary of Defense (Manpower). After a year on the job, he was given a political appointment as deputy assistant secretary of defense (reserve affairs). The most significant event during this period was the Cuban Missile Crisis. Hollingsworth was responsible for the call up of Reserve and National Guard units to support a possible invasion of Cuba. He opposed the mobilization of reserve forces since he believed they were not ready, but he was overruled. Fortunately, the crisis ended before any ground forces were committed. His last year in the Pentagon was spent in the Office of the Chief of Staff of the Army. Hollingsworth was promoted to brigadier general on December 1, 1965. Volunteering for a combat assignment, he left Washington in February 1966 and reported for duty with the 1st Infantry Division in Vietnam (see map 11). The division, known as the "Big Red One," was one of the most famous units in the US Army. At the time, it was heavily engaged with Vietcong and North Vietnamese Army (NVA) forces in the area between Saigon and the Cambodian border.[19]

Arriving in Indochina, Hollingsworth was assigned as the deputy division commander for maneuver under Maj. Gen. William E. Depuy. As such he was responsible for all military action and maneuver of the 1st Division, a job that kept him in the field most of the time and in the middle of the fighting. His radio call sign was "Danger 79er," which he would use throughout the rest of his military career.

His second Distinguished Service Cross was awarded for actions during the period November 5–8, 1966. On November 5 "three Special Forces units were attacked by a numerically superior Vietcong force. To gain an accurate knowledge of the fluid ground situation, he had his pilot fly repeated low level passes over the insurgent positions while receiving intense hostile fire. He ordered air strikes and artillery barrages on the Vietcong emplacements and enabled the friendly units to repel the large enemy force. On November 8 one of his battalions engaged several Vietcong units. Immediately upon arriving at the scene, Hollingsworth moved about the area issuing orders, maintaining fire discipline, and encouraging the men to fight with renewed efforts. He continuously exposed himself to the concentrated Vietcong fire to coordinate all facets of the battle. Faced with overwhelming firepower, the enemy withdrew."[20]

Hollingsworth had the wide respect of the enlisted men who served with him. He often flew into the thick of battle to rescue wounded soldiers who could not be evacuated immediately by the "dust-off" helicopters. The general was often seen in the chow line with the troops, tasting the food to see if it was fit for his men.

On March 20, 1967, "while serving as acting division commander, an artillery support base came under intense enemy mortar attack.

Hollingsworth flew to the besieged unit and, despite devastating ground fire directed at his aircraft, he ordered the pilot to make repeated low level passes over the area while he reconnoitered" the enemy positions. He ordered air strikes and "guided the aircraft in their bombing and strafing runs." At 5:00 a.m., when the enemy began a massive ground attack, he "flew directly over the assaulting force and adjusted artillery fire on the charging Vietcong. The aggressive defense repulsed the fanatical enemy."[21]

An example of Hollingsworth aggressiveness occurred when he was standing by a battalion commander on the Cambodian border. After the infantry officer's radioman was killed by fire from across the border, the general told him to call in artillery against the enemy. When the officer said he could not fire into Cambodia because it was against policy, Hollingsworth grabbed a radio and ordered the artillery barrage himself. Prince Sihanouk, the leader of Cambodia, later reported to the US Department of State that American forces had fired artillery into his country. The president asked for a report on the incident. When questioned, Hollingsworth said he ordered the artillery barrage and would not stand by and let the enemy kill his men without firing back. US policy was changed the next day to allow units to return fire when fired upon even if the enemy was in a sanctuary area.[22]

The general's tour of duty in Vietnam was not without controversy. He was the subject of a *London Sunday Times* article titled "The General goes Zapping Charlie Cong," which portrayed him as a Texas redneck who took pleasure in shooting Vietcong from his helicopter. Many people turned against him after the piece was published, and some government officials in Washington referred to him as an "unguided missile" or a "hip shooter." Hollingsworth thought he was portrayed unfairly and insisted that he was only doing "what I have done throughout my military career—saving as many lives as possible while destroying the enemy."[23]

After fifteen months in Vietnam, he returned to the States to serve as deputy commanding general, US Army Test and Evaluation Command, at Aberdeen Proving Ground, Maryland. In May 1968 he was reassigned to Fort Jackson, South Carolina, where he served as deputy commanding general until December 1968, when he became the commanding general. When five dissident soldiers tried to start an antiwar riot, Hollingsworth ordered military police to arrest them and place them in the stockade. When the men were scheduled to be tried in a closed military court, the American Civil Liberties Union and several leftist organizations protested. The secretary of defense sent an officer to Fort Jackson to tell Hollingsworth that the trial should be held in open court. The general told him that the court would be closed and if the authorities in Washington did not like it, he should be relieved. The trial was conducted in a closed court and the five soldiers, known in the press as the "Fort Jackson Five," were convicted. Hollingsworth and the secretary of the army were later sued in federal court for denying the men their First Amendment rights. The court in its ruling in favor of the defendants stated that a military force could not operate as a common ordinary civilian organization.[24]

Hollingsworth's next assignment was as commanding general, US Army Alaska, with headquarters at Fort Richardson. One of his first challenges was to clean out a civilian mafia that had penetrated the aviation supply company at Fairbanks and was stealing, with the assistance of some military personnel, thousands of dollars' worth of supplies. With help from Washington, he assembled fifteen special army auditors and about the same number of trained investigative agents. The Criminal Investigation Division men, assisted by the FBI, penetrated the business. This broke up the criminal organization and led to federal charges against the perpetrators.[25]

Experimenting with new equipment and developing techniques and tactics for operating in the extreme cold of the Arctic required much of the general's attention. He personally designed his own uniform using waterproof and windproof material that weighed only four pounds. In contrast, the clothing then typically issued to a soldier for survival at temperatures of minus-75 degrees weighed ninety-six pounds. The material worn by Hollingsworth is today known as Gore-Tex.[26]

After a series of military disasters in Vietnam as US forces were in the process of withdrawing from the country during 1971, Hollingsworth was called by the chief of staff of the army and told he had seven days to get to Indochina because Gen. Creighton Abrams needed him. This was soon followed by a call from Abrams himself, who said that he needed the "meanest man in the world" to sort things out for him in Vietnam. As an example, he noted that an artillery unit had a large number of soldiers killed by an enemy rocket while the troops were gathered in the unit mess hall. In another incident Fire Base Mary

Ann was overrun and suffered high casualties. Hollingsworth quickly wrapped up his activities in Alaska, sent his wife back to the States, and departed for Vietnam. Abrams assigned him as deputy commander of the XXIV Corps in the northern part of South Vietnam.

Hollingsworth was given a free hand by the corps commander and proceeded to inspect the units in the area. He found the men of one artillery battery so hopped up on drugs that rather than try to retrain the unit, he deactivated it. On another occasion, while inspecting a fire base, he discovered rusty weapons. This was an embarrassment to all of the division, brigade, and battalion commanders present. After tearing through the corps units, he was once again called by Abrams and told that a Vietnamese corps commander just outside Saigon had been relieved. The general wanted Hollingsworth to come to Saigon to serve as the commander of the Third Regional Assistance Command. He needed the "meanest man in the world" to help resolve another crisis.[27]

The Third Military Region comprised the eleven provinces surrounding Saigon between the Central Highlands and the Mekong Delta. On the morning of April 2, 1972, two NVA regiments using captured M-41 tanks attacked elements of the 25th Army of Vietnam (ARVN) Division in several firebases near the Cambodian border in northern Tay Ninh Province. Three days later three NVA divisions moved into Binh Long Province toward the capital, An Loc, which was only sixty-five miles north of Saigon. This was part of the North Vietnamese spring campaign, better known as the Easter Offensive, a coordinated three-prong attack designed to strike a knockout blow against the South Vietnamese government and military. The main attack came on March 30 when three NVA divisions struck across the Demilitarized Zone toward Quang Tri and Hue. The second prong was when NVA forces crossed from Cambodia into the Central Highlands, attacking toward Kontum. The third prong was the thrust in Binh Long Province.[28]

Instead of being the senior advisor to the South Vietnamese corps, Hollingsworth, in effect, became the corps commander once combat began. The Vietnamese general in command had been fighting the war for twenty years and had been wounded seven or eight times, but now was so sick and frightened that he could not eat or sleep. The Texan knew that he was not prepared to handle a major battle.[29]

Loc Ninh in Binh Long Province was attacked the morning of April 5 by the 5th Viet Cong Division. Loc Ninh was defended by approxi-

Hollingsworth with military advisors at An Loc. *Courtesy Frank Muller*

mately one thousand South Vietnam troops and their American advisers. The NVA violent attack was supported by artillery, mortars, and rockets. At least one tank also supported the attack. American advisers directed tactical air strikes that prevented the town from being overrun.

The intensity of the attack convinced Hollingsworth that this was the launch of a major offensive to capture An Loc and open the road to Saigon. He directed all available air support to assist the forces defending Loc Ninh. ARVN units and their American advisors fought desperately, but on April 7 were overrun and Loc Ninh captured. Fewer than one hundred defenders escaped to An Loc, the rest, ARVN and US advisors alike, either killed or captured.[30]

South Vietnamese president Nguyen Van Thieu made the decision to hold An Loc at all costs. He "radioed the senior ARVN officers in An Loc that the city would be defended to the death." Civilian and military officials all realized that if An Loc fell to the enemy, there would be little to stop the North Vietnamese from reaching Saigon. Hollingsworth was aware that when the enemy offensive started in Quang Tri, some American advisors had been pulled out. This had a disastrous effect on the morale of the South Vietnamese forces in the region. He was determined that this would not happen in his area and notified the advisers in Loc Ninh that they would not be evacuated and that they were there for the duration of the battle.[31]

Hollingsworth was in the air daily over the battlefield, often directing air strikes. He made it a point to speak by radio to the American advisors every day as well to get a sense of the situation on the ground and to offer encouragement. The general arranged for use of B-52 bombers in a tactical role by hitting targets in close support of the defenders. When it looked like the city would be overrun, he went to see Abrams to request that the air groups of two aircraft carriers offshore be dedicated to the fight for An Loc. Hollingsworth warned that unless he could get the additional air support, the NVA would be in Saigon in a few days. Abrams granted this request, and An Loc's defenders thereafter enjoyed constant close air support.[32]

Always a colorful figure, Hollingsworth vowed to his fellow advisers at An Loc: "Hold them and I'll kill them with airpower; give me something to bomb and I'll win." When the remarks became public, General Abrams chastised the Texan for the statement, concerned that the remarks suggested that he was taking over what should be a South Vietnamese show.

By the end of May, there was a lull in the fighting. The around-the-clock air strikes had devastated the attackers. As supplies and reinforcement began to arrive, ARVN troops began to expand the perimeter. On June 18 the siege of An Loc was declared over. ARVN forces and their American advisers, with the help of massive air support, had won a decisive victory over three enemy divisions in a desperate contest.[33]

At An Loc on April 6, Hollingsworth suffered an eye wound from rocket fire. There was no ophthalmologist available, so the eye went untreated until August 31. After an examination, a recently arrived

Lt. Gen. James F. Hollingsworth. *Official US Army Photo*

ophthalmologist had the general medically evacuated to Walter Reed Hospital in Washington, DC, where he stayed until December 22. He eventually regained use of the eye.

While in Walter Reed, Hollingsworth was visited by General Abrams, now the army chief of staff. Lying in bed with his injured eye covered with a black patch, he mentioned that he was thinking about retiring since he had only one eye. Abrams replied that he would rather have Hollingsworth with one eye than most anyone with three. He then said that he was sending the Texan to take over I Corps Group in Korea, which would mean a third star.[34]

After release from the hospital, Hollingsworth was sent to Fort Sam Houston, Texas, where he served as the deputy commanding general of the Fourth Army from March to July 1973. In July he assumed command of I Corps (US/ROK) Group in Korea (see map 5), a force of

250,000 soldiers. At that time the plan for the defense of South Korea was to fall back on successive lines, with the last line on the outskirts of Seoul. With the support of Pres. Richard Nixon, an offensive plan that called for massive artillery and air attacks was adopted, though it was opposed by the US ambassador and the State Department. Hollingsworth established a personal relationship with the Republic of Korea's president, Park Chung Hee. After the collapse of South Vietnam, Park asked the general if the United States would support his nation in case of attack. Hollingsworth assured him: "Mr. President, I came over here and said I would fight and die with your units out here and defend this country. And that is what I intend to do. I worked to change this strategy in which you supported me. We've got ammunition in here. We've got the air power so we know we can get it in here. I just want you to know that I am totally convinced that we will live up to our treaty in the case of Korea."

The South Koreans called the general Ho Lim Soo, "the dignified tiger in the forest." His forward-defense strategy opened up thousands of acres of fallow land behind the Demilitarized Zone for planting rice. In addition, Hollingsworth started a reforestation program. The forests had been damaged during the war, and after the war local villagers had cut down the remaining trees for heating and cooking purposes. Soldiers in each corps area provided the manpower to plant between 15 and 20 million pine seedlings, which enjoyed a growth rate of between 80 and 90 percent.[35]

After more than two and a half years in Korea, Hollingsworth returned to the States and was assigned as special assistant to the army chief of staff. As a result of Sen. Sam Nunn's interest in NATO and the inadequacies he observed during visits to Europe, Hollingsworth was tasked to conduct a study of the alliance in the Central Europe region. *The Hollingsworth Report: Central Europe Assessment* was provided to the Senate Armed Forces Committee during its hearing on the subject, NATO and the New Soviet Threat. Senator Nunn noted that the study was of great value to the committee. This investigation resulted in approving the buildup of US Army forces in Europe. This no doubt influenced greatly events leading to the fall of the Berlin Wall, the demise of the Warsaw Pact, and the shortening of the Cold War.[36]

Lt. Gen. James F. Hollingsworth's military decorations include the Distinguished Service Cross with Two Oak Leaf Clusters, Distinguished

Hollingsworth statue in the corps area on the campus of Texas A&M. *Courtesy Lisa Kalmus, Sanders Corps of Cadets Center*

Service Medal with Three Oak Leaf Clusters, Silver Star with Three Oak Leaf Clusters, Legion of Merit with Two Oak Leaf Clusters, Distinguished Flying Cross with Two Oak Leaf Clusters, Soldier's Medal, Bronze Star with Valor device and Three Oak Leaf Clusters, Air Medal with Valor device and 37 Oak Leaf Clusters, Army Commendation Medal, Purple Heart with Five Oak Leaf Clusters, Distinguished Unit Citation, and the Meritorious Unit Commendation Medal with Oak

Leaf Cluster. Belgium awarded the Fourragere and Croix de Guerre. The Republic of Vietnam awarded the National Order of Vietnam (Third, Fourth, and Fifth Class), Distinguished Service Order First Class, Cross of Gallantry with Five Palms, and Chung My Medal First Class. From the Republic of Korea, he received the Order of National Security Merit Tong-II Medal and Order of Merit Chung Mu.[37]

Retiring from the army on August 25, 1976, he founded a consulting company, Hollingsworth Consulting, Inc., based in Washington, DC. His primary clients were corporations in the defense industry. The general also served on several corporate boards in the aerospace and technology industries.[38]

In 1999 Hollingsworth was honored at a ceremony on the campus of Texas A&M University, where a seven-foot statue of his image was unveiled. The statue, *Danger 79er*, depicts the general in battle gear, complete with sidearm, and is located in the Corps of Cadets area. In 2013 a display of his military decorations and other memorabilia was placed in the Sanders Corps of Cadets Center on the A&M campus.

General Hollingsworth died at the age of ninety-one on March 2, 2010, in San Antonio, Texas. He was buried with full military honors at Arlington National Cemetery.

★ 10 ★
Aggie Ace of Aces

JAY T. ROBBINS
CLASS OF 1940

Jay Thorpe Robbins was born on September 16, 1919, in Coolidge, Texas. His father, Jacob Isaiah Robbins Jr., was a blacksmith who owned 750–1,000 acres divided among four farms. Three of these grew principally cotton, corn, and grain feeds. The fourth was pastureland that supported Jacob's cattle and sheep herds. His mother, Mary Douglas Thorpe Robbins, was an accomplished pianist, songwriter, and poet. The whole family was musically inclined and would have songfests on Sunday afternoons. Religion also played a role in the family's life, especially for Robbins's mother, who was a member of the Church of Christ, and insisted that he and his younger brother, Jack, go to Sunday school and church every week.

Robbins's father used sharecroppers to work his land while he spent most of his time in the blacksmith shop. From the time he was big enough, young Jay also worked on the farms, where among other things he learned to plow using mules. During the winter, when the sheep were lambing, he would stay up during the night working with those that had difficultly birthing. He also worked on weekends running the big stone gristmill behind his father's shop, grinding corn, barley, or wheat for local farmers.

As with many people during the Great Depression, the Robbins family experienced financial problems. His father had borrowed money to buy some of the farms and could not make the interest payments. He tried to turn the farms back to the insurance companies, but they were more than happy to let him keep the farms without making payments, knowing he was a dependable man who would pay when he could.

The town of Coolidge is located seventy-two miles south of Dallas and thirty-two miles northeast of Waco in northern Limestone County. It is an agricultural community whose population in 1919 was between 900 and 1,000 people; by the early 1930s this had risen to 1,169. The community experienced a serious setback in 1942 when the railroad decided to abandon its track through the town, but the resulting population decline proved to be moderate.

Robbins attended Coolidge public schools, and during his first year he finished two grades. When he entered high school, one of his favorite teachers proved to be a graduate of Texas A&M. During his sophomore year, he visited the A&M campus to compete in a soil-conservation contest. He enjoyed the event and after seeing the campus decided that he wanted to attend A&M. Robbins also participated in football, baseball, softball, basketball, track, and tennis and was the captain of the softball and tennis teams. He was also the president of the school's Future Farmers of America chapter. He graduated second in his class of forty from Coolidge High School in May 1936.[1]

Robbins showed an interest in aviation at a young age by building model airplanes. He was especially interested in flying models—those made of balsa wood and tissues with a windup rubber-band propulsion. He also built a gasoline-powered model that he would fly.[2]

The six-foot one-inch, 138-pound Robbins enrolled in Texas A&M in September 1936 at the age of fifteen, selecting agriculture as his academic major and infantry for his required military science. He was assigned to Company E, Infantry, in the Corps of Cadets. The college enrollment that year was 5,136 students, with 4,130 of them in the corps.[3]

Robbins enjoyed his four years in the cadet corps and believed that the self-discipline, mutual respect, integrity, and willingness to take on responsibilities helped him in his military career. His cadet company included several members of the baseball team and football All-American John Kimbrough. Robbins was a cadet sergeant during his junior year and a first lieutenant his senior year, serving as the company executive officer in the spring semester. Graduating with a bachelor of science in agriculture on May 31, 1940, he could not be commissioned until his twenty-first birthday in September.[4]

During his cadet years at A&M, Robbins took a tour of Randolph Field, Texas, which rekindled his interest in flying. When the war in Europe started, he considered becoming an aviation cadet and took a physical at A&M to see if he qualified. The examination disclosed that his heart periodically missed a beat. He decided not to enlist in the service but to continue his education and get a degree.

After graduation he spent a few months working for Bewley Mills, a feed and flour company, as a feed salesman. In addition to sales, he was a public-relations representative for the company. Robbins visited farmers in the area around Waco and helped them worm hogs and castrate pigs as well as helping them tend to their chickens, goats, sheep, and cattle. The job only lasted until July 1941, when he was called to active duty with the Army Air Corps at Randolph Field. When that branch changed a policy to permit officers to go through flight training in grade, Robbins applied and was accepted; his heart condition did not show up during this physical. He went to Corsicana, Texas, for primary flight training. The airfield was only a thirty-minute drive to his home, so he spent his weekends at home. His next stop was Randolph for basic flying training, then on to Victoria Army Air Field in Victoria, Texas, for advance flying training. While at Victoria he held the air-gunnery record, later attributing his gunnery skill to his early experience bird hunting with his father, which gave him an appreciation of space and speed.

In July 1942 Robbins received his pilot wings and began training in fighter aircraft as a member of the 55th Fighter Squadron at Morris Field, North Carolina, and Drew Field, Florida. From Florida he went to San Francisco to await air transportation to the South Pacific. The passengers on his flight were all fighter pilots, one of whom, Richard Bong, would become the top scoring ace in World War II with forty victories. Arriving in Brisbane, Australia, Robbins had another wait before finally arriving at his destination, Port Moresby, New Guinea, in September (see map 10). Reporting to the 8th Fighter Group, he was assigned to the 80th Fighter Squadron, later known as the "Headhunters." The group contained three fighter squadrons—the 35th, 36th, and 80th. All flew the Bell P-39 Airacobra, whose armament was one 37-mm cannon and four .50-caliber machine guns.

The squadron was based on an airstrip near Port Moresby. All personnel lived in tents with dirt floors. Their food varied from fair to poor, with canned beef and flour with weevils the main fare, supplemented by dehydrated potatoes, carrots, and eggs. Frozen food was rare because of the lack of refrigeration equipment. A major problem for the squadron was the high rate of malaria, which struck most everyone at some point or another; half of the pilots were sick with it at times. Robbins had malaria nine times while in the Pacific and suffered a reoccurrence two years after returning to the States.

Robbins's first combat mission was a fighter sweep over the Owen Stanley Mountains to the area of Lae and Salamaua. His mission was to look for enemy barges carrying supplies, which were found and strafed. The flight also strafed a military facility and landing wharfs in the area.

After eight or nine missions, Robbins's annual physical examination was due. During the examination his heart problem was detected again. Since there was no EKG machine available, the flight surgeon sent him to the 4th General Hospital in Melbourne, Australia, where he stayed four or five weeks while undergoing various tests on his heart before finally being cleared to fly again. During his stay at the hospital, Robbins met an army nurse, Ina Louise Priest of Winchendon, Massachusetts, who would later become his wife.[5]

When he returned from Australia, his squadron was in the process of moving to Milne Bay on the southeastern tip of New Guinea. After the squadron had been there a short while, they were hit by a daylight air raid. Robbins was in one of the four or five P-39s that managed to get airborne. Both he and Lt. Gerald Rogers claimed to have shot down the same enemy airplane. Robbins was sure he had destroyed it, but during debriefing by intelligence officers, they could not determine who should get the credit. Fifth Air Force practice was to not recognize divided victories, so the matter was decided by a coin flip, which Rogers won, giving him his second confirmed victory.[6]

After a brief stay at Milne Bay, the squadron went to Mareba in northern Australia to be equipped with the Lockheed P-38 Lighting. The P-38 was a twin-engine fighter armed with a 20-mm cannon and

Lockheed P-38 Lightning. *Official US Army Photo*

four .50-caliber machine guns. During this time the pilots trained in the P-38 while the ground crews learned how to maintain the new aircraft. Robbins painted "Jandina"—taking the "J" from his name, using Ina's name, and combining them with "and" in between—in bright colors on the nose of his P-38. Returning to Port Moresby for a short time, the squadron then moved to the other side of the island.[7]

From this new location, the 80th Fighter Squadron flew raids against Rabaul, New Britain, the major Japanese naval and air base in the South Pacific. With five airfields, Rabaul was the nerve center for all the enemy's southern operations for both the army and navy. The Headhunters' missions were either fighter sweeps over Japanese air bases, where the enemy fighters would be engaged in air-to-air combat, or bomber escort. The policy for fighter escorts early on was to stick close to the bombers and not engage in air-to-air combat, the main objective being to get the bombers through to the target and then get them back to base without any losses. This was later revised to allow the fighters to engage enemy aircraft away from (and not necessarily attacking) the bomber formation.[8]

Robbins by his P-38, Jandina. *Courtesy Cushing Memorial Library and Archives, Texas A&M University*

After flying thirty or forty combat missions involving bomber and cargo escort, strafing, and dive bombing, Robbins's first real air-to-air test came on July 21, 1943, near Bogadjim, New Guinea. As leader of a flight of four P-38s, he destroyed three enemy fighters and damaged two others. The other pilots in the flight destroyed eight other Japanese aircraft. This was the start of a long string of aerial victories for Robbins and the squadron.[9]

The Texan was awarded his first Distinguished Service Cross for actions on September 4. That day the squadron put up sixteen Lightnings, with Robbins leading a flight of four, flying over the mountains to an advanced fighter strip at Dobodura. Several hours passed before they were off to the Salamaua and Lae area, where Allied ships were discharging men and supplies in support of a major amphibious operation. The fighters were over the area for more than an hour before a pilot in the second flight blurted, "Bandits—ten o'clock high."

Robbins turned his flight into the incoming gaggle of thirty Zeke fighters. Then he saw five Val dive bombers below his formation at about 12,000 feet and flying in the same direction as the Zekes. He decided to go for the fighters instead of the easier targets below. As the Lightnings pulled up almost in front the enemy, they began to turn out in various directions. As Robbins was going after one Zeke, he noticed several others had come in behind his own ship and decided to go after his target before the planes behind him could close. The lone Zeke nosed down in an effort to outdive Robbins, who by then had pulled up behind the fighter. Firing his cannon and four machine guns, the target began to smoke and then its right wing tore off. The enemy plane flipped over and began a vertical dive—victory number one.

As he pulled out of his dive, Robbins turned right and began to climb. The enemy planes were no longer behind him. At that moment he noticed one Lightning that fifteen or twenty Zekes had boxed in and were firing away at with a good chance of shooting down. The Texan headed straight for the dogfight. Robbins aimed the nose of Jandina for the pack of Japanese fighters. Several of the enemy broke away and turned into him head on. Though facing fire from several fighters, he held his fire until they were in range, missing as they flew by. One of the Zekes still pursuing the imperiled Lightning broke off and headed for Jandina. Robbins maneuvered his craft into a firing position, but the enemy hit Jandina before Robbins could open up. Now it was his turn to fire, and the oncoming Zeke began to take hits. It soon pulled up, dragging a trail of heavy smoke, then went into a spin, falling fast—victory number two.

These three encounters had used some ammunition, but Robbins did not know how much. Jandina had taken several hits, though none apparently serious since the engines were running smoothly. As he watched his second kill plunge down, a second cluster of holes appeared in his right wing. Caught from behind, Jandina now shuddered distressingly as Robbins pushed the wheel forward to dive away from the pursuer. The weight of the Lightning and the initial diving speed quickly came into play and were too much for the Zeke.

Pulling away and still diving, Robbins spotted a Zeke down low at about 5,000 feet. There were enemy aircraft on each side of him. The lone enemy tried to turn in behind the Lightning, and Robbins turned left. This caught the Japanese pilot by surprise, and Robbins lined up the gray aircraft in the sight ring for a deflection shot. He pressed the gun button and the Zeke began to disintegrate—victory number three.

Japanese planes closed in from every direction. Several enemy fighters flew in his path, making head-on attacks. Robbins again waited until one was in range. When he pressed the button this time, only some of his guns fired. *Jandina* shuttered, hit again, but the enemy also showed hits. As the Zeke passed by, Robbins's plight was getting desperate. He pressed his mike button and called for help, but no answer came. Another Zeke bobbed up straight ahead, and Robbins fired a short burst. Afterward, he dipped his nose and headed for the coastline. The engines had performed very well, but the strain was beginning to tell, his right engine starting to cut in and out.

Another Zeke appeared ahead, and Robbins waited until it was in range, then concentrated his rounds into the aircraft's belly. As the Zeke turned away, the Texan banked after him and made a deflection shot that threw shells into the wing. It separated from the fuselage, and a brilliant orange fire enveloped the stricken enemy—victory number four.

Almost out of ammunition and nursing his crippled plane, Robbins knew that his only chance was to get to the coast before an engine quit. He encountered several enemy fighters along the way, each time turning into his attacker to simulate a counterattack. On one pass Jandina was hit again. He noticed some vessels to his right and turned in that direction, a last effort to survive. As he approached the warships, they began to fire. Robbins turned left, displaying the belly silhouette of the P-38. Fortunately, the ships' spotters identified him as an American fighter. Recognizing that the single-engine craft were Japanese, they directed their antiaircraft fire accordingly.

Even though his aircraft was badly damaged, Robbins decided to try to make it to his home base across the mountains. He found the mountain pass and flew through at 11,000 feet. With no radio, he passed over the field and wondered if his wheels would come down. He pulled the lever, and they lowered slower than usual but finally locked down. The crash truck, an ambulance, and ground crewmen headed for the runway in preparation for his landing. Coming over the end of the strip, Robbins cut the throttle, and Jandina hit and bounced. The landing gear held secure, and the P-38 rolled normally. Once the aircraft stopped, Robbins climbed out and flopped to the ground. After the intelligence debriefing, he made a request to the squadron commander—he wanted ten days' leave to get away from it all and to see Ina. The request was granted, and he soon headed for Australia aboard a C-47.[10]

Robbins's second Distinguished Service Cross was awarded for actions on October 24 during a mission over Rabaul. The 80th was one of four P-38 squadrons scheduled to participate in a low-level bombing and strafing attack against Rapapo Airstrip, a main Japanese fighter base near Rabaul. The sixteen 80th Squadron fighters would escort B-25s bristling with forward-firing .50 calibers and carrying para-frags (parachute-fragmentation bombs). Their mission was to neutralize or at least suppress the enemy fighter force. This preliminary strike was in support of an upcoming effort by B-24 heavy bombers and US Navy carrier aircraft to attack air bases, supply depots, port facilities, and enemy shipping in or near Rabaul Harbor.

Japanese fighters were first spotted at 11:30 a.m. They seemed to be everywhere, with at least 150 already airborne. Others were still taking off or preparing to do so from Ramapo. The B-25s flashed over the airstrip, strafing the planes attempting to take off and dropping their bombs on the facility. Ramapo soon sparkled like a Fourth of July display.

Robbins's first kill was a deflection shot of about thirty degrees on a Hamp (Japanese Navy fighter) that was attacking a B-25 formation. There were so many targets that squadron and flight integrity was difficult to maintain. The Americans were so badly outnumbered that it was obvious each pilot must fight his own battle, although they tried to operate in pairs.

The Texan's second kill came at about 7,000 feet as he climbed to engage additional Hamps at a higher altitude. One enemy fighter was scoring hits on a P-38 when Robbins came up on his rear and fired a deflection shot that blew off its right wing in flames. His third kill was a head-on attack against a Hamp whose pilot seemed intent on ramming Robbins. The enemy fighter was hit dead center and disintegrated.

Robbins then saw some Hamps circling a large cloud, with P-38s chasing them. He calculated a pursuit curve that would come out of the cloud just behind the enemy. Holding a steady curve through the cloud for a couple of minutes, when he broke out he missed a Hamp by no more than ten feet. His fourth kill came a few moments later as he was collecting his wits after this near midair collision. Robbins achieved a high-angle deflection shot on a Hamp in a tight diving turn, getting solid hits and causing it to burst into flames. Unfortunately, he began to take hits from another fighter he had not noticed on his tail but was able to lose it by diving through the clouds and making a reverse turn while in them.

What Robbins thought was his fifth kill came as he was thinking of leaving the target area. Spotting three Hamps about 2,000 feet below, he told his wingman to take the one on the right while he took the one on the left. Robbins scored solid hits on his target, whose left wing blew off; the pilot bailed out. His wingman closed on his Hamp, and it too went down in flames. Robbins did not realize that he had run out of gun-camera film, so he did not get credit for the kill.

Low on fuel and ammunition, the two Americans headed for home. But there were four Zekes between them and their exit route. Slowing down, the P-38s started a slow dive toward them. When in range, they opened fire. The wingman got some hits that sent pieces flying off a Zeke. Robbins got solid hits that blew off large pieces of his target, then his guns went silent. Out of ammunition, soon one of his engines began malfunctioning as well. Seeing some B-24s, Robbins and his wingman joined them for added protection in case other enemy fighters were encountered. They stayed with the bombers until nearing a remote Australian airstrip in northeastern New Guinea. Seeking to get his plane back on the ground, Robbins made a single-engine landing.

Since he had not returned to his home base as scheduled, word went around that Robbins had been shot down. Poor communications in the area prevented the home base from knowing that he had landed at another airstrip. His fiancé, now stationed at a hospital near Port Moresby, was heartbroken when she heard the news. But Ina could not believe that he had been shot down and kept hoping he was safe somewhere. She was overjoyed when he returned to the squadron a few days later.[11]

On December 26, 1943, the Headhunters flew two missions to cover an assault landing at Cape Gloucester on New Britain. This operation would complete the isolation of Rabaul, and the Japanese reacted with particular ferocity. Robbins was credited with two victories, but it was a sad day for the squadron because their commander, Maj. Edward Cragg, was killed in action. The next day Robbins, now the leading ace in the squadron with thirteen confirmed victories, was selected to command the 80th. His style of command was somewhat more conventional than Cragg's. Robbins continued to fly combat missions, but not as often due to his squadron-command duties.

During the summer of 1944, the 80th was visited by Charles Lindbergh in his role as a civilian technician. He worked with the pilots to increase the range of their P-38s by setting the RPMs low and the manifold pressure high. This resulted in the engines consuming less fuel, extending the range of the aircraft and contributing to a significant expansion of American airpower in the Pacific. Lindbergh also worked individually with Robbins on reducing the drag on Jandina. He helped polish the airplane so that it encountered less air resistance. This increased not only its range but also its airspeed by four or five knots.

In September 1944 Robbins became operations officer for the 8th Fighter Group. He was in that position for a short time before he became deputy commander. In November he returned to the United States after more than two years in New Guinea. Flying 607 hours on 181 combat missions and scoring twenty-two confirmed victories, he had done his bit. He was the fourth-highest ace of all US fighter pilots in the Pacific War.[12]

After a thirty-day trip across the Pacific aboard a troop transport, he arrived in California. He was appointed troop commander of a train bound for San Antonio, carrying troops returning from overseas. Most were going to the Texas city, but some were dropped off along the way.

Robbins was preceded to the States by Ina, whom he had married in Melbourne, Australia, in January 1944. She visited her new in-laws and went with them to meet her husband when he arrived in San Antonio. After enjoying a prolonged leave with his family, he then went to a rest-and-rehabilitation center in Southern California. While there he made guest appearances on radio shows and went on short trips with entertainers such as Carole Landis, Bob Hope, Eddie Cantor, Sammy Kaye, and Arthur Godfrey to sell war bonds.[13]

Robbins's next assignment was as commander of the 434th Army Air Forces Base Unit at Santa Rosa Field, California, from February to November 1945. When the war ended, he was commander of a P-38 training squadron designed to prepare replacement pilots for Lightnings in the combat zones. He was then selected to be the commander of a provisional P-38 squadron composed of pilots from various units on the West Coast to provide air-defense coverage for the first meeting of the United Nations in San Francisco.

He transferred to March Field, California, to serve as squadron operations officer with the 412th Fighter Group. The group was the first unit in the Air Force to be equipped with the Lockheed F-80 jet fighter. While at March Field, Robbins received an opportunity from the air force to obtain a regular commission and remain on active duty. After discussing the offer with Ina, he decided to stay in the military.[14]

In June 1947 Robbins was assigned to the Twelfth Air Force Headquarters at March Field as the chief of the fighter branch. He helped establish policy and procedures for all fighter units in the Twelfth Air Force. From there he went to a comparable job with the Tactical Air Command at Langley Air Force Base near Hampton, Virginia. Now he was involved with an entire air-force command developing standard procedures, operational requirements, flight-time protocols for pilots, and training guidelines.

In 1949 he served in operational posts at Twelfth Air Force Headquarters, now located at Brooks Air Force Base in San Antonio. Early the following year he attended the Air Command and Staff School at Maxwell Air Force Base, Alabama, returning to the Twelfth Air Force after graduation in June. He next was assigned to Mitchel Air Force Base, Long Island, New York, in August 1950, where he served as assistant chief, Tactical Air Operations Branch at the Continental Air Command. Robbins then transferred to Ent Air Force Base, Colorado Springs, Colorado, in January 1951, where he was assigned to the operational staff of the newly established Air Defense Command. This new command's mission was to provide for the air defense of the continental United States and involved the development of radar systems and the application of fighter interceptors, surface-to-air missiles, and anything else that would enable the country to counter the Soviet Union's strategic air capability.[15]

From June 1953 to September 1955, he was assigned to Headquarters, US Air Force, Washington, DC, where he served as plans and programs officer of the War Plans Division, Directorate Plans. Remaining in the Pentagon, he became a member of the Joint Strategic Plans Group of the Joint Chiefs of Staff. One of his responsibilities was to represent

Lt. Gen. Jay T. Robbins. *Courtesy National Museum of the US Air Force*

the Joint Chiefs of Staff on a special continental defense subcommittee of the National Security Council. On several occasions he was called upon to brief Pres. Dwight D. Eisenhower in the White House on continental defense.

His four years in the Pentagon was a grueling experience. Robbins normally worked seven days a week and would often be in his office until after midnight. There were times when he worked 100–150 hours per week, his office essentially open twenty-four hours a day. He was very happy to get orders for England, returning to regular flying and leaving the administrative problems he was working on. He was ready for something different.[16]

In July 1957 Robbins and his family moved to Britain, where he was assigned to the 20th Tactical Fighter Wing as deputy commander and later commander. He enjoyed the opportunity to get back to flying fighter aircraft and to be with a tactical unit. The wing was stationed at a Royal Air Force Base near the village of Weathersville, about an hour's drive north of London. With no on-base housing available, the Robbins family lived in the local community, where they got to know the British people. When he received this assignment, the 20th was in the process of converting from F-84s to F-100s, which was one of the most advanced fighters at that time. The wing was committed to NATO, with target assignments in East Germany.

Robbins left England in August 1961 to return to Washington, DC, where he attended the National War College. While there he was promoted to brigadier general. After graduation he was named director of flight safety at Norton Air Base near San Bernardino, California, and in January 1963 became director of aerospace safety. While director, the US Air Force established two consecutive record years in low worldwide aircraft accident rates. Robbins received his second star while serving at Norton Air Base.[17]

In July 1965 he became commander of the 313th Air Division on Okinawa. The command had a tactical fighter wing, a reconnaissance squadron, an airlift wing, and a refueling wing operating KC-135s. It was deeply involved in supporting the war in Vietnam, initially sending squadrons on rotation to Vietnam and Thailand. Later several of the units were stationed in Vietnam, and Robbins made several trips to both there and to Thailand to visit them. Another of his responsibilities was to take necessary precautions in the event of typhoons, which threatened Okinawa about two or three times a year. These required the evacuation of the aircraft to either Guam or the Philippines, depending on the typhoons' track.

Robbins was assigned to be chief of staff, Pacific Air Forces, headquartered at Hickam Air Force Base, Hawaii, in March 1967. As the number-three man in that command, he supervised the way the staff functioned and ensured that it provided the kind of staff work expected by the commanding general. Pacific Air Forces included all of the air-force units in Vietnam, Okinawa, Korea, Guam, and the Philippines.[18]

In July 1968 Robbins was named commander of the Twelfth Air Force, with headquarters at Connally Air Force Base near Waco. Stationed near his hometown, with his parents still alive and his two sons attending Texas A&M, he was happy to be back in Texas. But the Twelfth Air Force soon moved to Bergstrom Air Force Base in Austin. His command included most of the tactical forces west of the Mississippi River, including airlift wings, fighter wings, reconnaissance wings, and the weapons-center program at Nellis Air Force Base, Nevada. While at Bergstrom, Robbins was selected for promotion to lieutenant general.

During his time with the Twelfth Air Force, he attended home football games at Texas A&M and several times served as reviewing officer at the Corps of Cadets march-in prior to the game. On one visit he addressed the corps seniors.[19]

The editor of the *Austin American-Statesman* was from Coolidge, and because of Robbins's war background and the move of the Twelfth Air Force to Austin, the paper published a big Sunday supplement on the general and his command. Pres. Lyndon B. Johnson was at his ranch that weekend and read a copy of the supplement; he was impressed. Since the commander of the reconnaissance wing at Bergstrom had previously been Johnson's pilot on Air Force One, the president called and asked him to contact Robbins, informing the general that he and his wife were going to be invited to a state dinner for the prime minister of Barbados sometime in the near future. Not long afterward, Robbins received a call from the White House. The president extended the invitation for the general and his wife to be his guests at the state dinner for the prime minister. Of course, Robbins was most happy to accept. He and his wife flew to Washington in a T-39. They checked into their quarters at Bolling Air Base and were getting dressed for the dinner when the phone rang. It was Lady Bird Johnson's secretary saying that the Johnsons would like to invite them to spend the night in the White House. They hurriedly repacked and were ready when the car from the White House picked them up. That night they were seated at the table with the prime minister and his wife, Secretary of State and Mrs. Dean Rusk, and President and Mrs. Johnson. In his oral history Robbins said he had a good time but felt like a duck out of water.

The next morning they had coffee with Lady Bird, who hoped that the president would join them. When she learned that he would be a little late, she took the Robbins on a tour of the White House. When the president did show up, he wanted to talk about Texas, raising cattle, and the life of a rancher, spending over an hour with them. It was a memorable day for the general and his wife.

In February 1970 Robbins was named vice commander of the Tactical Air Command, headquartered at Langley Air Force Base, Virginia. He was given responsibility for the supervision and management of the Air Force Reserve and National Guard forces. Those units were located all over the country, and he spent much of his time visiting the scattered units.[20]

In August 1972 he was appointed vice commander of the Military Airlift Command. Several major operations were conducted during his time there. In 1973 Operation Homecoming brought home the prisoners of war from Vietnam. A major surge for the command came during the Yom Kippur War in 1973, when it flew vital supplies and ammunition to Israel.

At the age of fifty-five, with over thirty-three years' service and five thousand flying hours, Robbins retired in 1974 and moved to San Antonio. He had intended to retire in the Austin area, but the real-estate market was tight, and he could not find a house to suit his needs. He and his wife stayed at a house on Canyon Lake owned by his veterinarian brother while looking for their retirement home. Finally, the couple settled on San Antonio because of their many friends in the area and the military facilities, such as hospitals, commissaries, and base exchanges, available in the area.

Robbins had a number of offers from aircraft companies that wanted him as a consultant for partial or full-time work, but this would mean living in Washington, New York, or on the West Coast. He had promised himself that when he retired, he would not get himself tied down with a full-time job even if the money was good.

At his retirement Robbins was honored with a parade and formal retirement ceremony, including a flyover of F-100s from a National Guard unit. There was a big party at the Officers Club after the ceremony. The guests included officers from his World War II fighter squadron and people from the various assignments throughout his career. The Catholic priest who married Robbins and his wife in Australia also was invited as a surprise to the couple. His two sons, by then in the air force, flew in from their duty stations in Europe.

Lt. Gen. Jay T. Robbins's military decorations include the Distinguished Service Cross with Oak Leaf Cluster, Distinguished Service

Medal with Oak Leaf Cluster, Silver Star with Oak Leaf Cluster, Legion of Merit with Oak Leaf Cluster, Distinguished Flying Cross with Three Oak Leaf Clusters, Air Medal with Six Oak Leaf Clusters, and Air Force Commendation Medal with Oak Leaf Cluster.

Robbins died on March 3, 2001, in San Antonio, Texas. He was buried at the Fort Sam Houston National Cemetery.[21]

★ 11 ★

Kyle Field Star, Battlefield Hero

MARION CONDY "DOOKIE" PUGH

CLASS OF 1941

Fort Worth's North Side High School boasts several notable graduates, including Bob Schieffer, veteran television journalist; Johnny Rutherford, three-time Indianapolis 500 champion; Yale Lary, NFL Hall of Famer; Darrow Hooper, Olympic Gold Medalist; and Marion Pugh, quarterback of the Texas A&M 1939 National Championship football team.

Marion Condy "Dookie" Pugh was born on September 6, 1919, in Fort Worth to John Joseph and Ida G. Elmore Pugh. His father had attended Marion Military Institute in Marion, Alabama, while his mother had attended Livingston Teachers College in Livingston, Alabama. Sometime between 1914 and 1919, the family moved to Fort Worth, where his father opened a grocery store on the north side. Marion was the second child in the family; his sister, Julia Inez, was born in Alabama in 1913.

As a youth Pugh was interested in the outdoors and enjoyed hunting and fishing. He also enjoyed all kinds of sports, especially football, baseball, basketball, and track. One of his early ambitions was to be an all-state football player. During his three years at North Side High School, he was the first-string quarterback and was named to the All-District Team in 1935 and 1936. Pugh was named to the All-State Team his senior year and was co-captain of the football team that same year. An all-round athlete, he lettered in football, basketball, baseball, and track each year in high school.

Pugh was also active in other student activities. He served on the staff of the school's yearbook for three years. A popular student, he was elected president of the senior class and president of the student body. In the summer after graduation, he worked in the oil fields and decided that he wanted to study petroleum engineering in college. But in his freshman year at Texas A&M, he enrolled in liberal arts, with a goal of becoming a radio sports announcer. The following year he changed his major to agriculture.[1]

While Pugh was enjoying his high school senior year, the A&M football coach, Homer Norton, was developing a plan to build a national championship team. Norton knew that success depended on recruiting outstanding athletes, and he developed a list of who he considered the top-forty high school football players in the state. Most were poor and could not go to A&M without a scholarship. The coach determined that he needed $25,000 to make his plan work. If he signed twenty-five players, he could provide scholarships that would cover each for four years. Norton contacted Bert Pfaff, a prominent former student who was a successful oilman and builder. Pfaff agreed to meet Norton and Lil Dimmitt, the Aggies' trainer and ace recruiter, at a Dallas bank. A bank officer thought that Norton was there to make a payment on an outstanding loan and was surprised when the coach asked for a $25,000 loan. At first the banker refused, but when Pfaff threatened to close his account, the man relented and agreed to the loan.

After securing the funds, Dimmitt immediately drove to Fort Worth and signed his first recruit from the list—quarterback Marion Pugh. By the end of the day, Tommie Vaughn and Bill Miller were signed as well. Of the targeted forty players, thirty-seven signed and twenty-three reported as promised. Coach Norton had his core of talented athletes. In 1937 the freshman team was undefeated, and Norton was in charge of his own budget for the first time. E. J. Kyle, dean of the School of Agriculture and chairman of the Athletic Council, silenced some of the rumblings on campus by extending the coach's contract another five years. Among those rooting for the Aggies' success was a happy loan officer in Dallas, for the borrowers had started paying back the loans.[2]

Pugh entered A&M in September 1937, and even though he had requested coast artillery as his required military science, he was assigned to the infantry. Initially assigned to the Infantry Regiment Headquarters Company, he transferred to Company I, Infantry, the following year when his original unit was disbanded.

By 1938 the twenty-three talented scholarship signees were sophomores, and several, including Pugh, earned playing time. The record for the 1938 Aggie team was four wins, four losses, and one tie. One loss was to Texas Christian University, which won the conference that year and was declared national champions after beating Carnegie Tech in the Sugar Bowl. The Aggie fans had received a taste of the future when John Kimbrough, a future All-American, entered the TCU game and gave a stellar performance. Thereafter, he started every game. Kimbrough was among those recruited in 1937, but he had elected to attend Tulane to study medicine. After a disagreement with the Tulane coach, Kimbrough contacted Norton about transferring to A&M. Norton replied by sending him a train ticket to College Station.[3]

The sports section of the *1939 Longhorn* commented beside Pugh's picture: "A triple threat and a four-sports man is Marion Pugh. He labors in the backfield and knows how to pound away at a line. He can pass to receivers with regularity and is capable of good punting." The Aggies' time in the sun finally came in the 1939 football season, when they were undefeated in the regular season and won the Sugar Bowl in a close game (14–13) with Tulane. This was A&M's first (and thus far only) national championship in football. Pugh, who was the passer, shared quarterback duties with Charles "Cotton" Price. During his athletic career at A&M, Pugh won four freshman numerals, then added three varsity letters each in football and baseball. He was voted most valuable player in football in 1940 and All–Southwest Conference in baseball in 1941.[4]

With a war raging in Europe, Congress passed the Selective Service Act of 1940, causing coaches some concern about losing players to the military draft. Fortunately, advanced military students at senior ROTC schools would be exempt under provisions of a bill pending in Congress. Many athletes like Kimbrough and Vaughn were already under military contract in the ROTC, but some like Pugh and Marshall

Pugh played quarterback on the national-championship team in 1939. *Courtesy Texas A&M Yearbook*

Robnett had completed their required two years of military science and elected not to complete the two years of advanced ROTC leading to a commission. Coaches quickly reviewed the status of each player and encouraged those who did not have an advanced ROTC contract to sign up.[5]

Pugh married Helen Ruth Braselton in 1940 while still a student; they would live on campus in married-student housing. Helen graduated from North Side High School a year before Pugh. Her father gave the newlyweds a new car as a wedding present. After the ceremony they were driving to Dallas in the new car and did not know that Helen's brother had reported the car stolen. Unfortunately, the road from North Fort Worth to Dallas passed the jail in downtown Fort Worth. A policeman who had just heard the report of the stolen car was standing in front of the building, saw the car, and ordered it to stop. Pugh was taken into the jail, where he claimed the car was his but had no proof of ownership. Finally, someone recognized him, and he was released. As the couple left Fort Worth, they were driving on the Dallas Pike when a car pulled up behind him and started flashing its headlights. Pugh pulled to the side of the road, thinking he was going to be arrested again. When his brother-in-law got out of the car, he and his new bride were not amused. Years later it made for a good story.

During his senior year at A&M, Pugh became associated with the College Station agency of Seaboard Life Insurance Company. Others in the office were Aggies H. E. Burgess (Class of 1929), Sid Loveless (Class of 1938), and Paul Martin (Class of 1939).

In the fall of 1941, even though he had not graduated from A&M, Pugh played professional football for the New York Giants. He returned to college for the spring semester of 1942 and graduated in May. Having completed the requirements for a commission in the army, he was commissioned a second lieutenant and immediately called to active duty along with the other graduates.[6]

Pugh and several other Aggie athletes on active duty were detailed to play football on the army's all-star team. Their first game was against the Washington Redskins in the Rose Bowl in Pasadena, California. After playing a short series of exhibition games, Pugh reported to Camp Hood, Texas, to attend the Tank Destroyer Officers' Orientation Course conducted by the Tank Destroyer Tactical and Firing Center. Following completion of the course, he remained at Camp Hood and was assigned to the 893rd Tank Destroyer Battalion.

The battalion consisted of a headquarters company, three tank-destroyer gun companies of three platoons each, and a reconnaissance company of three platoons. Each battalion was authorized thirty-six commissioned officers, two warrant officers, and 636 enlisted men. A lieutenant colonel commanded the battalion, captains commanded the companies, and lieutenants led the platoons.

The 893rd Tank Destroyer Battalion was activated on December 13, 1941, at Fort Meade, Maryland. It was one of fifty-two tank-destroyer battalions the US Army activated that month.[7]

Pugh's unit was the first to arrive at the Tank Destroyer Tactical and Firing Center, located near Killeen, Texas. The center was commanded by another Aggie, Brig. Gen. Andrew D. Bruce (see chapter 2). Construction on the new camp had not begun, and the troops established a temporary camp in the northern part of the military reservation near Gatesville. The battalion served as the prototype of the new tank-destroyer units and was the first to be issued the new T-12 halftrack, which mounted a 75-mm gun. During 1942, the 893rd served as school troops, conducting demonstrations and training for new formations being rotated through the center. The battalion was also used as a test unit for new tank-destroyer doctrine and tactics.

In January 1943 the 893rd was transferred to Camp Shelby, Mississippi, and began an intensive training program to include participation in the Louisiana Maneuvers in April and May. By this time Pugh was commander of Company C. While at Shelby, the now-obsolete T-12 halftracks were replaced by the full-tracked M10 tank destroyer. Following a year of training, the battalion moved to Camp Kilmer, New Jersey, to prepare for deployment overseas. On January 9, 1944, the men shipped out through the New York Port of Embarkation. After crossing the Atlantic, they arrived in Liverpool on the eighteenth. The 893rd moved by train to a camp at Chudleigh in Devon, where new equipment was awaiting the battalion in a huge abandoned rock quarry. In March the unit was transferred to Bridgeport in Dorset on the southern coast. The men trained hard in preparation for combat on the Continent.

The battalion boarded ships in Southampton soon after D-Day and landed at the Omaha beachhead on July 1, 1944. On July 17 the unit was placed in support of the 2nd Infantry Division, then engaged in the fighting in the Normandy hedgerow country. The hedgerows limited mobility until a new device was developed that would allow a tank to crash through them. This new device, called the "Rhino" hedge cutter, was welded to the battalion's M10s.[8]

In its first combat operations, the 893rd was primarily employed in augmenting the bombardments of divisional artillery with indirect fire. On July 28 Pugh's company was in Saint-Amand and fired twenty-eight rounds at the tower of a church being used by the enemy as an observation post, resulting in the position's destruction and the killing of two observers inside. The company also destroyed a German 88-mm gun in the same action.

Things changed in August, when the tank destroyers were in direct support of advancing infantry regiments and used to neutralize enemy ground targets on request. Pugh's company was attached to the 90th Infantry Division for three days in late August. On the twenty-third the battalion was attached to the 4th Infantry Division, which had just been alerted for an urgent mission to support the liberation of Paris and transferred to V Corps. In a driving rain the 4th and the attached 893rd rolled along the road to Paris all that night and the following day. Although the French Resistance had been battling Germans for several days inside the city, the capital still was surrounded by enemy forces. To bring support to the patriots, the 4th Infantry Division and the 2nd French Armored Division raced to clinch the liberation of Paris. The 4th bivouacked twelve miles south of the city as the Germans retreated across the Seine River. That evening the 2nd French Armored met strong opposition between Versailles and the capital. At midnight the 4th received orders to move into the city. The division, supported by the 893rd, liberated the northern part of the city and rode in a triumphal procession through streets jammed with thousands of joyous Parisians. The Americans did not linger long but were soon in pursuit of the retreating Germans. For the month of August, the battalion reported destruction of two self-propelled guns, two antitank guns, and one halftrack. They also killed 28 enemy soldiers and captured 185 others.[9]

Racing across northern France, the 4th entered Belgium on September 7. The Germans were withdrawing to their border fortifications and most of the fighting after Paris and into Belgium was against the enemy's rear guard. The division liberated the towns of Saint-Hubert, Houffalize, Bastogne, and Saint-Vith before crossing the border into Germany on September 11. During this period, the 893rd was in direct support of the advancing infantry and claimed their first enemy tanks destroyed. The monthly report for September lists four tanks, two self-propelled guns, and two halftracks knocked out. It also credits the battalion with 122 enemy troops killed and 155 captured. For actions during the period September 7–13, the 893rd was awarded the Belgium Fourragere.[10]

Soon after, American forces in Belgium and northern France encountered the German border and the West Wall, or Siegfried Line as it was called by the Allies. The Siegfried Line was a formidable defensive position consisting of concrete bunkers fronted by antitank obstacles and minefields. The resultant pause in the Allied offensive allowed the supply elements to catch up with the forward units.[11]

In September an operation that was soon to be of great significance to the 893rd was taking place in an area known as the Huertgen Forest. The battle there was the longest and one of the bloodiest engagements fought by American forces in Europe, but it has been largely overshadowed by the Battle of the Bulge, which began on December 16. The Huertgen Forest covers an area of over fifty square miles and is actually composed of three separate forests—Roetgen, Wenau, and Konigl—though American soldiers based their reference to the area on the town of Huertgen, one of their early objectives (see map 8). The region forms a rough triangle that begins about five miles south and east of Aachen and extends to Duren on one side and Monschau on the other. Hilly and densely wooded except for cleared ground on the ridges where the towns are located, the terrain limited vehicular movement to a few roads and tracks. Poor weather prevailed during the battle, with fog, clouds, rain, snow, and cold. A military force entering the forest forfeited its ability to effectively use air power, artillery, and armor support.

The American First Army was poised to continue the attack to the Rhine River but was concerned about its right flank along the Huertgen Forest. V Corps was given the mission to protect this sector by securing the forest. The battle began on September 14, when a regiment of the 9th Infantry Division attempted to breach the Siegfried Line and capture the Huertgen-Kleinau road network. The attacking unit withdrew after a brief but bloody encounter with German defenders. On October 6 the division again entered the forest, with the crossroads town of Schmidt as the objective. Two attacking regiments pushed some 3,000 yards into the forest at a cost of 4,500 casualties. The battered 9th Division was replaced in late October by the 28th Infantry Division, strongly reinforced with tanks, tank destroyers, and artillery.

The first two weeks of October the 893rd was in defensive positions and spent time maintaining and winterizing their vehicles. Wire camouflage netting was welded to the M10s. Those troops not directly engaged in indirect-fire missions conducted training. On October 29 the battalion was attached to the 28th Infantry Division, whose first mission afterward was to seize Vossenack in preparation for the attack into the forest to capture Schmidt, the division's primary objective. The plan of attack after seizing Vossenack was for the 109th Infantry Regiment to advance to the northwest toward the village of Huertgen,

M10 tank destroyers of the 893rd Tank Destroyer Battalion traverse the Kall Trail in November 1944. *Official US Army Photo*

thereby securing the left flank of the main attack by the 112th Infantry Regiment, whose mission was to seize Kommerscheidt and Schmidt. The 110th Infantry Regiment was to attack southward to take a nest of pillboxes at Raffelsbrand and be prepared to continue on order into the Monschau Corridor.[12]

After receiving word that the 893rd was attached to the 28th Division, Pugh moved his company into indirect-firing positions to support the attack that jumped off on November 2. Sometime before noon the next day, reports arrived of an enemy tank repair and maintenance shop operating in the town of Nideggen. This was beyond the range of Pugh's guns, so he suggested to the battalion commander that Company C displace forward to new positions from which Nideggen could be taken under fire. The suggestion was approved late in the evening, and early the next morning, November 4, Pugh made a reconnaissance of the new positions. Upon returning to his company command post, he learned that 1st Platoon, under Lt. Turney Leonard (A&M Class of 1943), and Lt. Goodwin McElroy's 3rd Platoon had been ordered to the vicinity of Vossenack to repel a reported German tank attack. Lt. Jack W. Fuller, leader of the reconnaissance platoon attached to Company C, having previously reconnoitered routes of advance for just such an emergency call, had led the two platoons forward. Pugh took Lt. Curtis M. Edmund's 2nd Platoon, now numbering three guns, to the new positions. After the expected German tanks failed to appear, Leonard's and McElroy's platoons were withdrawn to the indirect-fire area.

Shortly before midnight, Pugh was ordered to move his company to Kommerscheidt to support the 112th Infantry. Two hours later Lieutenant Fuller returned from a reconnaissance of the Kall Trail to report that the route was blocked by three or four tanks from the 707th Tank Battalion. The Kall Trail, chosen as the main supply route for the 28th Division by division staff, was a narrow, steep, unimproved track with hairpin turns running from Vossenack through the Kall River gorge to Kommerscheidt. Its selection was made after a map survey showed what appeared to be a road leading across the gorge. But this "road" was actually a footpath used by Catholics in Kommerscheidt to walk to Sunday services in Vossenack and had never been used for vehicular traffic.

At about 7:30 a.m. on November 5, Fuller radioed that the Kall Trail was finally cleared. Pugh ordered the lieutenant to take the 1st and 3rd Platoons through to Kommerscheidt, while he would follow with the 2nd Platoon, now down to two destroyers, having lost one to a mine. From the original twelve destroyers in Company C, Pugh now had only seven available in the Kommerscheidt area. He traveled to the top of the hill near town, where he came under a heavy enemy artillery barrage. Jumping out of his jeep, he and those with him took shelter off the road. Once the fire had lifted, the captain checked the disposition of his company. He saw a 3rd Platoon destroyer on the northern edge of Kommerscheidt, which was hit immediately by direct antitank fire, and two more destroyers from Leonard's command on the right flank of the town, with some tanks of the 707th Tank Battalion. Contacting the 1st Platoon by radio, he was told that Leonard had not been seen for some time. The 3rd Platoon reported that Lieutenant McElroy had not been seen for two hours. The captain then went forward to locate the two missing officers but could not find either of them.

That night Pugh returned to Vossenack for ammunition and water; he also sought a replacement officer for either Leonard or McElroy. With the supplies loaded aboard four jeeps, he arrived at the northern entrance to the trail but was unable to go forward. A considerable number of jeeps and M29 cargo carriers (called "Weasels") in a supply train were blocking the road. About 1:00 a.m. the column began to move, but when they reached the bottom of the gorge, there was a loud explosion and a tremendous amount of small-arms fire. The Germans had cut the road and controlled the bridge over the Kall River. Pugh returned to Vossenack to await another opportunity to cross the trail with the supplies for his company.

The next morning he again started to take his small supply train through, Lieutenant Fuller in the first jeep and Pugh in the second. When the convoy reached a point three hundred yards south of Vossenack, it ran into an ambush. Under the cover of darkness, about forty Germans, armed with machine guns and at least one rocket launcher, had worked their way to a position alongside the road. When the Germans opened up, Fuller returned fire with his machine gun as did Pugh with his, though it jammed after three rounds. The captain then bailed out of the left side of the jeep at about the same time a German rocket shell grazed the top of the windshield. A large enemy soldier came at Pugh with a bayonet, which the officer batted away with his hand, suffering cuts to three fingers. After firing at the German a couple of times and missing, Pugh ran back up the trail toward Vossenack. Arriving at the top of the gorge, he contacted an infantry unit and requested support to go down the trail and clean out the Germans. The request was denied, and a few minutes later Fuller came back up the trail, telling Pugh that two of his men were injured and that he wanted to go and get them. Just about then a platoon of tank destroyers from Company B came out of Vossenack. Pugh commandeered two destroyers and, with Fuller in the lead, went down the trail. The Germans were still in the area, and the two destroyers fired on them with .50-caliber machine guns. Several enemy troops were killed from these bursts, and the rest of the ambushers fled into the forest. Pugh found his jeep wrecked, while Fuller's jeep contained one man dead and another wounded.

Pugh moved to the vicinity of Kommerscheidt to determine the status of his company and to locate Leonard and McElroy. He found that only three destroyers were in good operating condition. Coordinating with the 112th's commander, Pugh was told that the Germans had recaptured Schmidt and the planned attack was cancelled. The captain ordered several crewmen from his disabled destroyers to dig in as infantry.

At 6:00 a.m. on November 7, the Germans commenced a coordinated attack on Kommerscheidt. It began with a thirty-minute artillery preparation and was closely followed by an estimated two battalions of infantry and eighteen to twenty tanks, supported by the direct fire of other tanks and self-propelled guns on the Schmidt ridge. Lieutenant Edmunds's destroyer knocked out a Mark VI at thirty yards as it came into the town. A second destroyer knocked out three more tanks and, firing their machine guns, killed or wounded about forty infantrymen. Both Edmunds's and the other destroyer were knocked out by enemy tanks. The lieutenant's destroyer was using a barn for concealment when it was hit and he was wounded. He crawled into a hole, treated his wounds, and remained there until captured.

The Americans withdrew from Kommerscheidt and took up positions in the forest north of town. Only two destroyers remained fully operational at this point, and they were ordered to help organize the position against a night attack. At 6:30 p.m. the enemy launched another tank-infantry assault, which was broken up by artillery fire one hundred yards from the infantry's position.

There was very little activity the morning of the eighth other than occasional artillery and small-arms fire. That afternoon the 112th Infantry ordered a withdrawal across the Kall gorge to the vicinity of Vossenack and the destruction of all vehicles and any equipment that could not be removed. Of the nine destroyers that had gotten through to Kommerscheidt, seven had been knocked out and the other two had to be abandoned. Company C had destroyed seventeen German tanks and killed 150 or more German infantrymen. The initial strength of Company C consisted of forty-five enlisted men and four officers, but only Pugh and twenty-seven others came out of Kommerscheidt. All three of his platoon leaders were either killed or captured. The survivors came out in three different parties: Pugh led one group while company sergeants led the other two. The Americans had to bypass enemy positions in the forest on the way to Vossenack.

Pugh came to an aid station in a dugout near the Kall Trail and learned that the Germans were in control of the area, even periodically visiting the station. Two American medical officers and two chaplains confirmed that the aid station had been captured but was still operating, treating both Americans and Germans. They warned Pugh to remove his pistol in case the Germans returned; he carefully laid it on the ground. The captain's group crawled into some nearby foxholes to spend the night and started out of the gorge early the next morning in the direction of Vossenack. They reached a road junction in friendly hands near Germeter shortly after 10:00 a.m. on November 9.

The battered Company C was sent to a rear area to receive replacement vehicles and personnel. Given five days to reorganize, the company was then sent to Vossenack, where they replaced Company B for five days. On November 18 the 28th Division was relieved by the 8th Infantry Division, but the 893rd remained in place, joining the 8th Division. On December 6 Company C moved to Bergstein to support the 2nd Ranger Battalion. On the tenth the battalion was attached to the 78th Infantry Division, which was just moving into the line for its initial combat. Pugh's company moved south to Monschau, where it was attached to the 38th Cavalry Squadron, 102nd Cavalry Group. Monschau was considered a "rest area" for the newly reorganized Company C until the morning of December 16, when artillery and mortars—and finally small-arms fire—came crashing in. The massed German forces began an offensive known as the Battle of the Bulge. The 38th Cavalry Squadron with the attached tank destroyers was spread over a wide area to act as a screening force. Initially, the Germans penetrated in several areas, but the defenders fought off most of their strikes. Cavalry units soon were able to consolidate a position on the north shoulder of the major enemy penetration. Pugh and the tank destroyers were withdrawn from the area on December 27 and returned to battalion control.[13]

The 78th Division and the attached 893rd spent most of January 1945 holding their positions in the front lines. During this period of relative inactivity, Pugh took the opportunity to submit a recommendation for the award of the Medal of Honor to Lieutenant Leonard for his actions in the defense of Kommerscheidt. The recommendation was approved, and the decoration was presented to his mother in 1945. Leonard was declared missing in action after the battle, and his body was not recovered until 1950.[14]

By the end of the month, the German "Bulge" ceased to be a threat, with remnant forces withdrawing from Belgium and reoccupying their border fortifications. On January 30 the 78th resumed its advance into

Germany. By the end of the day, the 774th Tank Battalion had suffered greatly going into Schmidt. Pugh's tank destroyers fared better, eliminating two pillboxes and one antitank gun and killing many enemy troops. They then returned to Kommerscheidt, where they had been badly mauled by superior German forces in November. The area was littered with unburied American and German bodies, abandoned equipment, and knocked out vehicles. While in Kommerscheidt, Pugh took the opportunity to search for Turney Leonard, with no success.

The 78th Division continued the attack and captured the Schwammenauel Dam that controlled the level of the Roer River. Allied forces crossed the river and advanced rapidly to the Rhine. On March 7 the 9th Armored Division captured the Ludendorff railroad bridge, spanning the Rhine from Remagen to Erpel, intact. Pugh crossed on March 9 with his company and supported the 78th in its drive north toward the Ruhr industrial region. The division, supported by the 893rd Tank Destroyer Battalion, was deployed in a defensive position with a 44,000-yard front along the Sieg River. It was a holding operation that protected the flank of the divisions attacking eastward into the heart of the German homeland. The 78th remained along the Sieg River from about March 22 to the end of April. The 78th was relieved by the 97th Infantry Division and joined the battle to reduce the Ruhr Pocket. Combat operations for the 893rd Tank Destroyer Battalion in Europe concluded with the close of the Ruhr operation. The end of the war found the 893rd in Altendorf, about twenty miles north of Frankfurt. American units now had to change almost overnight from combat operations to occupation duties: the German army had to be demobilized; refugees, concentration-camp prisoners, and former slave laborers needed help to return to their homes; and military-government activities had to be supported.[15]

The War Department plan was to demobilize individuals, not units. This was based on a point system that awarded a point for each month of service, another for each month overseas, five points for each campaign star or combat decoration, five points for a Purple Heart, and twelve points for having a child under eighteen. Anyone with eighty-five points or more had a good chance of being discharged in the fall of 1945. Pugh, with his two Bronze Stars, two Purple Hearts, five campaign stars, and credit for months in service and months overseas had accumulated enough points to be returned to the States, where he was discharged in August 1945.[16]

Marion C. Pugh was in the lumber business in College Station after World War II. *Courtesy Cushing Memorial Library and Archives, Texas A&M University*

Pugh left the army just in time for the 1945 professional football season, during which he played quarterback for the New York Giants. He played his final season of football the following year with the Miami Seahawks.[17]

In College Station he was once again associated with Hershel Burgess when they formed a construction company. By 1949 this enterprise had expanded into the Marion Pugh Lumber Company, located on what is now Marion Pugh Drive just south of Olsen Field, Texas A&M's baseball stadium. He also operated the Pugh Realty Company. In July 1949 A&M's athletic director, Bones Irwin, announced that Pugh had been employed on a part-time basis as the freshman football coach and would also serve the Aggies as a scout. Pugh continued his love of and involvement in football by officiating high school games and later Southwest Conference games. One of his officiating partners was Barney Welch, an A&M legend in his own right, having been the first Aggie to carry the ball across the goal line in Memorial Stadium in Austin, a touchdown against the University of Texas capping a seventy-one-yard punt return. Welch believes that he and Pugh are the only individuals to have played, coached, and officiated in the Southwest Conference.[18]

Pugh had the sad duty of serving as pallbearer at the funeral of his former platoon leader, Lieutenant Leonard, whose remains had been found in Kommerscheidt in November 1949 and positively identified in January 1950. Leonard was buried in Dallas on May 10. The lieutenant's Aggie ring was found by a young German clearing the fields after the battle of the Huertgen Forest and returned to Texas A&M by the finder's son-in-law on Veterans Day in 2000.[19]

In 1957 Pugh joined with several prominent businessmen, mostly Aggies, to publish a daily paper, the *Twin City Star*, in the Bryan–College Station area. Facing stiff competition from the *Bryan Eagle*, which lowered its advertising rates, the fledgling paper folded after several months of operation. Pugh was active in the Texas Lumbermen Association and was elected sergeant-at-arms at its convention in Fort Worth in 1959. He was also active in local politics, serving on the College Station City Council for two terms and in 1962 making an unsuccessful run for the state senate against longtime senator William T. "Bill" Moore.[20]

Marion C. Pugh's military decorations include two Bronze Stars, two Purple Hearts, and the Belgium Fourragere.

On November 20, 1976, the Pughs and another couple drove twenty-five miles west of College Station to the small town of Somerville to have dinner at a popular steakhouse. During the meal, Pugh choked on a bite of steak and was rushed to the hospital in Bryan, where he died at age fifty-seven. Burial was in the College Station City Cemetery on November 23.[21]

The legend of "Dookie" Pugh lives on at Texas A&M. In 1961 he was inducted into the Texas A&M Athletic Hall of Fame. Each year the university baseball team presents the Marion Pugh Most Valuable Player award to a player. Another, the Marion Pugh Spirit Award, is a coveted honor given to the baseball player who best exhibits the "Aggie spirit."

★ 12 ★

Three Tours Are Enough

ROBERT L. ACKLEN JR.

CLASS OF 1963

Vietnam was America's most unpopular war. More than two million servicemen and women served in the conflict, most honorably and bravely. Some were drafted and went reluctantly to Vietnam; a few fled to Canada or Sweden. Others volunteered, eager to experience war as had their fathers and grandfathers. Some, once they were in combat, extended their one-year tour of duty and remained for a second tour. A few even extended for a third tour. One of those few was Robert Livingston "Bob" Acklen Jr., who would become one of the most decorated soldiers of the Vietnam War.

Born in Nashville, Tennessee, on March 24, 1941, Bob Acklen was the son of Robert L. and Aimee Amelie Marie Lips Acklen. His father was an insurance executive and his mother was of Dutch descent, born on a coffee plantation in the Dutch East Indies. His parents met while students at the University of Toronto. After living in Tennessee, Louisiana, and New York, the family moved to Dallas, Texas, in 1956.

Acklen attended Thomas Jefferson High School there and graduated in 1959. He participated in many school activities such as the Latin Club and the Chess Club. His participation in the ROTC program included the military chorus, drill team, and rifle team. He was also a member of the wrestling team and played on the freshman football team.

Enlisting in the Army Reserve in May 1958, Acklen was assigned to the 355th Engineer Battalion in Dallas and attended basic training at Fort Leonard Wood from July to September 1958. He went to the US Army Engineer Center at Fort Belvoir, Virginia, where he completed training on December 16, 1959, then returned to Dallas to join his reserve unit. After admission to Texas A&M, he continued his reserve service with units in the Bryan area.[1]

Acklen enrolled in Texas A&M in the spring semester of 1960 and was assigned to Company A-2 in the Corps of Cadets. The five-foot-eight-inch, 145-pound freshman selected civil engineering as his course of study. He changed his major to history in the spring semester of 1962 but the following spring changed it to mathematics. During his time in the corps, Acklen participated in many activities. As a freshman he was a member of the Fish Drill Team and was the freshman intramural wrestling champion. The next year he was the company's guidon bearer and was selected as the best-drilled sophomore in Company A-2. He served as an officer in several student organizations and was a member of the university wrestling team and the varsity rifle team. During his senior year, Acklen was the assistant editor of the yearbook, *Aggieland 1963*, and was president of the Alpha Phi Omega service fraternity.[2]

Acklen left school after his senior year and enrolled at Arizona State University in Tempe, Arizona, for the fall semester 1964. While there he continued his involvement in student activities, including the student senate and as a member of Sigma Chi fraternity. He was also a member of the Blue Key Honor Society and was selected for Who's Who. Acklen told his close friend Bill Harrison that he wanted to return to Texas A&M to get his degree and military commission. After completing four semesters at Arizona State majoring in history, he was readmitted to Texas A&M in the fall of 1966, receiving his bachelor of arts degree in history on May 27, 1967. Having completed his degree and the ROTC program, he was commissioned a second lieutenant in the US Army on June 27.[3]

Acklen's UH-1C gunship in Vietnam.
Courtesy Carolyn Bender

Called to active duty, he was assigned to the Infantry School, Fort Benning, Georgia, to attend the nine-week infantry-officer basic course. Afterward he volunteered for flight training and was sent to the US Army Primary Helicopter School at Fort Wolters, Texas, for the sixteen-week officer rotary-wing aviation course. Fort Wolters, located near Mineral Wells, was an infantry training center that was deactivated after World War II. After reactivation in 1951, its mission shifted in 1956 to training thousands of army personnel as well as pilots for helicopter operations with the Marine Corps and air force. The next phase of Acklen's training encompassed sixteen weeks at the US Army Aviation School at Fort Rucker, Alabama. Upon completion of flight training, he was awarded his army-aviator wings on August 27, 1968. Acklen received orders for Vietnam and arrived in country on October 6.[4]

His first assignment was with the 189th Assault Helicopter Company, a part of the 52nd Combat Aviation Battalion, 17th Aviation Group, 1st Aviation Brigade, located at Pleiku in the Central Highlands (see map 11). The company was organized into two lift platoons flying the Bell UH-1H (troop and cargo carrier) and a gun platoon flying the Bell UH-1C (gunship.) The UH-1H carried a pilot, copilot, crew chief/gunner, and a gunner. It was armed with two 7.62-mm door-mounted machine guns and could carry ten passengers. The UH-1C was smaller than the H model but had the same crew configuration. The armament subsystem consisted of a nose-mounted M-75 automatic grenade launcher or two to four packages of 2.75-inch (70-mm) folding-fin aircraft rockets and two door-mounted 7.62-mm machine guns.[5]

Acklen did not have to wait long to get into action. On the night of October 15, he was flying a gunship on a mission to cover the extraction of an Army of Vietnam (ARVN) unit when he came under heavy fire from a bunker. He attacked and destroyed the enemy position, permitting the extraction helicopters to land and pick up the ARVN forces.[6]

When an O-1 fixed-wing aircraft was shot down in a landing zone west of Duc Co, Acklen flew to the area to locate and rescue the crew. He spotted the wreckage and the two injured men on the ground. While flying through intense hostile fire, he directed the door gunners to fire into the enemy positions, located within a hundred yards of the downed aircraft. Acklen hovered over the landing zone and saw that the injured crewmen were unable to board unassisted. He jumped to the ground and helped load them himself.[7]

On January 15, 1969, "Acklen was on a resupply mission to a detachment of the 5th Special Forces Group at Mang Buk. He notified the detachment that he was having a difficult time locating their compound due to poor visibility and unfamiliarity with the area. His contact then informed him that two ARVN soldiers had just been seriously wounded on a patrol and needed emergency medical evacuation. Realizing the seriousness of the situation, Acklen elected to fly to the area and pick up the wounded soldiers. Completely disregarding his own personal safety and knowing that no gun cover or chase ship would be available, he headed for the patrol's location as visibility steadily became worse. When he arrived on site and began to descend into the pickup zone, he did so through small-arms and automatic-weapons fire. Due to the thick underbrush and fallen trees on the jungle floor, he was unable to land and forced to hover the helicopter for twenty minutes. The ARVN troops were directed to the ship and the wounded soldiers loaded aboard. Acklen managed to reach the compound at Mang Buk before fog closed in. There the wounded soldiers received medical treatment that saved their lives.[8]

When the weather closed in making it impossible to fly back to his unit, Acklen decided to put his helicopter inside the compound rather than leave it on the runway. That night the camp endured incoming mortar rounds and small-arms fire. He ran to his ship to detach one of its M-60 machine guns and then moved to the perimeter to help defend the compound. When one enemy soldier crawled to the main gate and heaved a satchel charge near his helicopter, Acklen crossed the open compound, picked up the charge, and hurled it back over the wall; it exploded on the runway, causing no damage. Had it not been for his personal courage, his aircraft might have been destroyed and several men wounded or killed."[9]

In February 1969 Acklen was transferred to the 52nd Combat Aviation Battalion to serve on the staff as an assistant operations officer. After a little over a month, though, he was reassigned to the 57th Assault Helicopter Company in Kontum. The 57th provided support to the Military Assistance Command Vietnam Studies and Observation Group in their mission to send reconnaissance teams into Laos and Cambodia to locate and interdict North Vietnamese Army (NVA) infiltration routes and their sources of supply. The teams were inserted by helicopter and, if detected, were extracted, often under enemy fire. Because of the dense jungle canopy, extraction was often made by lowering a rope with harnesses to which team members would attach themselves. With the men dangling from the rope, the helicopter would fly to the nearest forward operating base in Vietnam.[10]

Two days after his promotion to captain on July 9, 1969, "the enemy began launching 122-mm rockets into the battalion's compound. Acklen and another officer gathered their gear and ran toward the gunship revetments more than 150 yards away. Although repeatedly exposed to hostile fire and exploding rockets, they continued across the open compound and reached their helicopter, which they immediately prepared for takeoff. Once in the air they began to place accurate and effective rocket fire on the enemy launching sites, resulting in at least one secondary explosion. Their courage and determination were instrumental in stopping the enemy attack and causing the enemy to retreat."[11]

The Kontum compound came under rocket attack again on July 31. Acklen again ran from his bunker toward the gunship revetments while exposed to small-arms fire and flying shrapnel. He took up his helicopter and again placed devastating fire on the launch sites. The enemy ceased firing and, by the time he had expended his ordnance, had retreated from the area.[12]

Extending for a second tour in Vietnam, Acklen requested assignment to an infantry unit and was sent to the 3rd Battalion (Airborne),

Capt. Robert L. Acklen Jr. *Courtesy Carolyn Bender*

506th Infantry Regiment, 101st Airborne Division. He reported in December 1969 and was assigned as commander of Company B. The battalion was under operational control of the 173rd Airborne Brigade, located at LZ English near Bong Son. Its area of operation was in Binh Dinh Province, where the troops conducted search-and-destroy missions in the Bong Son, An Khe, and Cheo Reo areas. In March 1970 Acklen was transferred to Company C of the 3rd Battalion.

On April 19 he set up his company in an ambush position and as an enemy force approached, he directed the fire of his men on the hostiles. Under intense fire, he assaulted the enemy position with grenades and automatic fire and was credited with routing the enemy without his company sustaining any casualties.[13] On a reconnaissance patrol near An Khe on May 2, 1970, Acklen observed some fresh footprints leading to a cave. Leaving the majority of his company to secure the area, he investigated the cave. Detecting two enemy soldiers behind some rocks, Acklen captured them and led them to the outside. Returning to investigate a noise, he encountered two more soldiers and, after a brief struggle, forced them to surrender.[14]

For the previous five years of the war, US and South Vietnamese forces, because of political restraints, had tolerated the enemy's sanctuary in Cambodia. Pres. Lyndon B. Johnson had never felt emboldened enough to approve the repeated requests of Gen. William C. Westmoreland (commander, US Military Assistance Command Vietnam, 1964–68) for full-scale military operations in Cambodia. Prince Norodom Sihanouk, premier of Cambodia, had turned a blind eye to the Vietcong and NVA base camps and supply dumps in his country, while the North Vietnamese claimed that they had no forces there. Following the coup by Lon Nol overthrowing the Sihanouk government, Pres. Richard Nixon gave permission to Westmoreland's replacement, Gen. Creighton W. Abrams, to conduct ground operations in the sanctuary areas inside Cambodia. Nixon had previously authorized secret bombings to "quarantine" these sites.

The offensive was launched from three military regions (MR-2, MR-3, and MR-4). The high-water mark had 29,000 South Vietnamese troops and 19,300 US troops operating inside Cambodia, and the results were impressive. One significant cache yielded 1,300 individual weapons and more than 200 crew-served weapons along with 1.5 million rounds of AK-47 ammunition. Also seized from another site were 329 tons of ammunition and 700 tons of rice. The incursion was an intelligence bonanza. More than a million pages and thirty-two cases of cryptographic material were captured. "The casualties inflicted on the enemy, 11,349 killed and 2,328 captured or rallied, were almost incidental to the logistical accomplishment." President Nixon had limited US forces to a depth of thirty kilometers (18 miles) across the border. He also set June 30 as the date for all US forces to be out of Cambodia.[15] The operations from MR-2 were conducted by the 4th Infantry Division.

The 3rd Battalion, 506th Airborne Infantry, was placed under operation control to the 1st Brigade, 4th Infantry Division on April 30,

Acklen leads his rifle company on a sweep of an enemy base camp in Cambodia. *Courtesy Carolyn Bender*

1970. On May 2 the battalion was in the field south of Highway 19 and southwest of An Khe when they received a warning order to cease operations and prepare for a major strike in another area. This came as a surprise since they had encountered an enemy patrol the day before and had discovered an enemy rest area. The companies were picked up by helicopter and moved to Camp Radcliff, where the men had a chance to shower and have some hot meals. Replacements were assigned to companies, and the troops performed maintenance on their weapons and equipment. Rumors about the new operation circulated among them. News of the April 30 ARVN attack in an area of Cambodia known as the Parrot's Beak, which was followed by word that on May 1 US troops had begun operations in a region farther north known as the Fish Hook.

On May 3 the battalion departed Camp Radcliff for Pleiku, moving by convoy on Highway 19 through the Man Yang Pass. As night fell, the column continued moving and drove with black-out lights. After one of the vehicles went off a decrepit narrow bridge, the convoy commander

Acklen displays a captured Vietcong flag in Cambodia.
Courtesy Carolyn Bender

decided to stop for the night. The trucks pulled into an abandoned ARVN airstrip and used the vehicles to form a defensive perimeter. The convoy reached Camp Holloway near Pleiku the following day. Brigade operations orders designated the 506th as the assault force for the division, which would be the first unit to land in Cambodia.

The battalion boarded sixty helicopters on the fifth for the move to the objective area in Cambodia. Approaching the designated landing zone, heavy incoming fire forced the combat assault to be aborted. The second-choice landing site also offered stiff enemy resistance. By now the transport helicopters were running low on fuel and the gunships were short on ammunition and rockets, so the insertion was abandoned and the force flew back to Vietnam. After refueling and rearming at New Plei Djereng, the helicopters took to the air and again headed west to Cambodia. After attempting to land the battalion at two other alternate sites, the gunships began to pepper the perimeter of a third landing zone. One company disembarked and secured the area, setting up a defensive perimeter to safeguard the landing site for the rest of the battalion. Acklen's company was on the ground by the early afternoon and immediately headed east in search of enemy troops and weapons caches. After moving about a mile they stopped to establish a nighttime defensive perimeter.[16]

On May 6 a reconnaissance patrol made contact with a hostile force. One soldier was seriously wounded and required an emergency medical extraction. After radioing for a helicopter, Acklen moved to the landing area to direct the pilot. Reaching the aircraft with the injured soldier, he came under intense rocket and small-arms fire but remained in the open area until the man was safely aboard. When the evacuation was completed, Acklen took cover and returned fire, calling for and directing artillery fire that routed the enemy.[17]

"On May 12 Company C was conducting a reconnaissance-in-force mission in the Se San River valley when it came upon a hostile village. Moving forward cautiously, Acklen spotted an enemy soldier, shouted a warning to his men, and fired at the adversary. With disregard for his personal safety, he repeatedly exposed himself to position his company properly. The captain then assaulted the closest hut, forcing its occupants to flee. Following his example, the company swept across the village, and the enemy retreated from the area."[18]

That afternoon Company C discovered the "mother lode" of enemy weapons caches for the Northern Cambodian Incursion. As the troops began to search the abandoned village, they discovered that the site was a huge, well-developed rear area for NVA soldiers, covering at least several hundred square yards. It was almost dark, and a complete search could not be made. Because of the significance of the discovery, continuous artillery support was available throughout the night. A search of the area the next day netted more than 500 tons of rice and more than 800 individual weapons. The troops cleared a landing zone about a thousand yards from the village and hauled the captured weapons there to be flown to Vietnam. What rice could not be removed was destroyed in place. Engineers placed timed explosive devices in and around the huge pile of munitions and, once the troops had departed, a tremendous explosion rocked the area.[19]

On May 15 Acklen was wounded in action, earning him a Purple Heart. After being treated, he returned to his company. The operation was completed on May 16 and the American troops extracted from Cambodia; ARVN forces remained in the vicinity of the cache sites discovered earlier. The 3rd Battalion, 506th Infantry, and 3rd Battalion, 8th Infantry, established fire bases on the Vietnamese side of the border from which they could provide support bombardments for the ARVN troops.[20] On May 19 Acklen's battalion was shifted from the 4th Infantry Division to I Field Force Vietnam. It moved to Ban Me Thuot and began operations in the vicinity.

Acklen extended for a third tour in Vietnam and requested an aviation assignment. On October 4, 1970, he reported to the 2nd Squadron, 17th Cavalry, 101st Airborne Division (Airmobile), at Camp Eagle near Phu Bai and was assigned to B Troop as a Bell AH-1G Cobra pilot. The squadron was organized with a troop headquarters (one UH-1H), flight-operations detachment, aero-scout platoon (ten OH-6A), aero-rifle platoon (five AH-1H), weapons platoon (nine AH-1G), and service platoon (two UH-1H).[21]

The AH-1G Cobra (Huey Cobra) was a two-seat attack helicopter armed with a three-barrel 20-mm cannon mounted under the nose and 2.75-inch Zuni air-to-ground rocket launchers. The crew consisted of a pilot in command in the rear seat and a gunner (who was also a pilot) in front. On most missions the Cobra worked as part of a two-ship team with a scout helicopter, the Hughes OH-6A Cayuse, also called the Loach (from the army's term "LOH" for light-observation helicopter).[22]

"While conducting an aerial reconnaissance in the A Shau Valley, an area of known enemy concentration, a Loach came under hostile fire from several enemy ground emplacements. Acklen immediately delivered accurate and effective suppressive fire, allowing the observation helicopter to withdraw. As the pilot of the Loach was attempting to make a damage assessment, he was wounded. Acklen returned to the area and provided additional covering fire so the wounded pilot could withdraw.

The following day, November 16, a ranger team radioed for an immediate extraction. Acklen responded and flew his Cobra into the contact area. Because of poor visibility, he was able to use only his turret gun to provide suppressive support. When the rescue helicopter came under hostile fire, Acklen moved his aircraft between the enemy position and the evacuation ship to draw enemy fire, allowing the successful extraction of the ranger team."[23]

On the seventeenth Acklen flew a support mission near Hue, despite extremely poor weather conditions, to aid beleaguered troops on the ground. Again providing accurate suppression fire on the enemy position, he enabled a much needed resupply helicopter to land. Acklen then provided cover for the departure of the supply ship.[24]

"While serving as copilot and gunner on an AH-1G armed helicopter during the extraction of a small reconnaissance team under attack by an unknown-size enemy force in Thua Thien Province, he volunteered to provide covering fire for the extraction. He piloted his aircraft through adverse weather conditions to the site and placed accurate suppressive fire on enemy positions surrounding the team so lift helicopters could make the extraction. Throughout the operation, he informed his aircraft commander of their exact position in relation to the dangerous terrain. Although it was now night and raining, his aircraft managed to return to base camp by use of instruments only."[25]

In April 1971 Acklen was transferred to the 52nd Combat Aviation Battalion at Pleiku Air Base, where he was involved in training South Vietnamese Air Force pilots. On May 8 his helicopter crashed while on a training mission near Cheo Reo, and he was seriously injured. Acklen was flown by a medical-evacuation helicopter to the army hospital in Qui Nhon. From there, he was sent to the US Air Force hospital at Clark Air Base in the Philippines. On June 16, 1971, the captain was evacuated to Brooke General Hospital in San Antonio, Texas. Told that he would probably never walk again, Acklen began a long period of medical treatment and physical therapy, using his spare time in the hospital to take correspondence courses at the University of Texas in Austin. Using credits from Texas A&M and Arizona State in combination with his credits at the University of Texas, Acklen was awarded a bachelor of business administration degree.

After twenty-two months at Brooke, he was released in March 1973 and returned to active duty. Sent to Fort Benning, Georgia, Acklen attended the thirty-six-week Infantry Officer Advance Course. Following graduation, he volunteered to attend the eight-week Ranger Course and was an honor graduate of the difficult and rigorous school. Ordered to Korea, he was assigned as commander of Company A, 1st Battalion, 9th Infantry Regiment, 2nd Infantry Division. After five months of command duty, the captain was transferred to battalion headquarters, where he served as the S-3 Air. He then had a short assignment as a rotary-wing aviator in the 2nd Aviation Battalion. Experiencing medical problems, Acklen returned to the States and was admitted as a patient at Darnall Army Hospital at Fort Hood, Texas. On

April 30, 1976, he was medically retired from the army with 70-percent disability.

Acklen had married Kathleen P. McDowell of San Antonio on December 23, 1973. When he returned from his tour in Korea, she presented him with divorce papers. On September 2, 1975, their divorce was granted.[26]

Once back in civilian life, Acklen became a commercial helicopter pilot and a private investigator. He attended the University of North Texas in Denton and earned a computer-science degree. Afterward, he taught a computer-science course at the university and wrote software programs for private companies. Remembering his service with the 506th Infantry, Acklen was a cofounder of the 506th Infantry Association and was active in reunions of the organization. He also produced a newsletter for the 101st Airborne Division Association. Other veteran organizations to which he belonged were the Vietnam Helicopter Pilots Association, Special Operations Association, Special Forces Association, US Army Ranger Association, Disabled American Veterans, and Veterans of Foreign Wars.

On a trip to Israel with a church group, he visited St. Johns Hospital in Jerusalem, which specialized in ophthalmology. During the visit, Acklen analyzed their computer needs and later made several trips to Israel, at his own expense, to provide assistance for their software. As a result of his humanitarian work, he was awarded the Order of Saints Maurice and Lazarus, an order of chivalry, by the House of Savoy. At the time of his death, Acklen was in the process of being nominated to become the only American ever presented the Special Gold Medal of the Royal House of Savoy. In November 1980 he went to New York City to participate in investiture ceremonies in which he was awarded the Most Venerable Order of the Hospital of St. John of Jerusalem for his support of the hospital. The honor was sanctioned by Queen Elizabeth II of England, the sovereign head of the order.

Acklen was active in several patriotic, scholarly, and civic organizations. He was a member of the prestigious Society of the Cincinnati, the nation's oldest patriotic organization, founded in 1783 by officers of the Continental Army. Membership is limited to male descendants of officers of the Continental Army or Navy. Other organizations he joined were the Sons of Confederate Veterans, Baronial Order of the Magna Charter, National Society Sons and Daughters of the Pilgrims, Hugue-

Acklen was active in charitable organizations after his medical discharge. *Courtesy Carolyn Bender*

not Society of the Founders of Manakin in the Colony of Virginia, Sons of the American Revolution, Lions Club, and Jaycees.[27]

Acklen was inducted into the Texas A&M University Corps of Cadets Hall of Honor in 2000. He was awarded the Distinguished Alumnus Award by the Texas A&M Association of Former Students in 2010.

Capt. Robert L. Acklen's decorations include the Silver Star, Distinguished Flying Cross, six Bronze Stars (four for Valor), thirty-nine Air Medals (four for Valor), Purple Heart, and four Army Commendation Medals (three for Valor). The Republic of Vietnam awarded him the Cross of Gallantry with Gold Star, Cross of Gallantry with Silver Star,

Armed Forces Honor Medal First Class, Staff Service Honor Medal First Class, and Technical Service Honor Medal First Class.[28]

Acklen died of a brain tumor at the Veterans Administration Medical Center in Dallas, Texas, on December 31, 1998. A memorial service was held at Park Cities Presbyterian Church. He was buried with military honors at Mount Olivet Cemetery in his hometown of Nashville, Tennessee.[29]

★ APPENDIX 1 ★

Citations

This appendix contains the medal citations, where available, for the twelve men featured in this book. The citations shown herein are for the Distinguished Service Cross, Navy Cross, Silver Star, and the Distinguished Flying Cross.

Following are the official qualifications for the award of each of these awards as stated by the Department of Defense and the US Air Force Personnel Center:

The **Distinguished Service Cross** is the second-highest military decoration that can be awarded to a member of the United States Army (and previously, the United States Army Air Forces). It is awarded for extraordinary heroism:

- While engaged in action against an enemy of the United States;
- While engaged in military operations involving conflict with an opposing foreign force; or
- While serving with friendly foreign forces engaged in an armed conflict against an opposing armed force in which the United States is not a belligerent party.

Actions that merit the Distinguished Service Cross must be of such a high degree that they are above those required for all other U.S. combat decorations but do not merit award of the Medal of Honor.

The **Navy Cross** is the second-highest military decoration that may be awarded to members of the United States Navy, U.S. Marine Corps, and to members of the Coast Guard when operating under the authority of the Department of the Navy. It is awarded for extraordinary heroism:

- While engaged in action against an enemy of the United States;
- While engaged in military operations involving conflict with an opposing foreign force; or
- While serving with friendly foreign forces engaged in an armed conflict against an opposing armed force in which the United States is not a belligerent party.

Actions that merit the Navy Cross must be of such a high degree that they are above those required for all other U.S. combat decorations that do not merit award of the Medal of Honor.

The **Silver Star** is the third-highest military combat decoration that can be awarded to a member of the United States Armed Forces. It is awarded for gallantry in action:

- While engaged in action against an enemy of the United States;
- While engaged in military operations involving conflict with an opposing foreign force; or
- While serving with friendly foreign forces engaged in an armed conflict against an opposing armed force in which the United States is not a belligerent party.

Actions that merit the Silver Star must be of such a high degree that they are above those required for all other U.S. combat decorations but do not merit award of the Medal of Honor or a Service Cross (Distinguished Service Cross, the Navy Cross, or the Air Force Cross).

The **Distinguished Flying Cross** is awarded to any officer or enlisted person of the Armed Forces of the United States who shall have distinguished her/himself in actual combat in support of operations by heroism or extraordinary achievement while participating in aerial flight, subsequent to November 11, 1918.

GEORGE F. MOORE

Harbor Defenses at Manila and Subic Bays

Distinguished Service Cross

Citation

The President of the United States of America, authorized by Act of Congress, July 9, 1918, takes pleasure in presenting the Distinguished Service Cross to Major General George F. Moore (ASN: 0–2677), United States Army, for extraordinary heroism in connection with military operations against an armed enemy while in charge of the Harbor Defenses at Manila and Subic Bays, Philippine Islands, during the months of March and April 1942. Major General Moore displayed great gallantry in continually visiting the most exposed elements in his command and repeatedly passed from one echelon to another during sustained hostile attacks, giving encouragement, directing operations, and by his courage and example inspiring the heroic efforts of his command. The splendid efficiency and dogged determination of this garrison was largely based on his efficiency, tenacity, and individual courage. Major General Moore's intrepid actions, personal bravery, and zealous devotion to duty exemplify the highest traditions of the military forces of the United States and reflect great credit upon himself and the United States Army.

ANDREW D. BRUCE
Major, 4th Machine Gun Battalion
Distinguished Service Cross
Citation

For extraordinary heroism in action near Vierzy, France, July 17–18, 1918, and near Blanc Mont, October 3–4, 1918. On the night of July 17–18, he made a personal reconnaissance ahead of his troops through heavy flanking machine-gun fire. He pushed forward to the outpost lines through heavy artillery and machine-gun fire to keep in touch with all [of] his platoons. On October 3–5, he made a personal reconnaissance on the left flank of his division through heavy shell fire and continual sniping, and gained information which enabled him to well place the battalion and cover an exposed flank.

JOHN A. HILGER
307th Bombardment Group
Silver Star
Citation

The President of the United States of America, authorized by Act of Congress, July 2, 1926, takes pleasure in presenting the Silver Star to Colonel John Allen Hilger, (ASN: 0–20437), United States Air Force, for gallantry in action near Sinuiju, Korea, on 8 November 1950. Serving as Commanding Officer of the 307th Bombardment Group, FIFTH Air Force, Colonel Hilger led an aerial attack against that strategically important enemy stronghold and temporary capitol of North Korea. Due to Sinuiju's extreme importance as a supply and communications center, the enemy was expected to defend it with all resources at his disposal. Because of its location only 666 yards across the Yalu River from [the] Manchurian city of An-Tung, it was considered highly probable that Colonel Hilger's group would be attacked by anti-aircraft fire from both sides of the river and conventional and jet fighter aircraft from the Manchurian side of the international boundary. In order to assure destruction of this vital enemy installation, as well as prevent international consequences which could arise from American aircraft passing over or bombs landing on Manchuria, Colonel Hilger personally led his group. His skillful technique assured maximum destruction of the target area and his courage served as an inspiration to the personnel of the group. The leadership and gallantry displayed by Colonel Hilger on this mission are in keeping with the highest traditions of the military service and reflect great credit upon himself and the United States Air Force.

JOHN A. HILGER
1st Special Aviation Project
Distinguished Flying Cross
Citation

The President of the United States of America, authorized by Act of Congress, July 2, 1928, takes pleasure in presenting the Distinguished Flying Cross to Lieutenant Colonel (Air Corps) John Allen Hilger (ASN: 0–20437), United States Army Air Forces, for extraordinary achievement as Pilot of a B-25 Bomber of the 1st Special Aviation Project (Doolittle Raider Force) while participating in a highly destructive raid on the Japanese mainline on 18 April 1942. Lieutenant Colonel Hilger with 79 other officers and enlisted men volunteered for this mission knowing full well that the chances of survival were extremely remote, and executed his part in it with great skill and daring. This achievement reflects high credit on himself and the military service.

JAMES E. RUDDER
2nd Ranger Infantry Battalion
Distinguished Service Cross
Citation

The President of the United States of America, authorized by Act of Congress, July 9, 1918, takes pleasure in presenting the Distinguished Service Cross to Lieutenant Colonel (Infantry) James Earl Rudder (ASN: 0–294916), United States Army, for extraordinary heroism in connection with military operations against an armed enemy while serving with the 2d Ranger Infantry Battalion, in action against enemy forces of 6 June 1944, at Normandy, France. Lieutenant Colonel Rudder, commanding Force "A" of the Rangers, landed on the beach with his unit which was immediately subjected to heavy rifle, machine gun, mortar, and artillery fire. Devastating fire was also directed from the cliffs overlooking the beach. Completely disregarding his own safety, Lieutenant Colonel Rudder immediately scaled the cliffs in order to better direct the attack. By his determined leadership and dauntlessness he inspired his men so that they successfully withstood three enemy counterattacks. Though wounded again he still refused to be evacuated. Lieutenant Colonel Rudder's heroic leadership, personal bravery, and zealous devotion to duty exemplify the highest traditions of the military forces of the United States and reflect great credit upon himself and the United States Army.

JAMES E. RUDDER
109th Infantry Regiment
Silver Star
Citation

The President of the United States of America, authorized by Act of Congress, July 9, 1918, takes pleasure in presenting the Silver Star Medal to Lieutenant Colonel (Infantry) James Earl Rudder (ASN: 0–294916), United States Army, for gallantry in action while Commanding the 109th Infantry Regiment, 28th Infantry Division, in action against the enemy from 16 to 27 December 1944, in Germany. Lieutenant Colonel Rudder's regiment was attacked by vastly superior numbers of enemy forces on extended positions held in the vicinity of Bastendorf, Vianden, and Brandenburg, Germany. Lieutenant Colonel Rudder, as Regimental Commander, quickly estimated the difficult situation at the beginning of the attack. Through the skillful handling of his troops he was able to direct numerous counter-thrusts against the forceful attacking enemy. At great personal risk to himself, Lieutenant Colonel Rudder also made frequent trips to subordinate units, through enemy-infiltrated territory and under heavy enemy artillery fire. After assigning new and more advantageous defensive positions to his Combat Team, Lieutenant Colonel Rudder directed, during heavy enemy shelling, the destruction of bridges in the path of the enemy after his troops had passed over them. His outstanding tactical ability permitted his Regiment to inflict high casualties on the enemy with a minimum loss to his own troops. During this action, he is also credited with stopping an enemy offensive that threatened a large area to the south and west of his defensive positions. By his gallant and skillful leadership, Lieutenant Colonel Rudder reflects great credit upon himself and [the] Armed Forces of the United States.

DAVID L. HILL
75th Fighter Squadron
Distinguished Service Cross
Citation

The President of the United States of America, authorized by Act of Congress, July 9, 1918, takes pleasure in presenting the Distinguished Service Cross to Major (Air Corps) David Lee "Tex" Hill (ASN 0–889015), United States Army Air Forces, for extraordinary heroism in connection with military operations against an armed enemy while serving as Pilot of a P-40 Fighter Airplane in the 75th Fighter Squadron, 23d Fighter Group, TENTH Air Force, in aerial combat against enemy forces on 25 October, 1942, while performing bomber escort duty over enemy-held territory in the China Theatre. On this date, Major Hill attacked, without hesitation, superior numbers of enemy aircraft that were rising to intercept United States B-24 bombers. Without hesitation, he turned his aircraft on its back for a high-speed dive and placed his aircraft between enemy fighters and the B-24 bombers. With exceptional flying ability, Major Hill forced enemy aircraft to turn from the attack and dive away. With skillful marksmanship, he destroyed one aircraft and severely damaged three others resulting in their probable destruction. Major Hill's leadership, spirit, and extraordinary heroism in action against enemy forces in carrying the attack to the enemy without thought of the odds against himself were an inspiration to all fighter pilots. By his intrepid direction, heroic leadership, and superior professional ability, Major Hill set an inspiring example to his fellow aviators. Major Hill's extraordinary heroism and zealous devotion to duty were in keeping with the highest traditions of the military service and reflect great credit upon himself, the Tenth Air Force, and the United States Army Air Forces.

DAVID L. HILL
23rd Fighter Squadron
Silver Star
Citation

On October 25, 1942, in a daylight escorting flight far over enemy-held territory, this officer attacked, without hesitation, superior numbers of enemy planes that were rising to intercept our bombers. With exceptional flying ability, he forced enemy planes to turn from the attack and dive away, and with skillful marksmanship destroyed one plane, with probable damage to three others. Major Hill's leadership, offensive spirit, and gallantry in action in carrying the attack to the enemy without thought of the odds against himself, is an inspiration to all fighter pilots.

DAVID L. HILL
American Volunteer Group
Distinguished Flying Cross
Citation

David Lee Hill distinguished himself by extraordinary achievement while participating in aerial flight in the South China and Southeast Asia theater, from 7 December 1941 to 18 July 1942. The American Volunteer Group, the Flying Tigers, compiled an unparalleled combat record under extremely hazardous conditions. This volunteer unit conducted aggressive counter-air, air defense, and close air support operations against a numerically superior enemy force occasionally 20 times larger. Members of the All Volunteer Group destroyed some 650 enemy aircraft while suffering minimal losses. Their extraordinary performance in the face of seemingly overwhelming odds was a major factor in defeating the enemy's invasion of South China. The professional competence, aerial skill, and devotion to duty displayed by David Lee Hill reflect great credit upon himself and the Armed Forces of the United States.

DAVID L. HILL
23rd Fighter Group
Distinguished Flying Cross (Oak Leaf Cluster)
Citation

Colonel Hill (then Lieutenant Colonel) demonstrated outstanding achievement in aerial flight on November 25, 1943, while participating in the first attack by American air units on the Island of Formosa. In this mission he led a flight of single-engine planes which were to cover the rear of the formation from attacks by enemy fighters. After flying over the open waters of the Formosa Straits, he brought his planes directly into the target area which had been alerted by the preceding flights. His fighters strafed the air base at a low altitude causing considerable damage and disrupting thoroughly enemy defenses. By the application of sound tactical principles, his squadron prevented interception attacks by enemy fighters on other flights of the formation participating in the mission. He personally shot down one enemy plane in the air and destroyed one on the ground in addition to one probably destroyed. His alertness and skillful handling of the planes under his command in the target area contributed greatly to the success of this mission in which forty-six enemy aircraft were destroyed as against no American losses. Colonel Hill distinguished himself by displaying excellent leadership and in striking the first telling blow on the Island of Formosa brought credit to his own record as well as that of the Army Air Forces.

OLIN E. TEAGUE
3rd Battalion, 314th Infantry Regiment
Silver Star
Citation

For gallantry in action as battalion commander in France. On 24 June 1944 Lieutenant Colonel TEAGUE made a personal reconnaissance of his battalion's objective, which took him deep into the enemy's lines. Next morning (24 June 1944) under heavy enemy artillery, mortar, and automatic weapons fire, he personally led his battalion against the objective. When some of the men faltered, Lieutenant Colonel TEAGUE coolly and courageously exposed himself to enemy fire and urged them to follow him forward. He was wounded slightly in the action, but the battalion objective was accomplished. On 3 July 1944 the battalion was advancing through heavy enemy machine gun and mortar fire when Lieutenant Colonel TEAGUE was wounded in the back. Because the operation was at a crucial phase, he disdained medical attention until the objective had been taken. Success of the action was due in large part to his display of heroic leadership and coolness under fire. His conduct in both of these actions reflect highest credit on himself and the military forces of the United States.

OLIN E. TEAGUE
3rd Battalion, 314th Infantry Regiment
Silver Star (Oak Leaf Cluster)
Citation

Pursuant to authority contained in AR 600–45, in addition to the Silver Star previously awarded, the Oak-Leaf Cluster is awarded to the following named officer: Lieutenant Colonel OLIN E. TEAGUE, 0294931, Infantry, United States Army, for gallantry in action against the enemy on 8 July 1944 in France. After requesting tanks for use in an assault on a stubbornly defended and strongly emplaced series of enemy strongpoints, Lieutenant Colonel TEAGUE proceeded to the foremost elements of his command to reconnoiter the most effective route of attack for the tanks. He accomplished this at great personal risk, being constantly exposed to enemy small arms, machine guns, and artillery fire. He remained with the most advanced elements throughout the action and his presence so inspired the men that in spite of numerous casualties and exceptionally intense enemy fire, the objective was achieved and a highly strategic position gained and held. For his gallantry and indomitable spirit of leadership at a critical time, Lieutenant Colonel TEAGUE reflects highest credit on himself and the armed forces of the United States.

OLIN E. TEAGUE
3rd Battalion, 314th Infantry Regiment
Silver Star (Second Oak Leaf Cluster)
Citation

For gallantry in action against the enemy on 13 December 1944 in France. In preparation for an attack by his unit, Lieutenant Colonel Teague, battalion commander, made a personal reconnaissance deep into enemy territory and then, although the battalion sector was under enemy artillery and mortar fire, returned to lead both assault companies and each supporting tank destroyer into position. Feeling that the battalion observation post did not offer adequate observation of the entire sector, Lieutenant Colonel Teague was making his way forward when he was caught in a heavy enemy artillery concentration and severely wounded; and as he crawled from the area he suffered two additional wounds. Although suffering intense pain by the time aid reached him, he disdained evacuation until he had left detailed instructions for the continuance of the attack. The great courage, integrity of purpose, and willing self-sacrifice displayed by Lieutenant Colonel Teague in the performance of duty reflect high credit on himself and the armed forces of the United States.

RAYMOND L. MURRAY
2nd Battalion, 6th Marine Regiment
Navy Cross
Citation

The President of the United States of America takes great pleasure in presenting the Navy Cross to Lieutenant Colonel Raymond Leroy Murray (MCSN: 0–5127), United States Marine Corps, for extraordinary heroism as Commanding Officer of the Second Battalion, Sixth Marines, SECOND Marine Division, in action against enemy Japanese forces during the assault on Saipan, Marianas Islands, on 15 June 1944. Although sustaining two severe and painful wounds which necessitated his crawling from place to place during the initial stages of the landing, Lieutenant Colonel Murray refused to be evacuated and continued to direct the operations of his Battalion until his condition became so serious from pain and loss of blood that he was ordered to return aboard ship by the Regimental Commander. By remaining at his post, seriously wounded though he was, during the initial and crucial stages of the assault, Lieutenant Colonel Murray set a fine example for his officers and men and aided materially in overcoming the handicaps resulting from the heavy initial casualties, thereby contributing materially to the success of the operations. His outstanding courage, determination, and devotion to duty were in keeping with the highest traditions of the United States Naval Service.

RAYMOND L. MURRAY
5th Marine Regiment
Distinguished Service Cross
Citation

The President of the United States of America, under the provisions of the Act of Congress approved July 9, 1918, takes pleasure in presenting the Distinguished Service Cross to Lieutenant Colonel Raymond Leroy Murray (MCSN: 0–5127), United States Marine Corps, for extraordinary heroism in connection with military operations against an armed enemy of the United Nations while Commanding the Fifth Marines, FIRST Marine Division (Reinforced), in action against enemy aggressor forces in Korea from 29 November to 4 December 1950. Charged with the tremendous responsibility of taking over the perimeter defense of Hagaru-ri and subsequently pressing the attack to Koto-ri in conjunction with another Marine regiment, (the then) Lieutenant Colonel Murray, with his ranks depleted by casualties and all his officers and men exhausted from several days of fierce fighting in sub-zero temperatures, launched vigorous attacks to the eastward to seize a vital enemy-held ridge and consolidate his positions. Affording protection for the airstrip where approximately one thousand vehicles containing division supplies, ammunition, and equipment were assembled, he remained until all the wounded had been evacuated before directing his regiment in forming a rear guard for the entire column. Throughout the night, he beat off vicious onslaughts continuously by the enemy and, on the following morning, carried out a brilliantly executed counter attack, taking two hundred prisoners and leaving an ineffective and decimated enemy in his wake as he continued on to his destination, arriving that evening with units intact and ready to continue the attack to the south which contributed materially to the successful breakthrough of United Nations Forces in the Chosin Reservoir area and are in keeping with the highest traditions of the military service.

RAYMOND L. MURRAY
5th Marine Regiment
Navy Cross (Gold Star)
Citation

The President of the United States of America takes pleasure in presenting a Gold Star in lieu of a Second Award of the Navy Cross to Lieutenant Colonel Raymond Leroy Murray (USMC: 0–5127), United States Marine Corps, for extraordinary heroism in connection with military operations against an armed enemy of the United Nations while serving as Commanding Officer of the Fifth Marines, FIRST Marine Division (Reinforced), in action against enemy aggressor forces in the Republic of Korea on 6 and 7 December 1950. Charged with the tremendous responsibility of taking over the perimeter defense of Hagaru-ri, and subsequently pressing the attack to Koto-ri in conjunction with another Marine regiment (the then) Lieutenant Colonel Murray, with his ranks depleted by casualties and all his officers and men exhausted from several days of fierce fighting in sub-zero temperatures, launched vigorous attacks to the eastward to seize a vital enemy-held ridge and consolidate his positions. Affording protection for the airstrip where approximately one thousand vehicles containing division supplies, ammunition, and equipment were assembled, he remained until all the wounded had been evacuated before directing his regiment in forming a rear guard for the entire column. Throughout the night, he beat off vicious onslaughts continuously launched by the enemy and, on the following morning, carried out a brilliantly executed counterattack, taking two hundred prisoners and leaving an ineffective and decimated enemy in his wake as he continued on to his destination, arriving that evening with units intact and ready to continue the attack to the south. By his great personal valor, daring combat tactics, and superb leadership throughout this bitter offensive and defensive action, Lieutenant Colonel Murray served as a constant inspiration to his regiment in completing this extremely hazardous mission against tremendous odds, and his courageous devotion to duty reflects the highest credit upon himself, his gallant officers and men, and the United States Naval Service.

RAYMOND L. MURRAY
2nd Battalion, 6th Marine Regiment
Silver Star
Citation

The President of the United States takes pleasure in presenting the Silver Star medal to Major Raymond L. Murray, U.S. Marine Corps for conspicuous gallantry and intrepidity as Commanding Officer of the Second Battalion, Sixth Marines, Reinforced, in action against enemy Japanese forces on Guadalcanal Island, Solomon Islands, January 26, 1943. When his battalion, maneuvering into a position in the vicinity of the Poha River and the Coast Road, suddenly encountered withering fire from an enemy strong point, Major Murray, with inspiring leadership and utter disregard for his own personal safety, directed the hazardous advance of his troops to their post and committed them to action. During the remainder of the day and night he was constantly in the most exposed front lines, despite hostile fire from the trees and concealed foxholes, and, through his splendid courage and excellent tactical skill, his command was responsible for the complete destruction or forced retreat of the enemy. Major Murray's heroic conduct and valiant devotion to duty contributed to the success of this vital mission and were in keeping with the highest traditions of the United States Naval Service.

RAYMOND L. MURRAY
2nd Battalion, 6th Marine Regiment
Silver Star (Gold Star)
Citation

In the name of the President of the United States, the Commander in Chief, United States Pacific Fleet, takes pleasure in presenting the Silver Star to Lieutenant Colonel Raymond L. Murray, United States Marine Corps, for conspicuous gallantry and intrepidity as a Battalion Commander during action against enemy Japanese forces in Tarawa Atoll, Gilbert Islands, during the period of November 24 to 28, 1943. He landed his battalion on a separate island and prevented the enemy from escaping from the eastern end of Betio Island. Later when that island had been secured, he, in spite of strong enemy opposition, led his battalion with great courage and superior skill against the enemy, forcing them to fall back from island to island until they were destroyed in action on the last island, completing the seizure of the Tarawa Atoll. All during this operation he constantly exposed himself to hostile fire, and his cool display of leadership was an inspiration to his men. His conspicuous gallantry, intrepidity, and devotion to duty were in keeping with the highest traditions of the United States Naval Service.

RAYMOND L. MURRAY
5th Marine Regiment
Silver Star Oak Leaf Cluster (Army)
Citation

The President of the United States of America, authorized by Act of Congress July 9, 1918, takes pleasure in presenting a Bronze Oak Leaf Cluster in addition to a previously awarded Gold Star in lieu of a Third Award of the Silver Star (Army Award) to Lieutenant Colonel Raymond Leroy Murray (MCSN: 0–5127), United States Marine Corps, for conspicuous gallantry and intrepidity while commanding the Fifth Marines, FIRST Marine Division (Reinforced), in action against enemy aggressor forces in the amphibious landing resulting in the capture of Inchon, Korea, on 15 September 1950 in the Inchon-Seoul operation. His actions contributed materially to the success of this operation and were in keeping with the highest traditions of the military service.

RAYMOND L. MURRAY
5th Marine Regiment
Silver Star Second Oak Leaf Cluster (Army)
Citation

The President of the United States of America, authorized by Act of Congress July 9, 1918, takes pleasure in presenting a Second Bronze Oak Leaf Cluster in addition to a previously awarded Gold Star in lieu of a Fourth Award of the Silver Star (Army Award) to Lieutenant Colonel Raymond Leroy Murray (MCSN: 0–5127), United States Marine Corps, for conspicuous gallantry and intrepidity in action against an armed enemy of the United Nations in Korea during the period 3 August to 6 September 1950. While serving as Commanding Officer of the Fifth Marine Regiment, FIRST Marine Division (Reinforced), Colonel Murray displayed exceptional ability in directing the operations of his regiment against organized enemy resistance of superior strength. With complete disregard for his own safety, Colonel Murray made numerous visits to forward elements of his assault battalions to obtain first hand information necessary for sound tactical judgment in the employment of his regiment. On 11 August, as the regiment was advancing along the road to Sachon, it was halted by heavy enemy fire directed from well concealed emplacements on high ground overlooking the route of movement. Moving up to the front, constantly exposed to enemy small arms fire, Colonel Murray personally directed the tactical employment of his troops until the situation became stabilized. His cool and positive control of the command, fearless determination, and indomitable courage were an inspirational propellant for his valiantly fighting men and furthered the United Nations campaign for peace. Colonel Murray through his valor and notable proficiency as a combat commander reflects great credit on himself and the military service.

GEORGE H. GAY JR.
Torpedo Squadron 8 (VT-8)
Navy Cross
Citation

The President of the United States of America takes pleasure in presenting the Navy Cross to Ensign George Henry Gay, Jr., United States Naval Reserve, for extraordinary heroism in operations against the enemy while serving as Pilot of a carrier-based Navy Torpedo Plane of Torpedo Squadron EIGHT (VT-8), attached to the U.S.S. HORNET (CV-8), during the "Air Battle of Midway," against enemy Japanese forces on 4 June 1942. Grimly aware of the hazardous consequences of flying without fighter protection, and with insufficient fuel to return to his carrier, Ensign Gay, resolutely and with no thought of his own life, delivered an effective torpedo attack against violent assaults of enemy Japanese aircraft and against an almost solid barrage of anti-aircraft fire. His courageous action, carried out with a gallant spirit of self-sacrifice and a conscientious devotion to the fulfillment of his mission, was a determining factor in the defeat of the enemy forces and was in keeping with the highest traditions of the United States Naval Service.

JAMES F. HOLLINGSWORTH
2nd Battalion, 67th Armored Regiment
Distinguished Service Cross
Citation

The President of the United States of America, authorized by Act of Congress, July 9, 1918, take pleasure in presenting the Distinguished Service Cross to Lieutenant Colonel (Infantry) James Francis Hollingsworth (ASN: 0–34155), United States Army, for extraordinary heroism in connection with military operations against an armed enemy while servicing with Headquarters, 67th Armored Regiment, in action against enemy forces on 11 April 1945, in Germany. Colonel Hollingsworth personally led, in a 1/4 ton truck, a Task Force of tanks and infantry for fourteen hours in a dash of seventy-one miles from Gr. Douren, Germany, to the Elbe River at Schonebeck, Germany. On three occasions during the day he went into towns with small forces mounted in 1/4 ton trucks and by surprise, affected a complete surrender without bloodshed of the German garrisons. When stopped by a road block in Schonebeck, near a bridge, he continued to direct the fight, although he was wounded twice and barely able to walk. Only after the bridge had been blown and all hope for its capture had vanished did he consent to evacuation for his wounds. Colonel Hollingsworth's heroic actions and aggressive leadership were directly responsible for the accomplishments of the Task Force under his command and are in keeping with the highest traditions of the armed forces.

JAMES F. HOLLINGSWORTH

1st Infantry Division

Distinguished Service Cross (Oak Leaf Cluster)

Citation

The President of the United States of America, authorized by Act of Congress, July 9, 1918 (amended by act of July 25, 1963) takes pleasure in presenting a Bronze Oak Leaf Cluster in lieu of a Second Award of the Distinguished Service Cross to Brigadier General James F. Hollingsworth (ASN 0–34155), United States Army, for extraordinary heroism in connection with military operation involving conflict with an armed hostile force in the Republic of Vietnam while serving with Headquarters, 1st Infantry Division. Brigadier General Hollingsworth distinguished himself by exceptional valorous action during the period 5 November 1966 to 8 November 1966 while serving as Assistant Division Commander of the 1st Infantry Division. On 5 November 1966, three Special Forces units attacked what unexpectedly turned out to be a numerically superior Viet Cong force. Within minutes, General Hollingsworth was airborne over the battle area in his command and control helicopter. To gain an accurate knowledge of the fluid ground situation, he had his pilot fly repeated low level passes over the insurgent positions. During these reconnaissance passes, while receiving intense hostile fire, General Hollingsworth formulated stratagems for the maneuver of the ground units, ordered devastating air strikes and artillery barrages on the Viet Cong emplacements, and enabled them to repel the numerically superior Viet Cong force. On 8 November, one of his battalions engaged several Viet Cong Units. Immediately upon arriving at the scene, General Hollingsworth fearlessly moved about the area of conflict issuing directions, maintaining fire discipline, and encouraging the men to fight with renewed efforts. With complete disregard for his personal safety, he continuously exposed himself to the concentrated Viet Cong fire to coordinate all facets of the battle. His masterful and unerring battle strategy accounted for one of the most significant victories in the current conflict. Brigadier General Hollingsworth's extraordinary heroism and inspiring leadership were in keeping with the finest traditions of [the] military service and reflect great credit upon himself, the 1st Infantry Division, and the United States Army.

JAMES F. HOLLINGSWORTH
1st Infantry Division
Distinguished Service Cross (Second Oak Leaf Cluster)
Citation

The President of the United States of America, authorized by Act of Congress, July 9, 1918 (amended by act of July 26, 1963), takes pleasure in presenting a Second Bronze Oak Leaf Cluster in lieu of a Third Award of the Distinguished Service Cross to Brigadier General James F. Hollingsworth (ASN: 0–34155), United States Army, for extraordinary heroism in connection with military operations involving conflict with an armed hostile force in the Republic of Vietnam, while serving with Headquarters, 1st Infantry Division. Brigadier General Hollingsworth distinguished himself by exceptionally valorous actions on 20 March 1967 while serving as Acting Commander, 1st Infantry Division, when the artillery support base at Bau Bang come under intense enemy mortar attack a few hours after midnight. Taking off in his command helicopter, following a briefing on the situation, General Hollingsworth immediately flew to the besieged unit. Despite the devastating ground fire directed at his aircraft, he ordered his pilot to make repeated low level passes over the ravaged area while he dauntlessly reconnoitered it. Realizing that an insurgent ground assault was imminent, General Hollingsworth called for air strikes as he continued to expose himself to the hail of bullets streaking through the darkness. When flare ships illuminated the battlefield, he located the Viet Cong assembly area and ignoring his vulnerable position, guided the support aircraft in their bombing and strafing runs. At 0500 hours, the insurgents began their mass attack. Contemptuous of the grave dangers, General Hollingsworth flew directly over the assaulting force and adjusted artillery fire into the charging Viet Cong. During the entire engagement, he continuously risked his own safety to best coordinate and direct the aggressive defense which finally repulsed the fanatical enemy. Through his boundless courage and tactical ingenuity, he was instrumental in the defeat of the Viet Cong regiment, in which over 250 insurgents were killed. Brigadier General Hollingsworth's extraordinary heroism and devotion to duty were in keeping with the highest traditions of the military service and reflect great credit himself, his unit, and the United States Army.

JAMES F. HOLLINGSWORTH
67th Armored Regiment
Silver Star
Citation

The President of the United States of America, authorized by Act of Congress July 9, 1918, takes pleasure in presenting the Silver Star to Major (Infantry) James Francis Hollingsworth (ASN: 0–34155), United States Army, for conspicuous gallantry and intrepidity while serving with the 67th Armored Regiment, 2d Armored Division, in Normandy, France, on 29 July 1944. On that date, at approximately 0100 hours, the service trains of Combat Command "B" were dispersed in the woods near Notre Dame-de-Centilly, France. There were approximately forty vehicles loaded with gasoline and lubricating oils for the support of combat elements advancing with the attack. These trains were under the command of Major Hollingsworth. The area was subjected to aerial bombardment and one of the gasoline vehicles was set afire, the force of the explosion splashing fuel for some distance around the vehicle. Without regard for his own safety, Major Hollingsworth mounted the cab of three nearby trucks in quick succession and drove them to a safer location away from the burning vehicle. During the period the area was still subjected to aerial bombardment by the enemy. His prompt action at this crucial hour resulted in the saving from destruction of the entire fuel supply for elements in close combat with a retreating enemy. During this action fifteen casualties were sustained among personnel in the service trains under Major Hollingsworth. Through the advance of Combat Command "B," Major Hollingsworth repeatedly supervised the evacuation of wrecked vehicles from the heads of advancing columns while under enemy sniper and artillery fire. His professional skill rendered under hazardous conditions was an inspiration to his command and aided materially in the successful accomplishment of the Combat Commander's mission.

JAMES F. HOLLINGSWORTH
67th Armored Regiment
Silver Star (Oak Leaf Cluster)
Citation

The President of the United States of America, authorized by Act of Congress July 9, 1918, takes pleasure in presenting a Bronze Oak Leaf

Cluster in lieu of a Second Award of the Silver Star to Major (Infantry) James Francis Hollingsworth (ASN: 0–34155), United States Army, for conspicuous gallantry and intrepidity while serving with the 67th Armored Regiment, 2d Armored Division, on 9 January 1945 in Belgium. On 4 January 1945, 2d Battalion, 67th Armored Regiment, with Major Hollingsworth as Task Force Commander, attacked south of Freineux, Belgium. After several attacks were unsuccessful, the Task Force was ordered to re-assemble and attack from Odeigne towards Samree. After getting into the woods about half way to the objective, the attack was halted due to stiff enemy resistance, radio and engine trouble with the tank commanded by the assault company commander stopped the advance forward. Major Hollingsworth sent his command tank to the assistance of this commander and took a position in another tank to direct his task force. He acted as a loader for the 75-mm gun in this tank, because its crew consisted of only four men, which enabled him to direct the attack also. After two attacks had failed the enemy launched a powerful counterattack. It was during the process of beating off the attack that the 75-mm gun recoiled against Major Hollingsworth's arm. Although in extreme pain from a possibly fractured arm, Major Hollingsworth continued to load the gun and would not let himself be evacuated after being ordered by the Combat Commander. The valor, courage, and devotion to duty displayed by Major Hollingsworth reflect great credit upon himself and are in keeping with the highest traditions of the Military Service.

JAMES F. HOLLINGSWORTH
67th Armored Regiment
Silver Star (Second Oak Leaf Cluster)
Citation

The President of the United States of America, authorized by Congress July 9, 1918, takes pleasure in presenting a Second Bronze Oak Leaf Cluster in lieu of a Third Award of the Silver Star to Major (Infantry) James Francis Hollingsworth (ASN: 0–34155), United States Army, for conspicuous gallantry and intrepidity while serving with the 67th Armored Regiment, 2d Armored Division, from 27 March 1945 to 14 April 1945 in Germany. During this period, Major Hollingsworth commanded a task force in the advance of Combat Command "B" to the Elbe River.

Throughout the advance he moved with the leading elements of his command through enemy opposition which, though sporadic, was heavy at times. On several occasions Major Hollingsworth moved over roads not previously reconnoitered or cleared by friendly troops in order that he might determine the necessity of placing blocks on the flanks, or for the purpose of placing such blocks.

JAY T. ROBBINS
80th Fighter Squadron
Distinguished Service Cross
Citation

First Lieutenant (Air Corps) Jay Thorpe Robbins (ASN: 0–405112), United States Army Air Forces, was awarded the Distinguished Service Cross for extraordinary heroism in connection with military operations against an armed enemy while serving as pilot of a P-38 Fighter Airplane in the 80th Fighter Squadron, 8th Fighter Group, FIFTH Air Force, in aerial combat against enemy forces on 4 September 1943. On this date First Lieutenant Robbins shot down four enemy aircraft in a single mission. First Lieutenant Robbins' unquestionable valor in aerial combat is in keeping with the highest traditions of the military service and reflects great credit upon himself, the FIFTH Air Force, and the United States Army Air Forces.

JAY T. ROBBINS
80th Fighter Squadron
Distinguished Service Cross (Oak Leaf Cluster)
Citation

First Lieutenant (Air Corps) Jay Thorpe Robbins (ASN: 0–405112), United States Army Air Forces, was awarded a Bronze Oak Leaf Cluster in lieu of a Second Award of the Distinguished Service Cross for extraordinary heroism in connection with military operations against an armed enemy while serving as Pilot of a P-38 Fighter Airplane in the 80th Fighter Squadron, 8th Fighter Group, FIFTH Air Force, in aerial combat against enemy forces on 24 October 1943. On this date, for the second time in less than two months, First Lieutenant Robbins shot down four enemy aircraft in a single mission. First Lieutenant Robbins' unquestionable valor in aerial combat is in keeping with the highest traditions of the military service and reflects great credit upon himself, the FIFTH Air Force, and the United States Army Air Forces.

ROBERT L. ACKLEN JR.
3rd Battalion, 506th Infantry
Silver Star
Citation

For gallantry in action while engaged in military operations against an armed hostile force in Cambodia. Captain Acklen distinguished himself while serving as Commanding Officer of Company C, 3rd Battalion, 506th Infantry, 101st Airborne Division, operationally attached to the 4th Infantry Division. On 12 May 1970, Company C was conducting a reconnaissance in force mission in the Se San area of Cambodia when an enemy village was encountered. Moving forward cautiously, Captain Acklen spotted an enemy soldier, shouted a warning to his men, and initiated fire. With complete disregard for his personal safety, Captain Acklen repeatedly exposed himself to strategically position his men. Pressing on, Captain Acklen courageously assaulted the first enemy hooch, forcing the occupants to flee. Following his example, the friendly element swept across the objective and sent the hostile force into retreat. Captain Acklen's personal bravery, outstanding leadership, and exemplary devotion to duty are in keeping with the highest traditions of military service and reflect great credit upon himself, his unit, and the United States Army.

ROBERT L. ACKLEN JR.
2nd Squadron, 17th Cavalry
Distinguished Flying Cross
Citation

For heroism while participating in aerial flight evidenced by voluntary action above and beyond the call of duty in the Republic of Vietnam. Captain Acklen distinguished himself on 15 February 1971 while serving as copilot and gunner on an AH-1G armed helicopter during the extraction of a small reconnaissance team under attack by an unknown size enemy force in Thua Thien Province, Republic of Vietnam. After volunteering to provide cover fire for the extraction, Captain Acklen piloted his aircraft through adverse weather conditions to the extraction site. There, he began placing accurate suppressive fire on enemy positions surrounding the team so lift helicopters could affect the extraction. Throughout the operation, he informed his aircraft commander of their exact position in relation to dangerous terrain. Although it was now night and raining, Captain Acklen managed to return by use of instruments only. Captain Acklen's outstanding flying ability and devotion to duty were in keeping with the highest traditions of the military service and reflect great credit upon himself, his unit, and the United States Army.

★ APPENDIX 2 ★

List of Texas Aggies Awarded the Nation's Second-Highest Award

This appendix presents a list of Texas Aggies whose award of the Distinguished Service Cross, Navy Cross, or Air Force Cross has been verified. It also includes a list of those whose award remains unverified. The names were compiled from several sources. The *1920 Longhorn* includes a narrative for each Texas Aggie who died in World War I that contains information on their service and notes their awards. In 1919 the college published the *Gold Book,* which also lists former students who died in World War I. At the time the college published the *Alumni Quarterly,* which was superseded by the *Texas Aggie* magazine after the formation of the Former Student Association.

A search of copies of the *Alumni Quarterly* and the *Texas Aggie* magazine, especially the Silver Taps (obituary) section, revealed many now included in the lists of this appendix. It appears that in some cases, the obituary writer confused the Distinguished Flying Cross with the Distinguished Service Cross. An article in the *Guidon,* published by the Corps of Cadets Association, lists individuals identified to date who had been awarded one of the medals and requested information on eligible Aggies not included. An article also appeared in the *Texas Aggie* requesting information. The two articles resulted in the gathering of a few more names.

The website Military Times Hall of Valor was used to verify each award and to obtain a copy of the citation. In 1927 the US Army published *Decorations, United States Army, 1862–1926.* That book was also used to verify World War I awards. In a few cases relatives provided a copy of the citation.

There was one case of "stolen valor" encountered during the search. A former student claimed that he had been awarded a Distinguished Service Cross in Vietnam and that he had served with Special Forces and the highly classified Studies and Observation Group (SOG). A request to a source at Fort Bragg, North Carolina, to verify the individual's service in Special Forces revealed that he had been a staff officer in

Vietnam and had never served with either Special Forces or SOG. The award of the Distinguished Service Cross thus could not be verified.

The information obtained on the individuals listed below will be placed in the Sanders Corps of Cadets Center on the campus of Texas A&M University. Meanwhile, the search for eligible individuals continues.

VERIFIED AWARDS

(Individuals listed alphabetically by class year.)

Legend:

USA—US Army	AFC—Air Force Cross
USN—US Navy	WW1—World War 1
USMC—US Marine Corps	WW2—World War 2
AAF—US Army Air Forces	Kor—Korea
AF—US Air Force	VN—Vietnam
DSC—Distinguished Service Cross	IF—Iraqi Freedom
NC—Navy Cross	

Bennet Puryear Jr. '06 USMC NC (WW1)
George F. Moore '08 USA DSC (WW2)
Jesse L. Easterwood '09 USN NC (WW1)
William P. Bourland '13 USA DSC (WW1)
Herbert N. Peters '13 USA DSC (WW1)
Harry L. Bennett Jr. '14 USA DSC (WW1)
Leslie W. Brown '15 USA DSC (WW1)
Charles F. Warren '15 USA DSC (WW1)
John H. Moore '15 USA DSC (WW1)
Mitchell H. Brown '16 USA DSC (WW1)
Andrew D. Bruce '16 USA DSC (WW1)
Herbert W. Whisenant '16 USA DSC (WW1)
Albert M. Bledsoe '17 USN NC (WW2)
Walter T. H. Galliford '17 USMC NC (WW1)
Ortho K. Morrison '17 USA DSC (WW1)
John T. Walker '17 USMC NC (WW2)
John C. McKimmey '18 USA DSC (WW1)
Welborn B. Griffith Jr. '23 USA DSC (WW2)
Robert B. Williams '23 USA DSC (WW2)
James E. Rudder '32 USA DSC (WW2)

Samuel S. Graham '34 USA DSC (WW2)
John R. Smith '34 USA DSC (WW2)
Henry V. Baushausen '35 USA DSC (WW2)
Odell M. Conoley '35 USMC NC (WW2)
Raymond L. Murray '35 USMC NC (WW2), NC (Kor), DSC (Kor)
Milton J. Landry '36 USA DSC (WW2)
Bruce W. Reagan '37 USA DSC (WW2)
Horace S. Carswell Jr. '38 AAF DSC (WW2)
Andrew R. Cheek '38 USA DSC (WW2)
Clem B. Connally '38 USN NC (WW2)
Edgar J. Crane '38 USMC NC (WW2)
Rudyard K. Grimes '38 USA DSC (WW2)
David L. Hill '38 AAF DSC (WW2)
George F. Singletary Jr. '38 USA DSC (WW2)
John M. Cook '39 USA DSC (Kor)
Dexter L. Hodge '39 AAF DSC (WW2)
Herbert M. Mills '39 USA DSC (WW2)
Harry L. Brown '40 USA DSC (WW2)
Glenn E. Duncan '40 AAF DSC (WW2)
George H. Gay Jr. '40 USN NC (WW2)
James F. Hollingsworth '40 USA DSC (WW2), 2 DSC (VN)
Jay T. Robbins '40 AAF 2 DSC (WW2)
Edwin A. DuBose III '41 USN NC (WW2)
Thomas M. Horne '41 USMC NC (WW2)
Frank M. Pool '41 USA DSC (WW2)
John M. Stevens Jr. '41 USA DSC (WW2)
Charles W. Hodges '42 AAF DSC (WW2)
Charles S. Martin Jr. '42 USA DSC (WW2)
Claude C. Nathan Jr. '42 USN NC (WW2)
Otheil J. Erlund '43 USA DSC (WW2)
Claude E. Lovett Jr. '43 USA DSC (WW2)
Robert S. Roberts '43 USA DSC (Kor)
Wesley M. Hays '44 USN NC (WW2)
William C. Knapp '44 USA DSC (Kor)
John K. Wells '44 USMC NC (WW2)
William L. Wathen '45 USA DSC (WW2)
William P. Brown Jr. '46 USMC NC (WW2), NC (Kor)
Guy S. Meloy III '52 USA DSC (VN)

James R. Taylor '59 USA DSC (VN)
Byron Stone '60 USA DSC (VN)
David B. Robinson '62 USN NC (VN)
Neil Keltner '65 USA DSC (VN)
Robert F. Wilke '65 AF AFC (VN)
Richard L. Poling '69 AF AFC (VN)
Eric A. Moser '07 USA DSC (IF)

UNVERIFIED AWARDS

This section lists in order of class year those Texas Aggies who were identified in various documents as having been awarded a Distinguished Service Cross or Navy Cross but could not be verified by the author. Information about each is included in the hope that a reader can confirm the award and produce documentation to the Sanders Corps of Cadets Center.

Robert W. Nolte '13 USA DSC (WW1)—*Gold Book:* Born at Bolivar, Tennessee, on October 1, 1892. Served with 2nd Engineer in 1918 in France. Killed in the Battle of Blanc Mont. Posthumously awarded the Distinguished Service Cross.

Haydn P. Mayers '14 USA DSC (WW1)—*Gold Book:* Born September 15, 1890, at San Antonio, Texas. Killed in action on April 12, 1918, while serving with the 60th Infantry Regiment. Awarded the Distinguished Service Cross.

George F. Wellage '16 USA DSC (WW1)—*Gold Book:* Born August 14, 1893, at San Antonio, Texas. Killed in action on September 12, 1918, in the St. Mihiel Drive while serving with the 23rd Infantry Regiment. Received the DSC for services in the Battle of the Marne. (Award of Silver Star verified.)

Hugh McFarland '17 USMC DSC (WW1)—*Alumni Quarterly:* Hometown was Brownwood, Texas. Cited for heroism by the French government while serving with 96th Company, 6th Marine Regiment, during the period October 3–9, 1918. (Award of two Silver Stars verified.)

James M. Tongate '21 USA DSC (WW1)—Silver Taps section, *Texas Aggie,* April 1987: Hometown was Waco, Texas. Veteran of World War I who was awarded the DSC, Purple Heart, and French Croix de Guerre.

Jaime S. Morris '39 USN NC (WW2)—Silver Taps section, *Texas Aggie,* March 1992. Hometown was Valley Mills. Served as a navy pilot aboard the USS *Enterprise* during the Battle of Midway and other naval battles. Awarded the Navy Cross.

Vernon G. Hunt '45 USA DSC (WW2)—Silver Taps section, *Texas Aggie,* July 2002: From Titus County, Texas. Served with the 133rd Infantry Regiment, 34th Infantry Division, in North Africa and Italy during World War II. Awards include the DSC, Silver Star, Bronze Star, and Purple Heart.

★ NOTES ★

CHAPTER 1

1. 1900 US Census, Fort Worth Ward 2, Tarrant County, Tex., Roll T624–1590, 8A; "George Fleming Moore (1822–1883)," Justices of Texas, 1836–1986, Tarlton Law Library, University of Texas School of Law, n.d., http://tarlton.law.utexas.edu/justices/profile/view/71 (assessed Feb. 20, 2011).

2. Perry, *Story of Texas A&M*, 233; *1905 Longhorn*, 102; *1907 Longhorn*, 100; *1908 Longhorn*, 104. The *Longhorn* was the name of Texas A&M's yearbook at this time.

3. *1908 Longhorn*, 104; "Texas General of Corregidor Shot to Death," *Dallas Morning News*, Dec. 4, 1949, 2.

4. 1920 Official Army Register, 462; 1948 Official Army Register, 1283; "General Freed from Prison Native Texas," *Dallas Morning News*, Sept. 5, 1945, 3.

5. Schultz, *Hero of Bataan*, 26.

6. Dethloff, *Texas Aggies Go to War*, 80–81; *1938 Longhorn*, n.p.; Adams, *Keepers of the Spirit*, 136–37, 142.

7. Adams, *Keepers of the Spirit*, 142, 144.

8. "A&M Given High Praise by Johnson," *Dallas Morning News*, Apr. 22, 1942, 8.

9. Morton, *Fall of the Philippines*, 22; Morris, *Corregidor*, 30: Belote and Belote, *Corregidor*, 18–20.

10. Morton, *Strategy and Command*, 97.

11. Beebe, *Prisoner of the Rising Sun*, 6.

12. Wainwright, *General Wainwright's Story*, 12–15.

13. Morton, *Fall of the Philippines*, 88.

14. Belote and Belote, *Corregidor*, 49; Beebe, *Prisoner of the Rising Sun*, 6.

15. Morris, *Corregidor*, 184.

16. Belote and Belote, *Corregidor*, 50; Morton, *Fall of the Philippines*, 236.

17. Morton, *Fall of the Philippines*, 247.

18. Liddell Hart, *History of the Second World War*, 222–23.

19. Schultz, *Hero of Bataan*, 173–74, 190, 211–12; Morton, *Fall of the Philippines*, 360–61.

20. Morton, *Fall of the Philippines*, 359–60; Belote and Belote, *Corregidor*, 100.

21. Schultz, *Hero of Bataan*, 210–11.

22. Morton, *Fall of the Philippines*, 47, 529.

23. Liddell Hart, *History of the Second World War*, 223; Schultz, *Hero of Bataan*, 248.

24. "Bones of Fighters Heaped on Silent Bataan Years after Defenders Tragic Surrender," *Oregonian*, Apr. 10, 1947, 4.

25. Schultz, *Hero of Bataan*, 248.

26. Adams, *Softly Call the Muster*, 20–21, 72.

27. Schultz, *Hero of Bataan*, 249, 256, 279, 281–82.

28. Ibid., 286; Kerr, *Surrender and Survival*, 69–70.

29. Kerr, *Surrender and Survival*, 74; Beebe, *Prisoner of the Rising Sun*, 8.

30. Wainwright, *General Wainwright's Story*, 157–58, 172, 187–88.

31. Kerr, *Surrender and Survival*, 107; Schultz, *Hero of Bataan*, 343–44; Beebe, *Prisoner of the Rising Sun*, 9.

32. Schultz, *Hero of Bataan*, 347.

33. Kerr, *Surrender and Survival*, 108.

34. Schultz, *Hero of Bataan*, 350, 365–67; Wainwright, *General Wainwright's Story*, 213, 215, 222.

35. Wainwright, *General Wainwright's Story*, 234–35, 237–39.

36. Ibid., 240, 385.

37. Schultz, *Hero of Bataan*, 390–91.

38. Ibid., 390–95.

39. Ibid., 388–89, 398; Wainwright, *General Wainwright's Story*, 259, 388, 390, 395.

40. "Maj. Gen. Moore to Leave for Manila," *Seattle Daily Times*, Aug. 30, 1945, 2.

41. "Manila Staff Undergoes Shift," *Oregonian*, Oct. 31, 1946, 1; "145 Convicted of Army Graft," ibid., May 10, 1947, 2; "Offices Sent to New Posts," *Oregonian*, Jan. 1, 1947, 4.

42. "Rites Mark Corregidor Transfer," *Dallas Morning News*, Oct. 13, 1947, 1.

43. "Heroic Corregidor Defender Kills Himself," *(Long Beach, CA) Independent*, Dec. 6, 1949, 7A; "Last Rites for Gen. Moore," *San Mateo (CA) Times*, Dec. 5, 1949, 1.

44. Schultz, *Hero of Bataan*, 386.

CHAPTER 2

1. Andrew D. Bruce, Student Record, n.d., Agricultural and Mechanical College of Texas (hereinafter cited as Texas A&M); Boykin, *General A. D. Bruce*, 1; *1913 Longhorn*, 167, 253; *1914 Longhorn*, 50, 199; *1915 Longhorn*, 131; *1916 Longhorn*, 50, 158, 183; Adams, *Keepers of the Spirit*, 55, 79, 81.

2. Clark, *Second Infantry Division in World War I*, 5, 9, 12, 193; Boykin, *General A. D. Bruce*, 2; Westover, *Suicide Battalions*, 12, 14, 41.

3. Clark, *Second Infantry Division in World War I*, 15–17, 22.

4. Westover, *Suicide Battalions*, 84–85.

5. Clark, *Second Infantry Division in World War I*, 27, 34, 37, 91, 194.

6. Ibid., 96; Bruce, Distinguished Service Cross citation, July 17–18, Oct. 3–4, 1918.

7. Boykin, *General A. D. Bruce*, 8; Clark, *Second Infantry Division in World War I*, 133.

8. Clark, *Second Infantry Division in World War I*, 142, 146–47, 152–53, 157; Bruce, Distinguished Service Cross citation.

9. Clark, *Second Infantry Division in World War I*, 179–80, 183.

10. Barbara LeUnes, "A History of Allen Academy, 1886–1968" (master's thesis, Texas A&M University, 1970), iii, 132–37; "War Dep't Gives Allen Academy Honor Rating," *Bryan (TX) Eagle*, June 8, 1927, 1; "Film to Be Shown in Local Theaters," ibid., May 6, 1927, sec. 5, 1; "Allen Academy Opens 45th Year Friday," ibid., Sept. 17, 1929, 1.

11. Boykin, *General A. D. Bruce*, 11–12.

12. Faulk and Faulk, *Fort Hood*, 15–21.

13. Ibid., 25, 32, 34, 61.

14. Ibid., 51, 53–54, 58, 69.

15. Ibid., 72, 74–75.

16. Ibid., 74; *Ours to Hold It High*, 9, 26, 30, 36–37, 39.

17. *Ours to Hold It High*, 40–43, 57, 61–62, 65, 74–75, 103; Stanton, *Order of Battle*, 144–45; Crowl, *Campaign in the Marianas*, 364–65.

18. Crowl, *Campaign in the Marianas*, 374, 390–91, 396–97, 436–37; *Ours to Hold It High*, 125, 145.

19. Cannon, *Leyte*, 1, 11; Gailey, *War in the Pacific*, 317.

20. *Ours to Hold It High*, 42, 145.

21. Ibid., 149, 154; Cannon, *Leyte*, 72, 286, 291–92.

22. Boykin, *General A. D. Bruce*, 29; *Ours to Hold It High*, 174–76; Gailey, *War in the Pacific*, 336.

23. Gailey, *War in the Pacific*, 336–37.

24. *Ours to Hold It High*, 225; Stanton, *Order of Battle*, 145.

25. Appleman et al., *Okinawa*, 7, 9.

26. Ibid., 24, 54–56; *Ours to Hold It High*, 229.

27. *Ours to Hold It High*, 253–55; Appleman et al., *Okinawa*, 72, 75, 99, 150–52.

28. Appleman et al., *Okinawa*, 163.

29. Ibid., 159–60, 163, 170, 173; *Ours to Hold It High*, 273, 276.

30. Appleman et al., *Okinawa*, 181–82; A. D. Bruce Aggie Muster Speech, Apr. 21, 1960.

31. Stanton, *Order of Battle*, 145; *Ours to Hold It High*, 293.

32. *Ours to Hold It High*, 389, 391, 413–15, 437.

33. Hastings, *Korean War*, 26–27, 30; Stanton, *Order of Battle*, 87.

34. Boykin, *General A. D. Bruce*, 77.

35. Ibid., 78; Nicholson, *In Time*, 324–27.

36. Nicholson, *In Time*, 348; Adair and Gutierrez, *University of Houston*, 11–13, 17, 36–37, 40.

37. Nicholson, *In Time*, 377; Adair and Gutierrez, *University of Houston*, 44, 46, 48.

38. Boykin, *General A. D. Bruce*, 85–87.

CHAPTER 3

1. John A. Hilger, Application for Admission to Texas A&M Univ., Sept. 3, 1926; *1925 Athenian* (high school yearbook), 83; *1926 Athenian*, 39.

2. Brian Hart, "Sherman, TX," Handbook of Texas Online, https://www.tshaonline.org/handbook/online/articles/hds03 (accessed Apr. 2, 2012); *1925 Athenian*, 83; *1926 Athenian*, 39; Adams, *Keepers of the Spirit*, 119, 126.

3. *1929 Longhorn*, 156; *1932 Longhorn*, 70.

4. John A. Hilger Official Biography, US Air Force, Sept. 14, 2010, http://www.af.mil/AboutUs/Biographies/Display/tabid/225/Article/106769/brigadier-general-john-a-hilger.aspx.

5. "Announcement," *Riverside (CA) Daily Press*, Mar. 15, 1937, 8; "Lieutenant's Death Confirmed by Navy," *Dallas Morning News*, Dec. 12, 1945, 9.

6. "Cronan Assigned to Pendleton Air Base," *Seattle Daily Times*, Mar. 20, 1941, 14; "Reconnaissance Group Here for Maneuvers," *Augusta (GA) Chronicle*, Nov. 4, 1941, 3.

7. Doolittle, *I Could Never Be So Lucky Again*, 216–17.

8. Ibid., 218.

9. Ibid., 225, 227; Merrill, *Target Tokyo*, 15–18; Dethloff, *Texas Aggies Go to War*, 117.

10. Merrill, *Target Tokyo*, 19–21.

11. Ibid., 25–27, 29, 37; Doolittle, *I Could Never Be So Lucky Again*, 238.

12. Jacob Eierman, "I Helped Bomb Japan," *Popular Science*, July 1943, 64.

13. Merrill, *Target Tokyo*, 34.

14. Doolittle, *I Could Never Be So Lucky Again*, 250, 253.

15. Ibid., 253–54; Merrill, *Target Tokyo*, 50; Eierman, "I Helped Bomb Japan," 66.

16. Doolittle, *I Could Never Be So Lucky Again*, 515; Eierman, "I Helped Bomb Japan," 66; Tom Macia (son of James Macia), email message to author, Sept. 1, 2012.

17. Eierman, "I Helped Bomb Japan," 66; Lawson, *Thirty Seconds over Tokyo*, 58.

18. Eierman, "I Helped Bomb Japan." 65–68

19. Ibid., 68; Merrill, *Target Tokyo*, 40; Doolittle, *I Could Never Be So Lucky Again*, 40–41.

20. Merrill, *Target Tokyo*, 94.

21. Eierman, "I Helped Bomb Japan," 68.

22. Merrill, *Target Tokyo*, 120.

23. Doolittle, *I Could Never Be So Lucky Again*, 260; Glines, *Doolittle Raid*, 252.

24. "Aggie Heroes Get Ovation at College Station," *Dallas Morning News*, July 12, 1943, 11.

25. Molesworth, *Wing to Wing*, 10–13, 185; Hilger Official Biography.

26. "Tokyo Raiders Set for Best Reunion," *Seattle Daily Times*, Apr. 19, 1963, 33; "'Doolittle Boys' Tamer, Grandpas," *New Orleans Times-Picayune*, Apr. 29, 1978, 79; "Reunion of Tokyo Raiders Casualty of Viet Nam War." *Omaha World Herald*, Apr. 19, 1966, 18; "Doolittle Raid," *Military Officer*, July 2012, 67.

27. "Last of Doolittle Raiders Make Final Toast in Ohio," *Houston Chronicle*, Nov. 10, 2013, A2; "We Owe Them Our Eternal Respect and Gratitude," *American Legion*, Jan. 2014, 44–45.

28. Hilger Official Biography; Hilger, Silver Star citation, Nov. 8, 1950; "SAC Bases: MacDill Air Force Base," http://www.strategic-air-command.com/bases/MacDill_AFB.htm (accessed Sept. 9, 2012).

29. Hilger Official Biography; Hilger eulogy given by James H. Macia Jr., Hilger's navigator on the Doolittle Raid, Macia Family Personal Collection.

CHAPTER 4

1. Biography of Pres. Earl Rudder, n.d., Texas A&M Univ. Archives (hereinafter cited as Rudder Official Biography); "History of Eden, Texas," http://edentexas.com/articles/view/history-of-eden-texas (accessed Sept. 3, 2013); Hatfield, *Rudder*, 21–23, 26; King, *John Tarleton College Story*, 128.

2. Hatfield, *Rudder*, 21–23, 42; *1932 Longhorn*, 39.

3. *1932 Longhorn*, 39; James Earl Rudder, Application for Admission to Texas A&M Univ., Sept. 15, 1930; Rudder Official Biography.

4. Hatfield, *Rudder*, 51; Rudder Official Biography; Stanton, *Order of Battle*, 153.

5. Lane, *Rudder's Rangers*, 12–13, 15, 16, 17, 21; Hatfield, *Rudder*, 73–74.

6. Lane, *Rudder's Rangers*, 22.

7. Ibid., 26–27, 30.

8. Ibid., 36, 38.

9. Ibid., 44, 46, 53; Black, *Battalion*, 53.

10. Black, *Battalion*, 54.

11. Ibid., 55.

12. Ibid., 57–58.

13. Ibid., 60.

14. Ibid., 64–73.

15. Historical Division, "Pointe du Hoc," 3; Lane, *Rudder's Rangers*, 74–75.

16. Black, *Battalion*, 79.

17. Lane, *Rudder's Rangers*, 76.

18. Ibid., 79–81.

19. Historical Division, "Pointe du Hoc," 8, 21.

20. Lane, *Rudder's Rangers*, 82.

21. Ibid., 118; Historical Division, "Pointe du Hoc," 26–28.

22. Black, *Battalion*, 130, 132.

23. Lane, *Rudder's Rangers*, 140–43; Ambrose, *Victors*, 155–56.

24. Lane, *Rudder's Rangers*, 17, 170–71; Ambrose, *Victors*, 156; Historical Division, "Pointe du Hoc," 43.

25. War Department, General Orders No. 10, Feb. 22, 1945, Washington, D.C., 12 Aggie Heroes File, Texas A&M Univ. Archives.

26. Black, *Battalion*, 158–59.

27. Ibid., 167–68.

28. Ibid., 171.

29. Ibid., 172–77, 178–83, 185.

30. Ibid., 192–93, 195.

31. Ibid., 208; McDonald and Mathews, *Three Battles*, 414.

32. Black, *Battalion*, 210–13.

33. Ibid., 219, 222; McDonald, *Siegfried Line Campaign*, 462–63.

34. Kemp, *Regiment*, 212; War Department, "Table of Organization and Equipment No. 7–11," Feb. 26, 1944, Medal of Honor Collection, Texas A&M Univ. Archives (hereinafter MOHC).

35. Dupuy, *St. Vith*, 11; Cole, *Ardennes*, 55–56.

36. Cole, *Ardennes*, 55, 137, 227–28; Kemp, *Regiment*, 212.

37. Kemp, *Regiment*, 212, 214; McManus, *Alamo in the Ardennes*, 13.

38. McManus, *Alamo in the Ardennes*, 29.

39. Ibid.; Dupuy, *St. Vith*, 21; Black, *Battalion*, 240; Cole, *Ardennes*, 2, 17, 192–93.

40. Kemp, *Regiment*, 219, 226–27, 241.

41. Ibid., 246.

42. Ibid., 246–47, 250–52, 255–56.

43. Ibid., 257, 273–74, 283–84.

44. Ibid., 285, 290, 293, 295, 296–97.

45. Ibid., 298–99, 312–13, 319.

46. Huie, *Execution of Private Slovik*, 12, 75–78, 84, 88, 90, 130.

47. Kemp, *Regiment*, 318–19, 320, 323, 326, 333, 335–36, 341–42.

48. Ibid., 349, 352–54, 356–57.

49. Rudder Official Biography; Hatfield, *Rudder*, 267–68, 274–75.

50. Rudder Official Biography; "Veteran Land Scandal Biggest in History," *Houston Chronicle*, Feb. 27, 1955, 1; "Saying 'No' Difficult Task for New Land Commissioner," *Dallas Morning News*, Jan. 9, 1955, 6; "Giles Held Guilty, Gets 3-Year Term," ibid., July 28, 1955, 9.

51. Ibid.; "Earl Rudder New Chief of A&M System," *Dallas Morning News*, Sept. 2, 1965, 4; Adams, *Keepers of the Spirit*, 204; Dethloff, *Centennial History of Texas A&M University*, 556–58; "Cadets Boo Rudder over Coed Admissions," *Dallas Morning News*, Apr. 30, 1963, 9.

52. Dethloff, *Centennial History of Texas A&M*, 571–72.

53. Adams, *Keepers of the Spirit*, 217–18; Dethloff, *Centennial History of Texas A&M*, 570.

54. Rudder Official Biography.

55. Rudder Official Biography; "A&M University Buries President," *Bryan (TX) Eagle*, Mar. 26, 1970, 1; Dethloff, *Pictorial History of Texas A&M*, 182.

CHAPTER 5

1. Hill, *"Tex" Hill,* 21–24.

2. Ibid., 27–32.

3. Ibid., 32–33.

4. Ibid., 36, 39–40, 43.

5. David Lee Hill, Application for Admission to Texas A&M Univ., Aug. 3, 1944; Perry, *Story of Texas A&M,* 233; Adams, *Keepers of the Spirit,* 126.

6. Hill, *"Tex" Hill,* 44–45; *1935 Longhorn,* n.p.; *1936 Longhorn,* n.p.

7. Hill, *"Tex" Hill,* 45–46.

8. Ibid., 51–52, 54, 59.

9. Ibid., 63–65, 66, 67.

10. Ibid., 69; Toland, *Flying Tigers,* 10–11.

11. Toland, *Flying Tigers,* 14–15, 17, 22–23.

12. Hill, *"Tex" Hill,* 69–71, 72.

13. Hill, *"Tex" Hill,* 78; Bond and Anderson, *Flying Tiger's Diary,* 18, 21.

14. Hill, *"Tex" Hill,* 95; Bond and Anderson, *Flying Tiger's Diary,* 37–39.

15. Hill, *"Tex" Hill,* 95; Toland, *Flying Tigers,* 38.

16. Hill, *"Tex" Hill,* 105; Bond and Anderson, *Flying Tiger's Diary,* 52–53.

17. Hill, *"Tex" Hill,* 105.

18. Ibid., 111.

19. Ibid., 115, 118–19.

20. Ibid., 122–26.

21. Ibid., 127–29, 131.

22. Ibid., 132–33, 140.

23. Toland, *Flying Tigers,* 111–13, 117; Ford, *Flying Tigers,* 294; Bond and Anderson, *Flying Tiger's Diary,* 170.

24. Bond and Anderson, *Flying Tiger's Diary,* 118; Cornelius and Short, *Ding Hao,* 141.

25. Hill, *"Tex" Hill,* 170–71, 174.

26. Ibid., 174–75; Craven and Cate, *Army Air Forces in World War II, The Pacific,* 505.

27. Craven and Cate, *Army Air Forces in World War II, The Pacific,* 267–68; Ford, *Flying Tigers,* 324.

28. Ford, *Flying Tigers,* 176–77; Toland, *Flying Tigers,* 120–22; Scott, *God Is My Copilot,* 154.

29. Toland, *Flying Tigers,* 125–27.

30. Hill, *"Tex" Hill,* 185.

31. Ibid., 192–95, 200–201.

32. Ibid., 202–3.

33. Ibid., 202, 204–5, 207–9, 212, 219.

34. Ibid., 224–26, 227.

35. Ibid., 230–31; Cornelius and Short, *Ding Hao,* 309–10.

36. Hill, *"Tex" Hill*, 236, 238, 240, 247–48; Cornelius and Short, *Ding Hao*, 286, 289.

37. Hill, *"Tex" Hill*, 249, 252, 254, 255–56.

38. Ibid., 259–60.

39. Ibid., 262–64.

40. Ibid., 268–70.

41. Ibid., 271, 274–76, 279.

42. Ibid., 293.

43. "Legendary Flying Tiger Tex Hill Passes Away," *Air Force Print News Today*, Oct. 15, 2007, Moody Air Force Base, http://www.moody.af.mil/news/story_print.asp?id=123071935 (accessed Mar. 5, 2010).

CHAPTER 6

1. Olin E. Teague, Certificate of Service, Adjutant General's Department, State of Arkansas, Jan. 9, 1943; Olin E. Teague, Application for Admission to Texas A&M Univ., Sept. 19, 1928; *1932 Longhorn*, 32.

2. "University Times Were Often Rough," *Bryan (TX) Eagle*, Sept. 17, 1978, F8.

3. Ibid.; Olin E. Teague, Academic Record, n.d., Texas A&M Univ.; John Teague, interview by author, Oct. 12, 2011.

4. Weekly Report, Company 3801 (C), Waco, Mar. 28, 1937. Personal collection, Jack Teague.

5. Headquarters, First Military Area, Special Orders 200, Oct. 1, 1940 San Antonio, Headquarters, Camp Hulen, Special Orders 19, Jan. 22, 1942; Amendment of Orders, Adjutant General's Office, Mar. 29, 1942; letter, Assignment of Officer under Provisions [of] WD Circular 226, 1943, to Commanding General, Army Ground Forces, Washington, D.C., Jan. 19, 1946, Teague Family Personal Collection.

6. War Department, "Table of Organization and Equipment No. 7–11," Feb. 26, 1944, MOHC; Stanton, *Order of Battle*, 148–49; *Cross of Lorraine*, 9.

7. *Cross of Lorraine*, 18, 20, 24–25, 27, 32, 35; Harrison, *Cross Channel Attack*, 416–21; Liddell Hart, *History of the Second World War*, 543; Teague, Silver Star citation, June 24, 1944.

8. Teague, Silver Star (First Oak Leaf Cluster) citation, July 8, 1944; Teague interview, Oct. 12, 2011.

9. *Cross of Lorraine*, 37, 39, 43.

10. Ibid., 44–48; Blumenson, *Breakout and Pursuit*, 573; Teague interview, Oct. 12, 2011.

11. *Cross of Lorraine*, 49, 56, 61, 68.

12. Ibid., 68–69, 72, 74.

13. Ibid., 83, 88–89.

14. Ibid., 89, 108, 133; Bonn, *When the Odds Were Even*, 6, 7, 207.

15. Western Union telegram to Mrs. Freddie D. Teague, Dec. 30, 1944, Teague Family Personal Collection.

16. Headquarters, 43rd General Hospital, APO 420, Apr. 19, 1945; Teague interview, Oct. 12, 2011.

17. Teague interview, Oct. 12, 2011.

18. "Olin Teague World War II Veteran," *Bryan (TX) Eagle*, Sept. 17, 1978, F9.

19. "Disabled Veteran Wanted to Be Active in Politics," ibid., Sept. 17, 1978, F5.

20. "Teague Blames LBJ for Violence," *Dallas Morning News*, Oct. 26, 1966, D1.

21. "Teague Takes Ted to Task," *Springfield (MA) Union*, May 28, 1969, 2.

22. "Teague Hotly Disputes Carter's Blanket Pardon," *Dallas Morning News*, Feb. 9, 1977, D3.

23. "Greeks Must Launch Offensive, Texan Finds after Tour of Front," ibid., Oct. 26, 1947, 12.

24. "Teague Suggests A-Bomb for Korea," ibid., Jan. 29, 1952, 3.

25. "Teague's Viet Nam Study Exhaustive and Exhausting," ibid., Nov. 26, 1965, 10.

26. Note to Congressional Staff, Feb. 1966, Teague Papers, Texas A&M Univ. Archives.

27. "Teague to Tour Vietnam at President's Request," *Dallas Morning News*, June 18, 1967, 5; "Mine Haiphong Harbor," ibid., June 22, 1967, 10.

28. File 151–1, Box 46, Teague Papers, Texas A&M Univ. Archives.

29. Travis B. Bryan to Department of the Air Force, Mar. 17, 1950, with attached study, "Why Bryan, Texas Would Qualify as the Ideal Location for the Proposed Dept. of the AF Air Academy," ibid.

30. "Teague Ends 32 Years in Congress," *Bryan (TX) Eagle*, Sept. 17, 1978, F4.

31. Bell County Historical Commission, *Story of Bell County*, 211; Teague interview, Oct. 12, 2011.

CHAPTER 7

1. Raymond L. Murray, Application for Admission to Texas A&M Univ., n.d.; Murray, *Highpockets*, 3, 6, 243; *1929 El Arroyo* (Harlingen High School yearbook), n.p.; *1930 El Arroyo*, 20; *1935 Longhorn*, n.p.

2. Bruno Hochmuth was a major general commanding the 3rd Marine Division in Vietnam when he was killed in November 1967 in a helicopter crash. Joe McHaney was the Corps of Cadets commander during his senior year at Texas A&M and retired from the Marine Corps as a colonel.

3. Murray, *Highpockets*, 7–8, 12–14, 16.

4. Donovan, *Outpost in the North Atlantic*, 1–8, 10, 13–14, 30–31; "Who's Who in the Marine Corps"; Murray, *Highpockets*, 1.

5. Johnston, *Follow Me!*, 13, 21; Gailey, *War in the Pacific*, 160.

6. Johnston, *Follow Me!*, 40; Gailey, *War in the Pacific*, 158, 162–63, 167.

7. Gailey, *War in the Pacific*, 162–64, 167.

8. Johnston, *Follow Me!*, 40, 46.

9. Gailey, *War in the Pacific*, 168, 171–72, 174, 182; Frank, *Guadalcanal*, 543.

10. Johnston, *Follow Me!*, 71–72, 79–81; "Who's Who in the Marine Corps"; Gailey, *War in the Pacific*, 184; Frank, *Guadalcanal*, 614.

11. Johnston, *Follow Me!*, 85, 88–89, 98.

12. Gailey, *War in the Pacific*, 229–30; Liddell Hart, *History of the Second World War*, 510; Gregg, *Tarawa*, 44, 76.

13. Gregg, *Tarawa*, 11, 57, 69, 74, 97; Johnston, *Follow Me!*, 119.

14. Gregg, *Tarawa*, 131, 162, 166–67; Graham, *Mantle of Heroism*, 249; Murray, *Highpockets*, 36.

15. Murray, *Highpockets*, 37, 51; Johnston, *Follow Me!*, 166.

16. Johnston, *Follow Me!*, 172; Gailey, *War in the Pacific*, 274.

17. Johnston, *Follow Me!*, 192; Gailey, *War in the Pacific*, 275–77, 280, 292–93; Murray, *Highpockets*, 53–54.

18. Murray, *Highpockets*, 54–56, 59; "Who's Who in the Marine Corps."

19. Appleman, *South to the Naktong, North to the Yalu*, 21, 35, 252–53.

20. Murray, *Highpockets*, 67, 69–79, 81; "Who's Who in the Marine Corps."

21. Murray, *Highpockets*, 86–88, 92, 95, 97.

22. Ibid., 100–101; Appleman, *South to the Naktong, North to the Yalu*, 514–16, 524, 537.

23. Murray, *Highpockets*, 109–10; Appleman, *South to the Naktong, North to the Yalu*, 610, 635, 684–85; Hammel, *Chosin*, 3, 8–9.

24. Hammel, *Chosin*, 9–10; Appleman, *South to the Naktong, North to the Yalu*, 772; Murray, *Highpockets*, 115.

25. Hammel, *Chosin*, 12, 14–15.

26. Ibid., 12, 14–15, 212, 216–17, 365; Murray, *Highpockets*, 132.

27. Murray, *Highpockets*, 142; Wilson, *RETREAT, HELL!*, 241, 282–83.

28. Hammel, *Chosin*, 365; Leckie, *Conflict*, 222; Murray, *Highpockets*, 146, 148; Wilson, *RETREAT, HELL!*, 318, 334.

29. Wilson, *RETREAT, HELL!*, 318, 334; Murray, *Highpockets*, 146, 148.

30. Blair, *Forgotten War*, 542–43; "Who's Who in the Marine Corps."

31. Blair, *Forgotten War*, 680; Murray, *Highpockets*, 154, 156; Hammel, *Chosin*, 415–16; Leckie, *Conflict*, 260.

32. Murray, *Highpockets*, 173–74, 176, 178.

33. Ibid., 178–79, 181–82, 187, 190; "Who's Who in the Marine Corps."

34. Murray, *Highpockets*, 191, 193, 196, 201.

35. Ibid., 208–9, 215–16; "Who's Who in the Marine Corps."

36. Murray, *Highpockets*, 222, 226, 231, 234, 236; "Who's Who in the Marine Corps."

CHAPTER 8

1. George H. Gay Jr., Application for Admission to Texas A&M Univ., July 2, 1936; Gay, *Sole Survivor*, 24–26, 31, 34–35.

2. Gay, *Sole Survivor*, 37–41, 46; Lord, *Incredible Victory*, 85.

3. Gay, *Sole Survivor*, 63–63, 122; John Domagalski. "The Heroic Flight of Torpedo Squadron 8," *World War II History* (Jan. 2010): 51.

4. Gay, *Sole Survivor*, 75–76, 81–83; Gailey, *War in the Pacific*, 131.

5. Domagalski, "Heroic Flight," 52.

6. W. Smith, *Midway*, 66–68, 164–66.

7. Prange, *Miracle at Midway*, 435.

8. Gay, *Sole Survivor*, 113–15, 117; Mrazek, *Dawn like Thunder*, 89.

9. Gay, *Sole Survivor*, 119–29.

10. W. Smith, *Midway*, 100–103, 133; Lord, *Incredible Victory*, 141, 160.

11. Gay, *Sole Survivor*, 128–32, 137, 141–42.

12. Ibid., 142–43, 147–48, 161, 168–69, 173.

13. Ibid., 179, 191, 195, 197–98.

14. Gailey, *War in the Pacific*, 160, 185; Gay, *Sole Survivor*, 199, 210.

15. Gay, *Sole Survivor*, 229, 233–37.

16. Ibid., 242, 245–46, 263, 266, 270, 275.

17. Ibid., 275–76, 288, 290, 293–95.

18. Mrazek, *Dawn like Thunder*, 432.

CHAPTER 9

1. James F. Hollingsworth, Application for Admission to Texas A&M Univ., Sept. 9, 1936; Victoria Elieson, director, Sanger, Tex., Public Library, phone interview by author, Oct. 22, 2012.

2. *1937 Longhorn*, n.p.; *1938 Longhorn*, n.p.; *1939 Longhorn*, n.p.

3. Houston, *Hell on Wheels*, 157, 189, 191, 195, 199; James F. Hollingsworth Oral History, Aug. 18–20, 1982, Texas A&M Univ. Oral History Collection, Texas A&M Univ. Archives, 13–16, 21–23.

4. Houston, *Hell on Wheels*, 200–204; S. Smith, *2nd Armored Division*, 36–40.

5. S. Smith, *2nd Armored Division*, 40–45; Hollingsworth, Silver Star citation, July 29, 1944.

6. Hollingsworth Oral History, 25; Ryan, *Last Battle*, 71; Harmon, *Combat Commander*, 214.

7. Harmon, *Combat Commander*, 230–32; Hollingsworth Oral History, 1–8; S. Smith, *2nd Armored Division*, 53.

8. Harmon, *Combat Commander*, 243–45; Hollingsworth, Silver Star citation, Jan. 9, 1945; Hollingsworth Oral History, 30–31.

9. Hollingsworth Oral History, 34; Ryan, *Last Battle*, 278–79.

10. Ryan, *Last Battle*, 270, 272, 278, 292–93, 294; Hollingsworth Oral History, 35–37.

11. Hollingsworth Oral History, 40–41; Ryan, *Last Battle*, 295–96; Houston, *Hell on Wheels*, 418–19, 423–25.

12. Hollingsworth Oral History, 41–43; Harmon, *Combat Commander*, 280, 286, 291.

13. Hollingsworth Oral History, 45–46, 50, 51.

14. Schwarzkopf, *It Doesn't Take a Hero*, 62–63.

15. Hollingsworth Oral History, 51.

16. Ibid., 52, 55; Jay M. Parker, "The Colonels' Revolt: Eisenhower, the Army, and the Politics of National Security," June 17, 1994, class paper, Naval War College, Newport, RI, 1, 31–32, 49, 72, 77.

17. Hollingsworth Oral History, 57–61.

18. Ibid., 56, 62.

19. Ibid., 66, 68.

20. Hollingsworth, Distinguished Service Cross with Oak Leaf Cluster citation, November 5–8, 1966.

21. Hollingsworth, Distinguished Service Cross with Second Oak Leaf Cluster citation, March 20, 1967.

22. Hollingsworth Oral History, 117–18.

23. "Tiger in the Forest," *Wall Street Journal*, Jan. 13, 1976, 1.

24. Hollingsworth Oral History, 81–84.

25. Ibid., 89–90.

26. Ibid., 86–87.

27. Ibid., 90–92.

28. Willbanks, *Thiet Giap!*, 3–5.

29. Ibid., 93.

30. Ibid., 14–18.

31. Ibid., 21.

32. Frank Muller, interview by author, Aug. 16, 2012; Willbanks, *Battle of An Loc*, 115.

33. Willbanks, *Battle of An Loc*, 66; Willbanks, *Thiet Giap!*, 57–58, 61.

34. Hollingsworth Oral History, 102–3.

35. Ibid., 130–34; "U.S. General Envisions 'a Short Violent War' if Korean Reds Attack," *Wall Street Journal*, Jan. 13, 1976, 1.

36. Hollingsworth Oral History, 140; *The Hollingsworth Report*, in US Congress, *Congressional Record* 123, no. 13 (Jan. 25, 1977).

37. Lt. Gen. James F. Hollingsworth, US Army Biographical Data, http://corps.tamu.edu/lieutenant-general-james-f-hollingsworth-40/.

38. Muller interview, Aug. 16, 2012.

CHAPTER 10

1. Jay T. Robbins Oral History, Aug. 14, 15, 1980, Texas A&M Univ. Oral History Collection, Texas A&M Univ. Archives, 1–8.

2. Ibid., 6.

3. Jay T. Robbins, Application for Admission to Texas A&M Univ., Sept. 1, 1936; *1937 Longhorn*, n.p.; Perry, *Story of Texas A&M*, 233; Adams, *Keepers of the Spirit*, 126.

4. Robbins Oral History, 20, 24–25.

5. Ibid., 28–33.

6. Stanaway and Hickey, *Attack & Conquer*, 96.

7. Ibid., 100; Robbins Oral History, 32; Sims, *American Aces*, 86.

8. Gailey, *War in the Pacific*, 127, 220; Robbins Oral History, 33.

9. Jay T. Robbins, autobiographical sketch, n.d., Texas A&M Univ. Archives.

10. Robbins, Distinguished Service Cross citation, Sept. 4, 1943; Sims, *American Aces*, 88–89, 92–101. In his oral history Robbins uses the term "Zeke" for all of the Japanese fighters he encountered. The official Allied reporting name was Zeke, although the use of the name "Zero" was later commonly adopted.

11. Robbins, Distinguished Service Cross with Oak Leaf Cluster citation, Oct. 24, 1943; Stanaway and Hickey, *Attack & Conquer*, 132–32; Robbins, autobiographical sketch, 4–6.

12. Stanaway and Hickey, *Attack & Conquer*, 136, 138, 192–93, 259, 314; Robbins Oral History, 22, 37–38; Sims, *American Aces*, 101; Robbins, autobiographical sketch, 2.

13. Robbins Oral History, 38.

14. Ibid., 52–54.

15. Ibid., 62; Jay T. Robbins Official Biography, US Air Force, http://www.af.mil/AboutUs/Biographies/Display/tabid/225/Article/105108/lieutenant-general-jay-t-robbins.aspx.

16. Robbins Oral History, 73, 78–79; Robbins Official Biography.

17. Robbins Oral History, 79, 88; "Air Force on Way to New Flying Safety Record, Says General," *Seattle Daily Times*, June 8, 1965, 1.

18. Robbins Oral History, 92–94, 96.

19. Ibid., 74, 97, 99–100; Robbins Official Biography.

20. Robbins Oral History, 75, 100; Robbins Official Biography.

21. Robbins Oral History, 102–5; Robbins Official Biography.

CHAPTER 11

1. Marion C. Pugh, Application for Admission to Texas A&M Univ., July 30, 1937; *1935 Lasso* (high school yearbook), 44, 60; *1937 Lasso*, n.p.; W. C. Kendrick, interview by author, Mar. 3, 2012.

2. Herskowitz, *1939 Texas Aggies*, 39–42.

3. Ibid., 41, 240; Perry, *Story of Texas A&M*, 249.

4. Perry, *Story of Texas A&M*, 244; *1939 Longhorn*, n.p.; *1940 Longhorn*, n.p.

5. "Texas Aggie Football Stars Exempt from Conscription," *Dallas Morning News*, Aug. 17, 1940, 5.

6. Marion Pugh, Academic Record, n.d., Texas A&M Univ.; *1939 Longhorn*, n.p.; W. C. Kendrick, interview by author, July 21, 2011; Herskowitz, *1939 Texas Aggies*, 244.

7. "Coach Wade May Divide Gridders into Two Groups," *Augusta (GA) Chronicle*, Aug. 27, 1942, 14; Gabel, *Seek, Strike, Destroy*, 45; Stanton, *Order of Battle*, 138.

8. Stanton, *Order of Battle*, 138; Gabel, *Seek, Strike, Destroy*, 45; Kerlin, *893d Tank Destroyer Battalion*, 19–20.

9. Headquarters, 893rd TD Battalion, After Action Report, Aug. 6, 1944, Combined Arms Research Library, Command and General Staff College, Ft. Leavenworth, KS (hereinafter After Action Report); After Action Report, Sept. 4, 1944.

10. After Action Report, Oct. 7, 1944; Information and Education Division, European Theater of Operations, *Famous Fourth* (Paris, 1945), 7–8; Stanton, *Order of Battle,* 81–82.

11. McDonald, *Siegfried Line Campaign,* 8–9.

12. Ibid., 343–47.

13. Marion Pugh, Combat Interview, Nov. 22, 1944; Kerlin, *893d Tank Destroyer Battalion,* 28–34; After Action Reports, Nov. 6, Dec. 6, 1944, Jan. 5, 1945.

14. Headquarters, 893rd TD Battalion, "Subject: Recommendation for Award," Jan. 5, 1945. The story of Turney Leonard can be found in Woodall, *Texas Aggie Medals of Honor.*

15. After Action Reports, Feb. 4, Mar. 2, Apr. 5, May 2, 1945; Kerlin, *893d Tank Destroyer Battalion,* 36–39, 41–44.

16. Kerlin, *893d Tank Destroyer Battalion,* 12–13; Perret, *There's a War to Be Won,* 533.

17. Herskowitz, *1939 Texas Aggies,* 244; "Pugh Ex-Aggie Passing Star, to Continue Pro Grid Career," *Dallas Morning News,* Nov. 26, 1945, sec. 2, 5.

18. Barney Welch, interview by author, Aug. 5, 2011; "Pugh Joins Aggie Staff," *Dallas Morning News,* July 7, 1949, 3.

19. Woodall, *Texas Aggie Medals of Honor,* 105–9.

20. "New Daily Paper Slated for Bryan," *Dallas Morning News,* Jan. 3, 1957, pt. 2, 2; "Two Old Aggies Tangle in State Senate Contest," ibid., May 4, 1962, 15; "Texas Lumbermen Favor General Retail Sales Tax," ibid., Apr. 21, 1959.

21. Welch interview, Aug. 5, 2011.

CHAPTER 12

1. Robert L. Acklen Jr., Application of Admission to Texas A&M Univ., May 14, 1959; "Acklen Family Favors Boxers," *Dallas Morning News,* A15; Robert L. Acklen Jr. Service Record, DA Form 24, 12 Aggie Heroes File, Texas A&M Univ. Archives.

2. *1963 Aggieland,* 240, 256, 266, 406.

3. Robert L. Acklen Jr., Academic Transcript, n.d., Arizona State Univ.; Robert L. Acklen Jr., Academic Transcript, n.d., Texas A&M Univ.; Robert L. Acklen Jr., Service Record, DA Form 2–1; *1966 Sahuaro* (Arizona State yearbook), 28, 346, 377, 426; William H. Harris Jr., interview by author, Mar. 25, 2014.

4. Robert L. Acklen Jr., DD Form 214; Acklen Service Record; "Camp Wolters," http://www.globalsecurity.org/military/facility/camp-wolters.htm (accessed Feb. 20, 2014).

5. Stanton, *Vietnam Order of Battle,* 114, 122; Dorr, *Chopper,* 95–96, 196.

6. Acklen, Vietnamese Gallantry Cross citation, Jan. 11, 1969.

7. Acklen, Army Commendation Medal for Heroism citation, Feb. 1, 1969.

8. Acklen, Air Medal for Heroism citation, Jan. 21, 1969.

9. Acklen, Bronze Star for Heroism citation, Sept. 16, 1969.

10. Acklen Service Record; Vaughn R. "Bobby" Ross, interview by author, Mar. 15, 2014.

11. Acklen, Army Commendation Medal for Heroism citation, Oct. 14, 1969.

12. Acklen, Army Commendation Medal for Heroism citation, Oct. 29, 1969.

13. Stanton, *Vietnam Order of Battle*, 159; Acklen, Bronze Star for Heroism citation, Sept. 10, 1970.

14. Acklen, Bronze Star for Heroism citation, Dec. 9, 1970.

15. Nolan, *Into Cambodia*, 69–70, 72; Sorley, *Better War*, 204, 208, 210.

16. Headquarters, 4th Infantry Division, "Operational Report—Lessons Learned for Period Ending July 31, 1970," Aug. 20, 1970; Berry, *Twelve Days in May*, 43, 61–63, 67–68, 86–87, 90, 243–44.

17. Acklen, Bronze Star for Heroism citation, Mar. 1, 1971.

18. Acklen, Silver Star citation, June 20, 1971.

19. Berry, *Twelve Days in May*, 253–55; 4th Infantry Division, "Operational Report," Aug. 20, 1970.

20. 4th Infantry Division, "Operational Report," Aug. 20, 1970.

21. "A History of the 2nd Squadron, 17th Cavalry from 1916 to 1976," Document 5440119001, Vietnam Center and Archives, Texas Tech Univ., Lubbock, 15.

22. Dorr, *Choppers*, 213, 240.

23. Acklen, Air Medal for Heroism citation, Dec. 10, 1970.

24. Acklen, Air Medal for Heroism citation, Dec. 24, 1970.

25. Acklen, Distinguished Flying Cross citation, June 13, 1971.

26. DD Form 214, Report of Separation from Active Duty, Apr. 30, 1976, 12 Aggie Heroes File, Texas A&M Univ. Archives; US Army Infantry School, Subject: Honor Graduate, May 23, 1974, ibid.; Carolyn Bender (Acklen's sister), interview by author, Mar. 13, 2014.

27. Carolyn Bender interview; "Acklen Admitted to Venerable Order," *Park Cities (TX) News*, Nov. 13, 1980, 3.

28. "He Never Talked about It," *Texas Aggie*, June 1999, 7; DD Form 214, Apr. 30, 1976.

29. "Vietnam Hero Bob Acklen Dies at 57," *Dallas Morning News*, Jan. 5, 1999, 18.

APPENDIX 1

The definitions of and qualifications for the Distinguished Service Cross, Navy Cross, Silver Star, and Distinguished Flying Cross are taken from "Description of Medals," Military Awards for Valor, Department of Defense, http://valor.defense.gov/DescriptionofAwards.aspx; and "Distinguished Flying Cross," US Air Force Personnel Center, Aug. 4, 2010, http://www.afpc.af.mil/library/factsheets/factsheet.asp?id=7767.

★ BIBLIOGRAPHY ★

Adair, Wendy, and Oscar Gutierrez. *University of Houston: Our Time: Celebrating 75 Years of Learning and Leading.* Virginia Beach: Donning, 2001.

Adams, John A., Jr. *Keepers of the Spirit: The Corps of Cadets at Texas A&M, 1876–2001.* College Station: Texas A&M University Press, 2001.

———. *Softly Call the Muster: The Evolution of a Texas Aggie Tradition.* College Station: Texas A&M University Press, 1994.

Ambrose, Stephen E. *The Victors: Eisenhower and His Boys: The Men of World War II.* New York: Simon & Schuster, 1998.

Appleman, Roy E. *South to the Naktong, North to the Yalu, June–November 1950.* US Army in the Korean War. Washington, D.C.: Center of Military History, US Army, 1986.

Appleman, Roy E., James M. Burns, Russell A. Gugeler, and John Stevens. *Okinawa: The Last Battle.* US Army in World War II: The War in the Pacific. Washington, D.C.: Historical Division, Department of the Army, 1948.

Beebe, John M. *Prisoner of the Rising Sun: The Lost Diary of Brig. Gen. Lewis Beebe.* College Station: Texas A&M University Press, 2006.

Bell County Historical Commission. *Story of Bell County, Texas, Volume I.* Austin, TX: Eakin, 1988.

Belote, James H., and William M. Belote. *Corregidor: The Stirring Saga of a Mighty Fortress.* New York: Berkley, 1984.

Berry, Jerald W. *Twelve Days in May: The Untold Story of the Northern Thrust into Cambodia by the 4th Infantry Division (Operation Binh Tay I), May 1970.* Libby, MT: by the author, 2010.

Black, Col. Robert W. *The Battalion: The Dramatic Story of the 2nd Ranger Battalion in World War II.* Mechanicsburg, PA: Stackpole, 2006.

Blair, Clay. *The Forgotten War: America in Korea, 1950–1953.* New York: Random House, 1987.

Blumenson, Martin. *Breakout and Pursuit.* US Army in World War II: The European Theater of Operations. Washington, D.C.: Center of Military History, US Army, 1989.

Bond, Charles R., Jr., and Terry H. Anderson. *A Flying Tiger's Diary.* College Station: Texas A&M University Press, 1984.

Bonn, Keith E. *When the Odds Were Even: The Vosges Mountains Campaign, October 1944–January 1945.* Novato, CA: Presidio, 1994.

Boykin, Calvin C., Jr. *General A. D. Bruce: Father of Fort Hood.* College Station, TX: C&R, 2002.

Bradley, Omar N. *A Soldier's Story.* New York: Henry Holt, 1951.

Cannon, M. Hamlin. *Leyte: The Return to the Philippines.* US Army in World War II: The War in the Pacific. Washington, D.C.: Chief of Military History, Department of the Army, 1954.

Clark, George B. *The Second Infantry Division in World War I: A History of the American Expeditionary Force Regulars, 1917–1919.* Jefferson, NC: McFarland, 2007.

Cole, Hugh M. *The Ardennes: Battle of the Bulge.* Washington, D.C.: US Army Center of Military History, 1965.

Cornelius, Wanda, and Thayne Short. *Ding Hao: America's Air War in China.* Gretna, LA: Pelican, 1980.

Craven, Wesley F., and James L. Cate, eds. *The Pacific: Guadalcanal to Saipan, August 1942 to July 1944.* Vol. 4 of *The Army Air Forces in World War II.* Washington, D.C.: Office of Air Force History, GPO, 1983.

———. *Plans and Early Operations, January 1939 to August 1942.* Vol. 1 of *The Army Air Forces in World War II.* Chicago: University of Chicago, 1948.

Cross of Lorraine: A Combat History of the 79th Infantry Division, June 1942–December 1945. Nashville, TN: Battery, 1986.

Crowl, Philip A. *Campaign in the Marianas.* US Army in World War II: The War in the Pacific. Washington, D.C.: Office of the Chief of Military History, Department of the Army, 1960.

Daniels, Ken. *China Bombers: The Chinese-American Composite Wing in World War II.* North Branch, MN: Specialty, 1998.

Dethloff, Henry C. *A Centennial History of Texas A&M University, 1876–1976.* 2 vols. College Station: Texas A&M University Press, 1975.

———. *A Pictorial History of Texas A&M University, 1876–1976.* College Station: Texas A&M University Press, 1975.

———. *Texas Aggies Go to War: In Service of Their Country.* With John A. Adams Jr. College Station: Texas A&M University Press, 2006.

Donovan, James A. *Outpost in the North Atlantic: Marines in the Defense of Iceland.* Washington, D.C.: Marine Corps Historical Center, 1992.

Doolittle, James H. *I Could Never Be So Lucky Again.* With Carroll V. Glines. New York: Bantam Books, 1992.

Dorr, Robert F. *Chopper: Firsthand Accounts of Helicopter Warfare, World War II to Iraq.* New York: Berkley Books, 2005.

Dupuy, Col. R. Ernest. *St. Vith: Lion in the Way; the 106th Infantry Division in World War II.* Washington, D.C.: Infantry Journal Press, 1949.

Faulk, Odie B., and Laura E. Faulk. *Fort Hood: The First Fifty Years.* Temple, TX: Frank W. Mayborn Foundation, 1990.

Ford, Daniel. *Flying Tigers: Claire Chennault and His American Volunteers, 1941–1942.* Washington, D.C.: Smithsonian Institution Press, 1991.

Frank, Richard B. *Guadalcanal: The Definitive Account of the Landmark Battle.* New York: Random House, 1990.

Gabel, Christopher R. *Seek, Strike, Destroy: U.S. Army Tank Destroyer Doctrine in World War II.* Fort Leavenworth, KS: Combat Studies Institute; Washington: GPO, 1986.

Gailey, Harry W. *War in the Pacific.* Novato, CA: Presidio, 1995.

Gay, George. *Sole Survivor.* Naples, FL: Midway, 1980.

Gill, Lonnie. *Tank Destroyer Forces, WWII.* Paducah, KY: Turner, 1992.

Glines, Carroll V. *Chennault's Forgotten Warriors: The Saga of the 308th Bomb Group in China.* Atglen, PA: Schiffer, 1995.

———. *The Doolittle Raid: America's Daring First Strike against Japan.* New York: Orion Books, 1988.

Graham, Michael B. *Mantle of Heroism: Tarawa and the Struggle for the Gilberts, November 1943.* Novata, CA: Presidio, 1993.

Gregg, Charles T. *Tarawa.* New York: Stein and Day, 1984.

Halberstam, David. *The Best and the Brightest.* New York: Random House, 1992.

Hammel, Eric. *Chosin: Heroic Ordeal of the Korean War.* Novato, CA: Presidio, 1994.

Harmon, E. N. *Combat Commander: Autobiography of a Soldier.* With Milton MacKaye and William Ross MacKaye. Englewood Cliff, NJ: Prentice-Hall 1970.

Harrison, Gordon A. *Cross-Channel Attack.* US Army in World War II: The European Theater of Operations. Washington D.C.: Office of the Chief of Military History, Department of the Army, 1951.

Hastings, Max. *The Korean War.* New York: Simon and Schuster. 1987.

Hatfield, Thomas M. *Rudder: From Leader to Legend.* College Station: Texas A&M University Press, 2011.

Herskowitz, Mickey. *The 1939 Texas Aggies: The Greatest Generation's Greatest Team.* Houston: Halcyon, 2006.

Hill, David "Tex." *"Tex" Hill: Flying Tiger.* With Reagan Schaupp. Spartanburg, SC: Honoribus, 2003.

Historical Section, US War Department. "Pointe du Hoc (2nd Ranger Battalion, 6 June 1944)." In *Small Unit Actions.* Washington, D.C., 1946.

Houston, Donald E. *Hell on Wheels: The 2d Armored Division.* Novato, CA: Presidio. 1986.

Huie, William B. *The Execution of Private Slovik.* New York: Signet, 1954.

Johnston, Richard W. *Follow Me! The Story of the Second Marine Division in World War II.* New York: Random House, 1948.

Kemp, Harry. *The Regiment: Let the Citizens Bear Arms.* Austin: Eakin, 1991.

Kerlin, Henry C., ed. *History of the 893d Tank Destroyer Battalion.* N.p., [1945].

Kerr, E. Bartlett. *Surrender and Survival: The Experience of American POWs in the Pacific, 1941–1945.* New York: William Morrow, 1985.

King, C. Richard. *The John Tarleton College Story: Golden Days of Purple & White.* Austin: Eakin, 1998.

Lane, Ronald. *Rudder's Rangers: The True Story of the 2nd Ranger Battalion D-Day Combat Action.* Manassas, Va.: Ranger Associates, 1979.

Lawson, Ted W. *Thirty Seconds over Tokyo.* New York: Random House, 1943.

Leckie, Robert. *Conflict: The History of the Korean War, 1950–53.* New York: G. P. Putnam's Sons, 1962.

Liddell Hart, B. H. *History of the Second World War.* New York: G. P. Putnam's Sons, 1970.

Lord, Walter. *Incredible Victory.* New York: Harper & Row, 1967.

McDonald, Charles B. *The Siegfried Line Campaign.* US Army in World War II: The European Theater of Operations. Washington, D.C.: GPO, 1963.

McDonald, Charles B., and Sidney T. Mathews. *Three Battles: Arnaville, Altuzzo, and Schmidt.* US Army in World War II: Special Studies. Washington, D.C.: GPO, 1952.

McManus, John C. *Alamo in the Ardennes: The Untold Story of the American Soldiers Who Made the Defense of Bastogne Possible.* Hoboken, NJ: Wiley & Sons, 2007.

Merrill, James M. *Target Tokyo: The Halsey-Doolittle Raid.* New York: Popular Library, 1964.

Molesworth, Carl. *Wing to Wing: Air Combat in China, 1943–45.* New York: Orion Books, 1990.

Morris, Eric. *Corregidor: The End of the Line.* New York: Stein and Day, 1981.

Morton, Louis. *The Fall of the Philippines.* US Army in World War II: The War in the Pacific. Washington, D.C.: US Army Center of Military History, 1995.

———. *Strategy and Command: The First Two Years.* US Army in World War II: The War in the Pacific. Washington, D.C.: US Army Center of Military History, 1962.

Mrazek, Robert J. *A Dawn like Thunder: The True Story of Torpedo Squadron Eight.* New York: Little, Brown, 2008.

Murray, Zona G. *Highpockets: The Man, the Marine, the Legend.* Direct2Press, 2009.

Nicholson, Patrick J. *In Time: An Anecdotal History of the First Fifty Years of the University of Houston.* Houston: Pacesetter, 1977.

Nolan, Keith W. *Into Cambodia: Spring Campaign, Summer Offensive, 1970.* Novato, CA: Presidio, 1990.

Official Army Register 1920. Washington, D.C.: GPO, 1920.

Official Army Register 1948. Washington, D.C.: GPO, 1948.

Ours to Hold It High: The History of the 77th Infantry Division in World War II. Washington, D.C.: Infantry Journal Press, 1947.

Perret, Geoffrey. *There's a War to Be Won: The United States Army in World War II.* New York: Random House, 1991.

Perry, George Sessions. *The Story of Texas A&M.* New York: McGraw-Hill, 1951.

Prange, Gordon W. *Miracle at Midway.* New York: McGraw-Hill, 1982.
Rust, Kenn C., and Stephen Must. *Fourteenth Air Force Story in World War II.* Temple City, CA: Historical Aviation, 1977.
Ryan, Cornelius. *Last Battle.* New York: Pocket Books, 1996.
Sawicki, James A. *Tank Battalions of the US Army.* Dumfries, VA: Wyvern, 1983.
Schultz, Duane. *The Doolittle Raid.* New York: St. Martin's, 1988.
———. *Hero of Bataan: The Story of General Jonathan M. Wainwright.* New York: St. Martin's, 1981.
Schwarzkopf, H. Norman. *It Doesn't Take a Hero.* New York: Bantam Books, 1992.
Sims, Edward H. *American Aces in Great Fighter Battles of World War II.* New York: Harper, 1958.
Smith, Steven. *2nd Armored Division "Hell on Wheels."* Hersham, UK: Compendium, 2003.
Smith, William W. *Midway: Turning Point of the Pacific.* New York: Thomas Y. Crowell, 1966.
Sorley, Lewis. *A Better War: The Unexamined Victories and Final Tragedy of America's Last Years in Vietnam.* New York: Harcourt Brace, 1999.
Stanaway, John. *P-38 Lighting Aces of the Pacific and CBI.* Oxford, UK: Osprey, 1997.
Stanaway, John C., and Lawrence J. Hickey. *Attack & Conquer: The 8th Fighter Group in World War II.* Atglen, PA: Schiffer, 1995.
Stanton, Shelby L. *Order of Battle U.S. Army, World War II.* Novata, CA: Presidio, 1984.
———. *Vietnam Order of Battle.* Mechanicsburg, PA: Stackpole, 2003.
Toland, John. *The Flying Tigers.* New York: Random House, 1963.
Wainwright, Jonathan M. *General Wainwright's Story: The Account of Four Years of Humiliating Defeat, Surrender, and Captivity.* Garden City, NY: Doubleday, 1946.
Westover, Wendell. *Suicide Battalions.* New York: G. P. Putnam's Sons, 1929.
Willbanks, James H. *The Battle of An Loc.* Bloomington: Indiana University Press, 2005.
———. *Thiet Giap! The Battle of An Loc, April 1972.* Fort Leavenworth, KS: US Army Command and General Staff College, 1993.
Wilson, Jim. *RETREAT, HELL! We're Just Attacking in Another Direction.* New York: William Morrow, 1988.
Woodall, James R. *Texas Aggie Medals of Honor: Seven Heroes of World War II.* College Station: Texas A&M University Press, 2010.

★ INDEX ★